MW01617792

In Pursuit of the Dragon

In Pursuit of the

TRADITIONS AND TRANSITIONS IN MING CERAMICS

AN EXHIBITION FROM THE IDEMITSU MUSEUM OF ARTS

Seattle Art Museum

Dragon

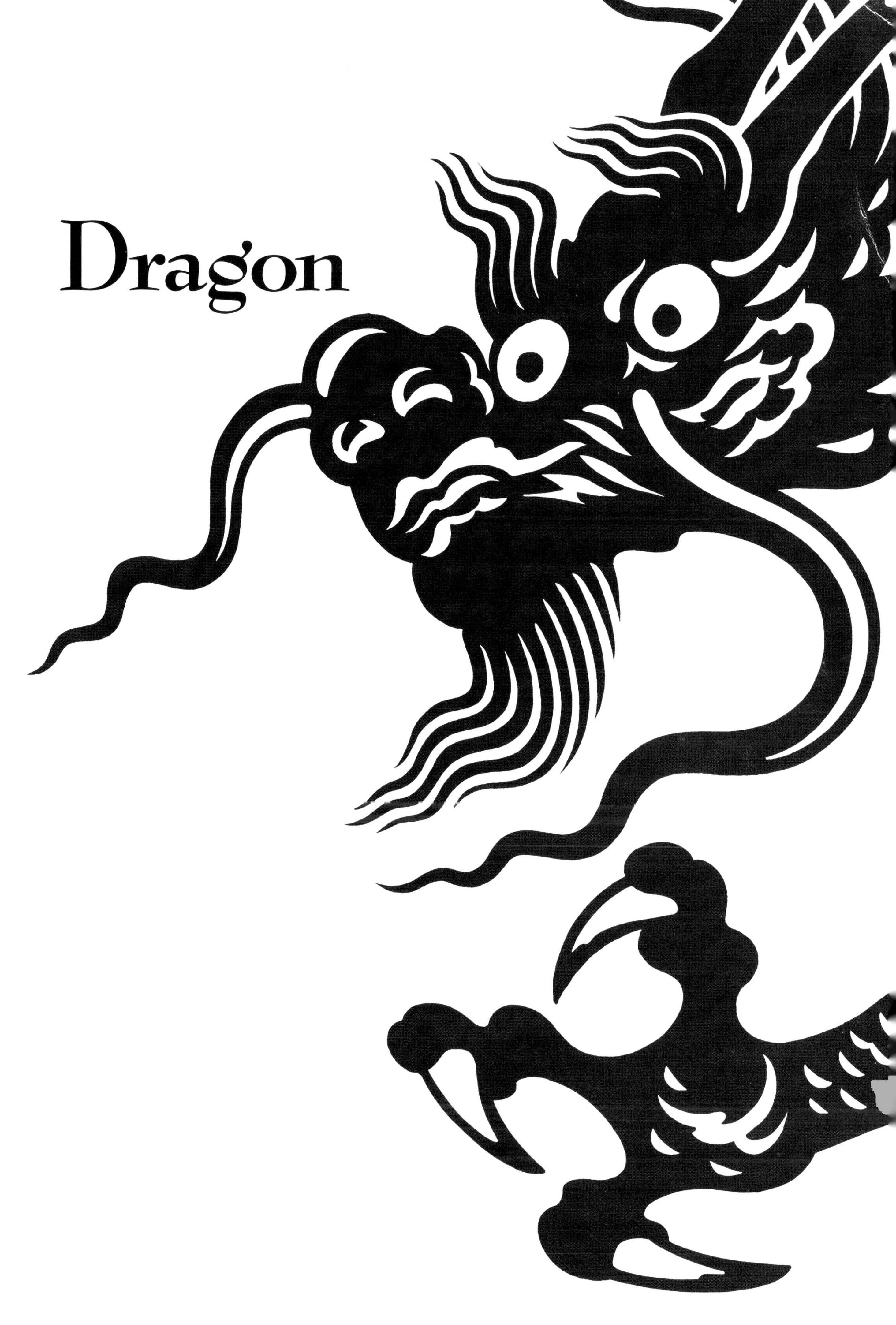

This project has been made possible through the generosity and cooperation of the Idemitsu Museum of Arts, Tokyo; and support from Northwest Airlines; PONCHO; the National Endowment for the Arts; the Metropolitan Center for Far Eastern Art Studies, Kyoto; the Asian Cultural Council; and the K. A. Baillargeon Endowment; and by a federal indemnity from the Federal Council on the Arts and the Humanities.

Exhibition venues:
Seattle Art Museum
Yale University Art Gallery, New Haven
Detroit Institute of Art
Carnegie Museum of Art, Pittsburgh
Birmingham Museum of Art
Los Angeles County Museum of Art
Honolulu Academy of Arts

Published by
Seattle Art Museum
Volunteer Park
Seattle, Washington 98112

Printed in Japan.

Managing editor: Helen Abbott
Editor: Suzanne Kotz
Design and production: Ed Marquand Book Design
Photography: Courtesy of the Idemitsu Museum of Arts

Front cover: Left to right, nos. 39, 1, 62, 47, and 44 (details).
Back cover: Large *guan* jar, Ming dynasty, Xuande period (1426–35), no. 21.

ISBN 0–932216–27–7
Library of Congress Catalogue Card Number: 88–11675

To avoid confusion, the use of Japanese terms has been limited in this catalogue. Japanese has been used only in the case of ware types such as *shonzui, kinrande,* and *kosometsuke* which are universally known by these terms, and in situations where there is no Chinese or English equivalent. All other italicized terms are in Chinese.

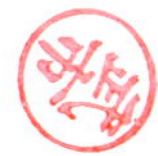

Contents

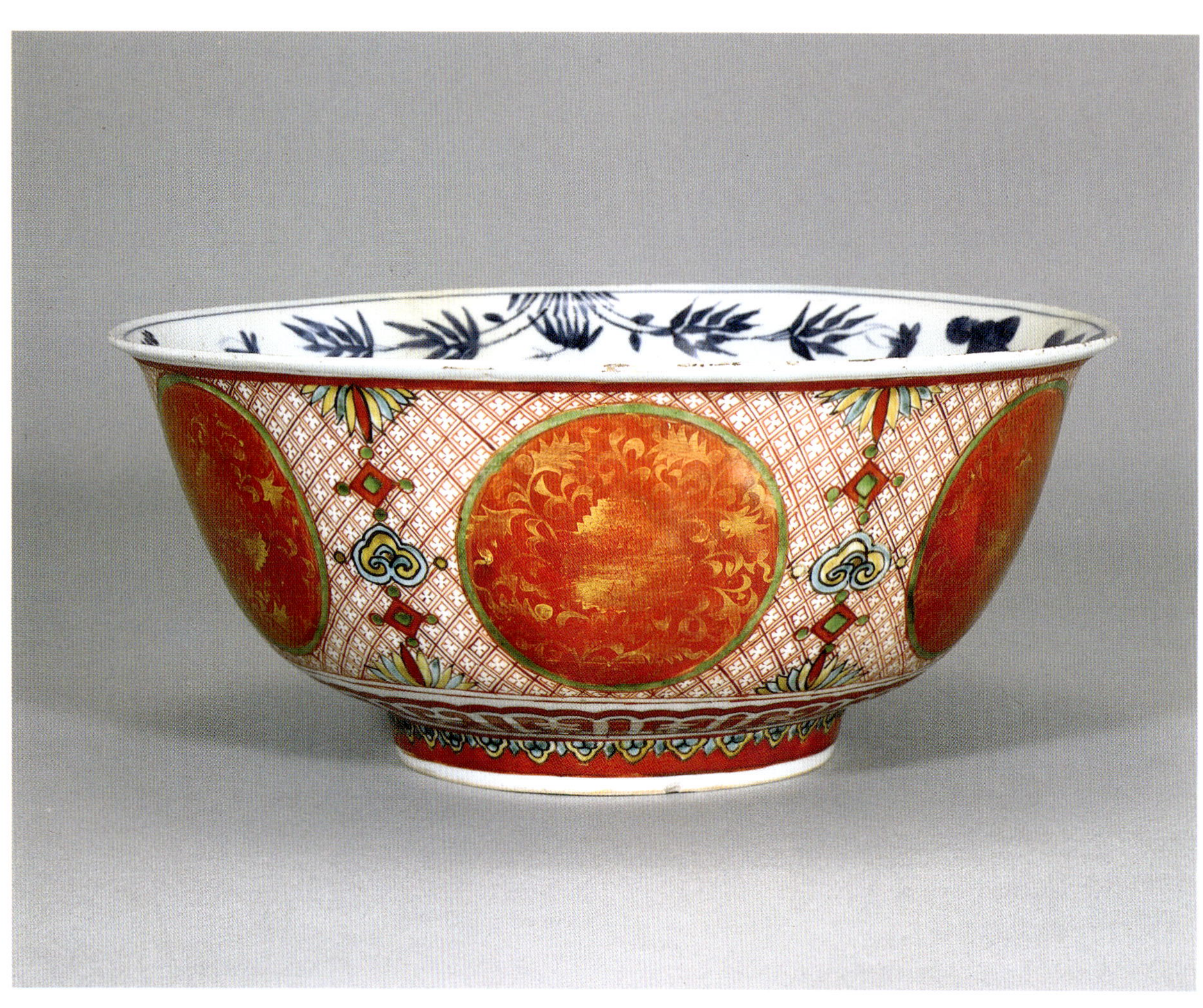

Large bowl, Ming dynasty,
Jiajing period (1522–66), no. 51

Foreword

In Pursuit of the Dragon: Traditions and Transitions in Ming Ceramics traces the development of ceramic styles from the Yuan to the Ming dynasties and documents the full flowering of Ming ceramics production. The exhibition, drawn from the collection of the Idemitsu Museum of Arts, is rich in materials that demonstrate developments in the manufacture of Chinese ceramics, affording us many opportunities to appreciate the potter's skill. This complementary catalogue, in particular, provides art historical and archaeological information to confirm dating and origins as well as insights into the materials, techniques, and motifs employed by Chinese artisans during the Yuan and Ming dynasties.

In the Eastern cyclical calendar, 1988 is the year of the dragon, an auspicious year to present the exhibition and this catalogue. Therefore, the evolution of the much-used dragon motif is of special interest. Its popularity is demonstrated by the fact that a full third of the objects in the exhibition have the dragon either as a main or secondary decorative motif; an even larger percentage of the pieces intended strictly for the Chinese market display this design.

Unlike the dragon in the West, the dragon in China is a propitious animal. Able to breathe both clouds and fire, the Chinese dragon is associated with rain and water and the season of spring. By legend it retires to the watery depths in the autumn and returns in the spring to ascend to the skies, bringing with it moisture vital to agriculture. Considered by the Chinese to be the chief of the scaled reptiles, this peculiar animal has nine basic components: the head of a camel, the horns of a deer, the eyes of a rabbit, the ears of a cow, the neck of a snake, the belly of a frog, the scales of a carp, the claws of a hawk, and the paws of a tiger. On each side of its mouth are long whiskers, and its chin is bearded.

The dragon appeared very early in Chinese art and beliefs and plays an important role in all Chinese religions. From at least as early as the Han dynasty (202 B.C.–A.D. 220), the dragon, in particular the five-clawed dragon, was an imperial symbol. Indeed, the emperor of China occupied the Dragon Throne. For this reason it was a favorite ornament in architecture and the decorative arts, particularly those associated with the imperial family.

Because the dragon was a purely mythical beast, the artists who rendered it could freely interpret it. Pursuing the dragon through the periods and ceramic styles presented in this exhibition provides an interesting look at the different types of dragon, the way its form evolved over time, and the different effects that could be achieved in this one motif with the various decorative techniques used. In a broader sense, the pursuit of the dragon can be seen as the pursuit of beauty and knowledge, a pursuit we trust will be aided by the exhibition and catalogue *In Pursuit of the Dragon.*

Jay Gates
Director
Seattle Art Museum

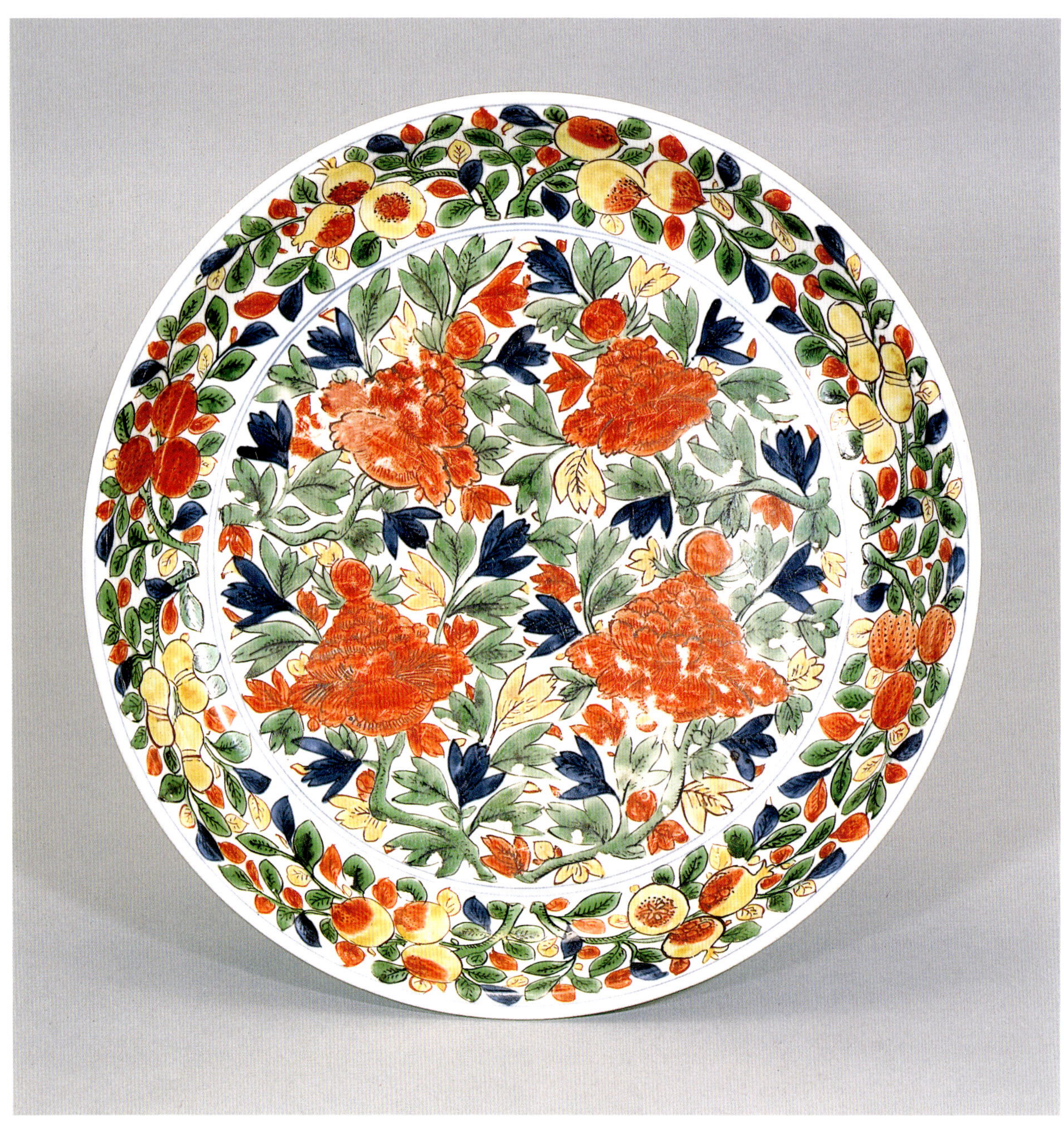

Large dish, Ming dynasty,
Wanli period (1573–1619), no. 71

Acknowledgments

The Idemitsu Museum of Arts since its inauguration in 1966 has been known throughout the world among academics and museum professionals, graduate students in Asian art history, and devotees of Asian art as the home of one of the world's most exciting and most beautiful collections of art. The staff is unfailingly hospitable to those of us who have come calling to learn from this great repository. This generosity was epitomized in the fraternal warmth and delightful good nature of Professor Tsugio Mikami, for many years a member of the Board of Directors and Advisor to the Idemitsu Museum of Arts before his death in 1987. Professor Mikami's frank and open attitude, good nature, scholarly discipline, and intellectual probity have come to represent the spirit of the Idemitsu Museum. Professor Mikami's death was a deeply felt loss, and in the field of Asian art history and archaeology a voice of great reason and integrity has been stilled. In appreciation of his immense contribution to the field and in a gesture of respect, this exhibition and catalogue are dedicated to his memory.

It has been almost a decade since the Idemitsu Museum of Arts, led by Professor Mikami, joined with the Seattle Art Museum to sponsor an exhibition of one hundred objects and paintings from the Idemitsu collection. Conceived as a broad ranging selection of treasures from the vast collection, the hundred pieces included material from China, Japan, Korea, and Southeast Asia. This was the first presentation in the United States of an exhibition based exclusively on material from the Idemitsu collection, and after opening at the Seattle Art Museum in the fall of 1981, it traveled to the Kimbell Art Museum, Fort Worth; Japan House Gallery, New York; and the Denver Art Museum, where public reaction registered unqualified approval.

Encouraged by the success of the first exhibition, Professor Mikami suggested a second, more focused project featuring an aspect of the Chinese ceramic collection. An inveterate archaeologist, Professor Mikami envisioned a project that would consider recent discoveries at the imperial kilns of Jingdezhen in relation to the development of the ceramic style of the Ming dynasty. Many new findings particularly germane to objects in the Idemitsu collection had come to light in recent years, and, Mikami argued, an exhibition would offer an excellent opportunity to bring this information to the public in connection with some of the most important representative examples. Further, additional material from the preceding Yuan dynasty would illustrate the stylistic debt of the Ming ceramists to the dynamic, international character of that relatively short period.

Henry Trubner, now Seattle Art Museum Senior Curator Emeritus, was a longtime friend and colleague of Professor Mikami. Mr. Trubner had led the Seattle Art Museum's organizing of the 1981 exhibition, and again in 1985, with Professor Mikami, he initiated the present exhibition and undertook to organize the tour in the United States. Mr. Trubner retired in 1987, but has remained as honorary curator for the exhibition and contributed an essay to the catalogue.

The successful completion of projects such as this, of immense complexity and covering a long period of time, requires the full support and cooperation of a multitude of persons. First to be acknowledged are the staff at the Idemitsu Museum of Arts, headed by the Director, Shosuke Idemitsu, and Ryosuke Suematsu, Deputy Director. Takashi Eto, Curatorial Manager, greatly assisted in the organizing and logistical planning. Assisting in this was Naganori Akui, Curator, who along with Tadanori Yuba, Curator of Chinese Art, accompanied the exhibition on tour as traveling curators. Mr. Yuba also contributed to the catalogue an insightful discourse on developments at Jingdezhen. Mary Ann Rogers, independent research specialist in Chinese ceramics, working with the staff at the Idemitsu Museum of Arts, provided the superb analyses accompanying the illustrations of the objects.

The Idemitsu Museum of Arts graciously assumed all the expenses for the printing of the catalogue. In addition to the financial contributions of the two organizing institutions, expenses for the exhibition and catalogue preparation have been underwritten by a number of grants. Foremost among these were grants from the National Endowment for the Arts, PONCHO, the Metropolitan Center for Far Eastern Art Studies, Kyoto, and the Asian Cultural Council, New York City, and a federal indemnity from the Federal Council on the Arts and the Humanities. In Seattle, material support for the project came from the K. A. Baillargeon Endowment. We gratefully acknowledge the donated services of Northwest Airlines in providing trans-Pacific transportation for these precious objects.

Seattle Art Museum Director Jay Gates cheerfully supported the project, which was long under way at the time he joined the staff in 1987. Bonnie Pitman-Gelles, Associate Director for Program, and Jill Rullkoetter, Head of Education, have provided stimulating and informative programming to complement the exhibition. Also we are grateful for the cooperative assistance of all the staff of the Museum Services Division, headed by Gail Joice. Particular thanks go to Michael McCafferty, Exhibitions Designer, and his crew for the sterling installation of the exhibition. Special Registrar Evelyn Klebanoff efficiently supervised the handling of the objects with great care and concern throughout the entire eighteen-month course of the exhibition.

The catalogue, a truly international cooperative effort, was skillfully guided through all its many stages by Helen Abbott, Publications Manager, and her capable staff. Our thanks go to the editor, Suzanne Kotz, who so expertly joined the texts prepared by many different hands, and to Willi Patzkowsky and Paula Thurman for tireless keyboarding and proofreading. We wish especially to take note of the fine essays. Mr. Trubner and Mr. Yuba were joined by John Ayers, former Keeper of the Far Eastern Department at the Victoria and Albert Museum, London. His excellent background essay, focusing on blue-and-white porcelain of the Yuan and Ming periods, provides a valuable overview of the complex development of ceramic art in China.

In the museum's Department of Asian Art, Associate Curator Michael Knight, upon Mr. Trubner's retirement, took on the duties of lead curator for the exhibition. Joined by Zora Nedoma, Administrative Assistant for the Curatorial Division, they addressed the complex organizational issues with equanimity and goodwill. The success of the exhibition is in no small part the result of their diligent efforts.

Finally, it is important to note with appreciation the interest and support of the six participating institutions. Without their unflagging enthusiasm, the exhibition would not have been possible. Situated as they are throughout the United States, their participation will insure the greatest possible opportunity for the American public to share in the richness of the Idemitsu Museum of Arts collection of Chinese ceramics.

William Jay Rathbun
Curator of Asian Art
Seattle Art Museum

Chronologies

Chronological Table of Dynasties

Shang	c. 1750–c. 1050 B.C.
Zhou	c. 1050–256
Qin	221–207
Han	202–A.D. 220
Three Kingdoms	221–265
Southern (Six Dynasties) and Northern Dynasties	265–581
Sui	581–618
Tang	618–907
Five Dynasties	907–960
Song	960–1279
Yuan	1260–1368
Ming	1368–1644
Qing	1644–1912
Republic	1912–1949
People's Republic	1949–

Reign Periods of the Ming Dynasty

Hongwu	1368–98
Jianwen	1399–1402
Yongle	1403–24
Xuande	1426–35
Zhengtong	1436–49
Jingtai	1450–56
Tianshun	1457–64
Chenghua	1465–87
Hongzhi	1488–1505
Zhengde	1506–21
Jiajing	1522–66
Longqing	1567–72
Wanli	1573–1619
Taichang	1620
Tianqi	1621–27
Chongzhen	1628–44

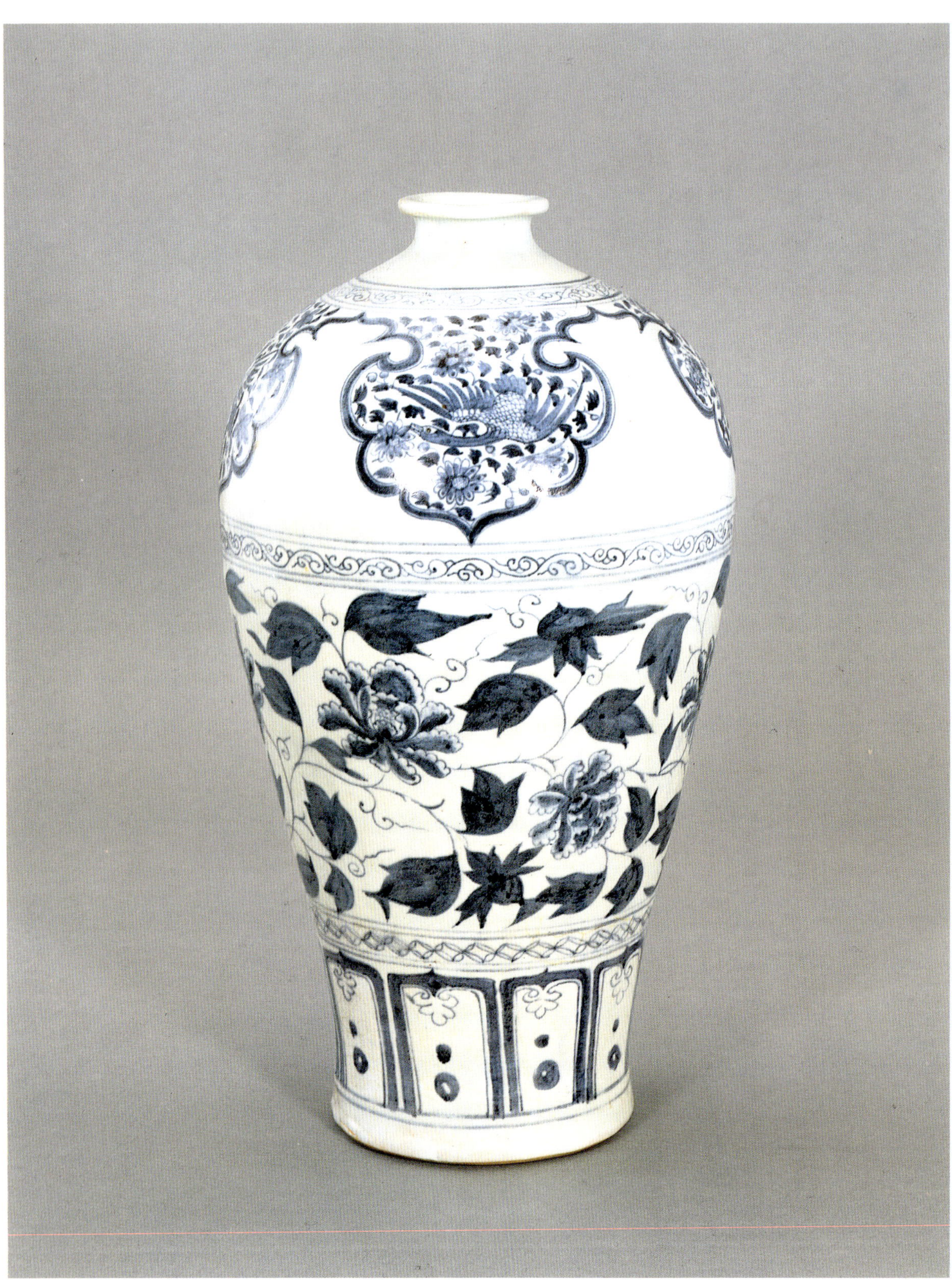

Meiping, Yuan dynasty,
third quarter 14th century, no. 11

Blue-and-White and the Origins of Ming Porcelain Style

JOHN AYERS

The worldwide reputation Chinese potters have enjoyed over the centuries might well be epitomized in their invention of porcelain. Examples of the hard, white, translucent ware, so near miraculous in character and far more sophisticated than any other form of pottery previously known, began to reach the Near East in the ninth century, not long after it was first made. Much later, early in the sixteenth century, when Portuguese ships first visited China, painted blue-and-white came increasingly to Europe. It was to emulate these imports that native European porcelain industries were finally set up in the eighteenth century, some two hundred years later. This Chinese preeminence can now be seen to have originated in their early manufacture of stoneware pottery, the beginnings of which can be traced to before 1000 B.C. Very much later, in developing and perfecting the high-temperature technology required for stonewares, the Chinese came on the one hand to create the finest of ceramic glazes and on the other, almost as if by chance, to make porcelain.

By the Song dynasty (960–1279) the craft of ceramic production was already acquiring a great range and power of expression, and a remarkable flowering of the art took place. Fresh and pleasing forms were created in stoneware and dressed in glazes of subtle color and texture, and other decoration, which might be carved, molded, or painted, was generally restrained in character. Much porcelain was also made, but because of its plain purity, as well as the current taste for restraint in design, painted decoration was not employed. Not until much later, in early Ming times, were painted porcelains to win the approval of the court. The general response, however, was then both swift and complete, and blue-and-white and enamel-painted or color-glazed styles were quick to develop. Located mainly in a small area of south-central China, the expanding porcelain industry, helped by a thriving foreign trade, entered a period of prosperity that has continued with few interruptions until modern times.

The first major symptom, if not the cause, of this great change in taste was the introduction of blue-and-white: the white porcelain ware whose surface was directly painted with a cobalt-oxide pigment before glazing. The blue color of the designs developed in baking the ware to its firing temperature, hence the technique was highly economical. Underglaze painting in red, employing a copper-oxide pigment, was also practiced, but this was less successful and hence only intermittently used. The experimental stages of these techniques cannot yet be fully documented and dated, but there is now little doubt as to when they occurred: the development of the new style as an economic product can be placed somewhere between the second and fourth decades of the fourteenth century. By that time China had been under the alien rule of the Yuan dynasty (1260–1368) for half a century. The Mongol regime brought suffering and disruption; however, it had the effect of reviving contacts with other parts of Asia that had long been lost, and it was apparently in this unusual climate that cobalt-oxide pigment was introduced to Jingdezhen, the great porcelain center in Jiangxi province. The use in the Near East of the substance for decorating pottery is well attested prior to this date.[1]

Although Yuan blue-and-white ware is today regarded as a glorious achievement in its own right and is highly prized, fifty years ago its nature was barely understood. Chinese records, so far as they were known, conveyed little about the origin of the style and had been incorrectly interpreted as ascribing it to the preceding Song period. Ceramic scholars in the West were mainly preoccupied with attempting to identify the outstanding blue-and-white of the early Ming fifteenth-century reigns which, by contrast, enjoyed a legendary esteem in China. As early as 1929, however, R. L. Hobson had published as genuine an unusual pair of tall altar vases, which according to their inscription were made for a temple in Jiangxi province in A.D. 1351. Although twenty years later there were still some who derided these as fakes, they are accepted now without question. Housed in the Percival David Foundation in London, they constitute one of the main cornerstones of the chronology of early blue-and-white.[2]

The Beginnings of Blue-and-White

Progress in identifying early blue-and-white was more rapid in the years following the Second World War. Especially notable are John Pope's studies into ancient surviving collections of these wares in the Near East. His analytical work, which appeared in 1952, published and placed on record what is still today the largest collection of such wares in existence: the no less than forty-one pieces in the Topkapi Saray, the imperial palace of the Ottoman sultans in Istanbul.[3] This and his more broadly based book published in 1956[4] on the important collection of the Safavid rulers at Ardebil in Iran clearly established the character of the early wares as a group and their close relationship with the dated David vases, thus putting the mid fourteenth-century date beyond doubt.

Wares such as those of the Percival David group provided evidence of a level of quality quite exceptional in the field of export ceramics, a subject that began to attract more attention. Meanwhile a growing interest in the Yuan period in ceramics generally was broadening the scholar's approach. Nearer to China—in countries such as the Philippines and Indonesia—other Jingdezhen wares were turning up, mainly as a result of uncoordinated excavations.[5] Apart from early blue-and-white, some of it different in character from the Near Eastern material, these included various kinds of white wares. Production of porcelains at Jingdezhen in Song times had been mainly in the *yingqing* style, which has a brilliant glaze with a bluish green tinge and decoration of fluent, sketchy, incised designs. This production continued during the Yuan dynasty, when the designs became increasingly schematized and representational in character, and other types were made with new forms of decoration in relief. In one distinctive type the designs are mold-impressed, and the porcelain is harder and finer grained with a semiopaque white glaze; this is *shufu* ware, which is recorded as having been made under the Yuan as an official ware. These finds increasingly showed that the *yingqing, shufu,* and underglaze-painted wares, whether in blue or in red, were closely linked, and more and more the Yuan period at Jingdezhen was seen as one of rich and germinal experiment in porcelain decoration.

In more recent years, partly from the excavation of datable pieces in China and elsewhere and partly through stylistic comparisons, the measure of uncertainty concerning the sequence and dating of these various wares has been sharply reduced. Important examples have provided a few more dates. Among them, for example, is a striking class of large *yingqing* figures of Buddhist deities, now in collections worldwide, of which one in Kansas City bears an inscribed date corresponding to A.D. 1298 or 1299. Links with these pieces have been noted among a class of *yingqing* wares with incised decoration and also among those having applied relief decoration, on some of which blue or red decoration also appears.[6]

The earliest wholly reliable evidence of underglaze-blue painted designs on porcelain is that of a blue-and-white covered vase with a peony scroll design which was found in a tomb at

Jiujiang, Jiangxi province, with evidence of its burial in 1319. Compared with other known material, the shape and decoration of this work appears unskilled and tentative.[7]

A vast amount of new information was provided by the discovery in 1976 on the seabed off Sinan, in southwest Korea, of an entire sunken shipload of porcelain. Apart from quantities of celadon, there were many *yingqing* wares with Yuan shapes and designs and *shufu*-type wares with molded decoration. On the internal evidence of inscribed wooden labels, the shipment itself can be dated to the year 1323 or immediately thereafter, and we can deduce that most, if not all, were manufactured shortly before that date.[8] No blue-and-white was found at Sinan, although it is perhaps significant that a few pieces were found decorated in copper red and in the even rarer iron-oxide brown. All this is in accord with the theory of a tentative production still in its infancy at the time, a production that can be contrasted with the evident maturity and expertise shown by the David vases, with their associated date of 1351.

A further reference point is found in the form of a white porcelain dish in the David Foundation collection. Decorated with phoenixes and clouds in molded relief, it bears an obscure incised reign date matching the year 1328. Its quality and decorative style link it on the one hand with Yuan *shufu* ware and on the other with certain early Ming wares.[9]

Early to Mid Fourteenth-Century Wares

No better starting point could be found for considering the relationships of the wares of this early period than the porcelain vase with *yingqing* glaze covering carved decoration (no. 5). Its form, with its bulbous, swelling shoulder, exemplifies the powerful if somewhat tentative shapes of the mid Yuan period. The design is presented in three zones, with a dragon incised in the main central band, flanked by a floral scroll above and lotus petal panels below—a scheme indicative of a new taste for contained naturalism. The piece is almost identical to one found in the Sinan shipwreck, and confirmation of its date is offered by another such piece excavated from a tomb in Jiangxi province dated to 1325.[10] The bottle with painting in underglaze copper-red (no. 7) is of similar material and construction and shows a transference of the same decorative intentions into the painted medium. Designs in this group are still sketchy, consisting here of a single plainly outlined spray of the sacred *lingzhi* fungus with triangular panels above. The piece represents an early, yet successful experiment in this newly invented technique.

By the second quarter of the fourteenth century, therefore, the new mid to late Yuan decorative style was emerging. A decade or more might have elapsed before the manufacture of the blue-and-white bottle (no. 8) and the *meiping* (no. 11). In each case the handling of the forms has developed greater assurance. The *meiping* in particular has a fuller shoulder and anticipates the characteristic tapering neck of the mid-fourteenth century. The blue decoration, which is in a rich violet-toned cobalt, reveals a considerable advance and elaboration of style, with a fuller scheme now introducing narrow borders between the main bands and designs sometimes on the neck and foot. A broad peony scroll and panels with geese flying among chrysanthemums are done in a manner employing broad, washlike strokes as well as drawn outlines. The bottle is decorated with a rare anecdotal subject of a legendary figure—as shown by the cloud frames surrounding him—enticing a deer, which holds in its mouth a spray of fungus. It is painted with skill and a fine sense of humor.

The large dish with foliated rim (no. 9) introduces another technical device in its use of molded relief work to highlight designs such as the peony band and chrysanthemum border, which are also given a solid blue ground. Four shaped panels in the center depict lotus floating

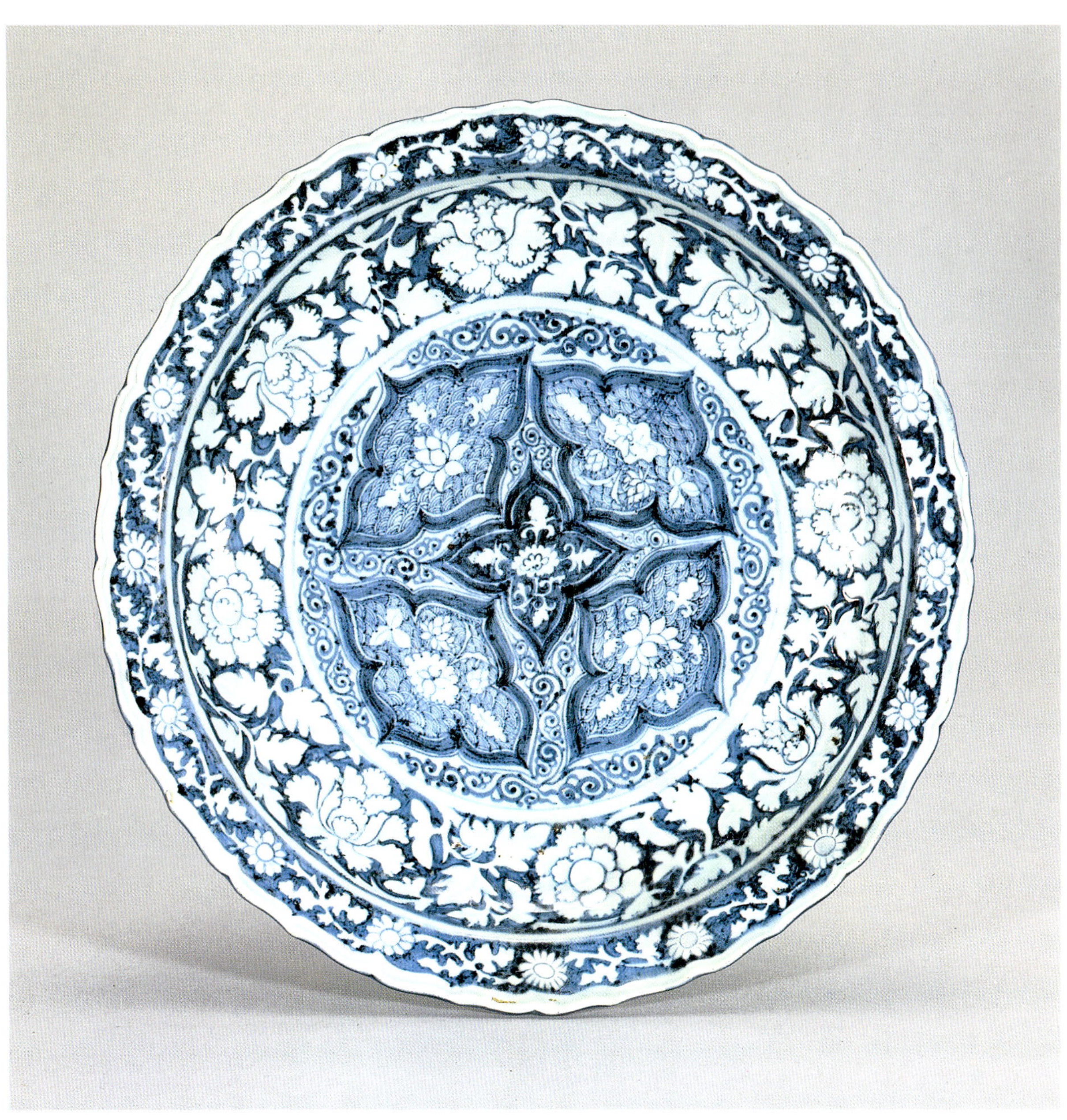

Large foliate-rimmed dish, Yuan dynasty,
mid 14th century, no. 9

on water, and the entire design is treated with a characteristic vigor and individuality. The porcelain has now become noticeably denser and whiter, the glaze at the same time losing some of its softer *yingqing* character and color. The somewhat brittle Song *yingqing* body had been made almost exclusively of mined "China stone" or *cishi*—the petuntse described in the letters of the Jesuit missionary Père d'Entrecolles in the eighteenth century; in his time, however, as he tells us, it was combined with kaolin clay. Perhaps, as has been suggested, it was in Yuan times that this practice was adopted in order to make a stronger and more highly fired ware, a helpful feature for *shufu* ware and for the new, large blue-and-white dishes, bowls, and vases required by the foreign trade. As the Sinan wreck has shown, large dishes of Longquan celadon, with its different and coarser body material, were exported in great quantities at what must have been an even earlier date.

Barely another decade can separate the large dish with foliated rim from the magnificent large jar (no. 10), which represents the full maturity of the Yuan blue-and-white style. The nobility and vigor of the decoration of the wares of this mid fourteenth-century group is unsurpassed in the history of painting on porcelain. In its boldness of conception and confident drawing the jar reveals the hand of a master, who may be the painter of the 1351 David vases, for the long dragon pursuing the flaming pearl and supporting motifs such as the breaking wave border around the neck correspond on both and are similarly treated.

Mid to Late Fourteenth-Century Wares

A different and somewhat more formal approach is displayed in a dish painted in a grayish underglaze red (no. 14). Pieces of this family are found equally painted in blue or in red: a new development. The regular, four-pointed central motif, when compared with that of the earlier dish (no. 9), is altogether more orderly in design. The very systematic and neat arrangement of flowers in the molded and bracketed well and the weak version of the famous wave border are also noteworthy. There are significant differences in shape in this family. Some students see here the beginnings of a new style, one associated with the Ming dynasty, which regained power from the Mongols in 1368. Others believe it is a late development of the Yuan; more evidence is needed, but the weight of opinion nowadays favors the later date.[11]

The first emperor of the Ming dynasty was Zhu Yuanzhang, a successful leader of the revolt against the Mongols, who adopted the reign name of Hongwu (1368–98). It is possible that, having established his campaign in Jiangxi province, he later set up factories at Jingdezhen to supply porcelain for his court, but accounts are conflicting. There is no proof as yet that he did so. No wares are known bearing the genuine Hongwu reign mark, although excavations at the site of the palace at Nanjing have unearthed porcelain fragments that seem indicative. They include some small dishes with a design of five-clawed dragons surrounding cloud designs, a type that is found in blue-and-white, or with monochrome glazes of blue, red, white, or brown covering partly molded and partly incised designs, sometimes with two colors on the same piece.[12] Evidently not made for export, these wares in some respects continue the official *shufu* tradition of the Yuan and might possibly represent a comparable ware of Hongwu's time.

Two pieces from the Idemitsu collection represent this tradition: the small white dish (no. 6) and the bowl with both red and blue glazes (no. 13). In each case dating is somewhat problematic and differing opinions have been expressed. Thinly potted and quite translucent, the white dish displays a pair of phoenixes in a band of molded relief around the inside. In this it can be compared with the dish in the David Foundation with its incised date of 1328. Here, however, the style is different, and the phoenix motif does not continue across the center, which displays

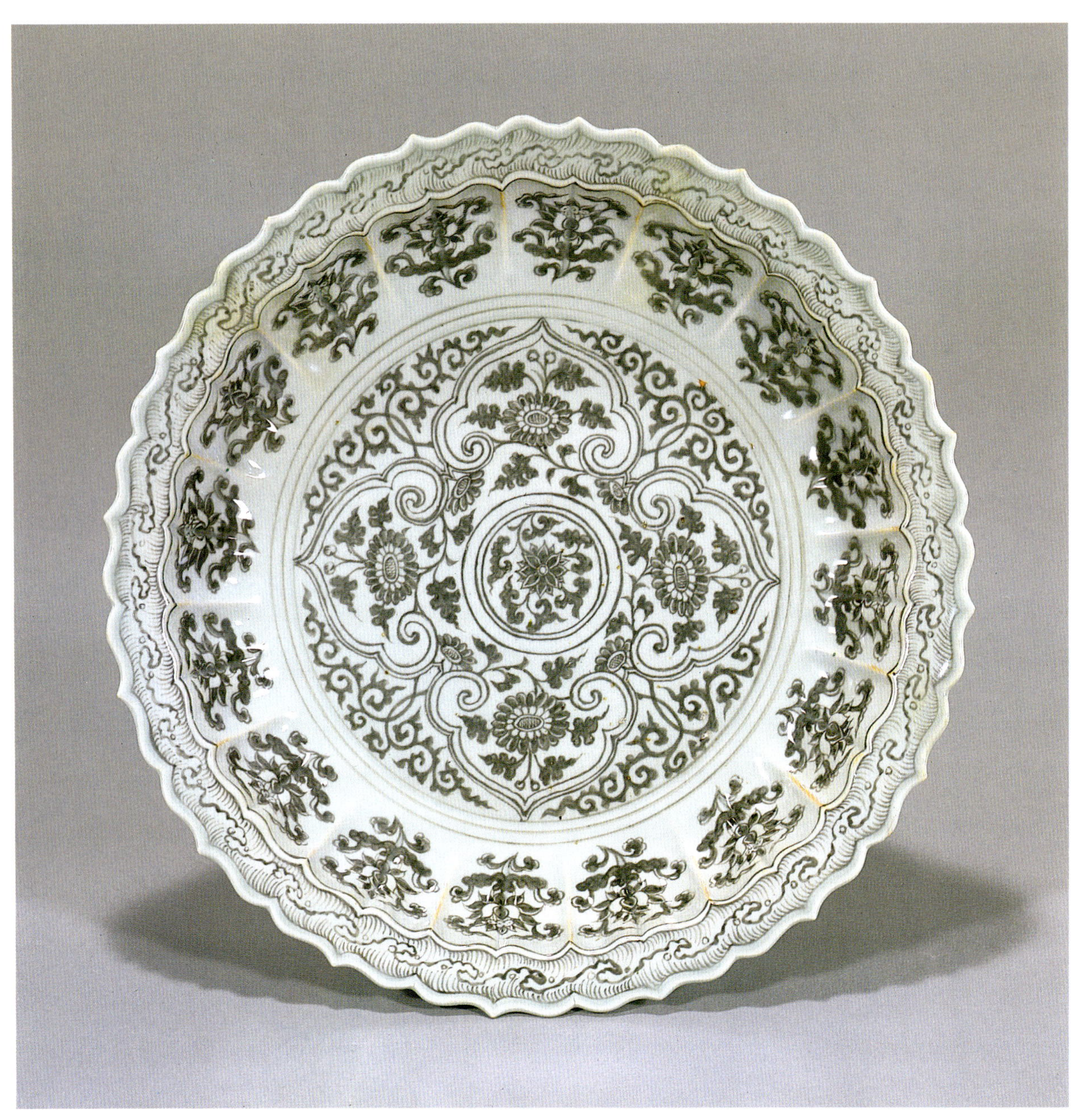

Large foliate-rimmed dish, Ming dynasty,
Hongwu period (1368–98), no. 14

an incised three-cloud design, one not associated with other Yuan types, although it was still current in subsequent Ming reigns. In some respects the piece anticipates the white wares of the following reign of Yongle (1403–24)—also often thinly made and relief-molded, with a fine glaze, silky to the touch, which has a slight greenish tinge where it runs thick.

The red and blue bowl is a heavily made piece with a high and massive foot. The blue glaze covering the outside is plain except for the ring of incised lotus-petal panels around the foot; the red glaze inside covers a relief-molded design of two dragons and a single incised cloud in the center. In form this bowl bears some relationship to a plain white bowl found in the tomb of Song Sheng, marquis of Xining (died 1407), or those with interior relief designs from the tomb of his wife, who died in 1418.[13] Closer still is the parallel with a bowl in the Yamato Bunkakan near Nara which has the same decorative scheme[14] but with a white glaze outside and brown glaze inside; this strongly links it with the group of small dishes, perhaps of Hongwu date, to which we have referred.

Fifteenth-Century Wares

There is much less uncertainty concerning the Ming wares of the early fifteenth century. The reigns of Hongwu's fourth son, Yongle (1403–24), and grandson Xuande (1426–35) are among the most celebrated in ceramic history. Renowned as a patron of the arts in general and as a builder of the Forbidden City in Beijing which superseded the older Yuan palace, Yongle left everywhere the mark of his fine and energetic talent. Porcelains probably made for his court include some especially refined wares in monochrome white or red, and two stem cups (nos. 15, 16) are examples of this very rare sort. In each case the bowl has a mold-impressed interior decoration of five-clawed dragons among clouds—a now-traditional formula; the sides were then so thinly pared that the glaze provides much of their substance, an effect the Chinese call *tuotai* (bodiless). The half-concealed dragons on such pieces were called *anhua* (secret decoration). These cups were made not to drink from but for ritual use; they probably contained pure water and stood on altars. Each cup bears in the center the four-character reign mark *Yongle nian zhi,* or "made in the Yongle period." This constitutes virtually the first use of the imperial period name *(nian hao)* as an indication of date, a frequent if never wholly standard practice from that time forward.

The blue-and-white wares are perhaps the most immediately impressive of these two famous reigns. Court influence on the factories aimed at sustaining high standards in all departments. The materials used were pure and refined, and the cobalt pigment rich and intense; much attention was paid to the perfection of forms, which were greatly extended in range. An ambitious repertoire of designs was adopted, and these often display a high painterly quality as well as a more disciplined approach. A magnificent example is the large dish (no. 18), over two feet in diameter, which depicts a garden landscape. A composition of fine trees, plants, ornamental rocks, and water is executed in a superior technique employing superimposed ("heaped-and-piled") strokes to achieve a strikingly vivid and realistic effect.[15] Another dish with a grapevine design (no. 19) conveys a similar spirit of naturalistic invention; as with so many of these wares, systematic use is made of flower-and-fruit sprays for the border and panel designs.

Unlike the monochrome pieces just described, virtually none of the blue-and-white ascribed to the Yongle period bears a reign mark. In the Xuande period, however, it is found more regularly; this has helped materially to distinguish the similar products of the two reigns. Many Xuande wares in fact have a sumptuous glaze rich in tiny bubbles with a marked "orange-skin" surface and an especially rich, purplish tone of cobalt; analyses have shown that in this

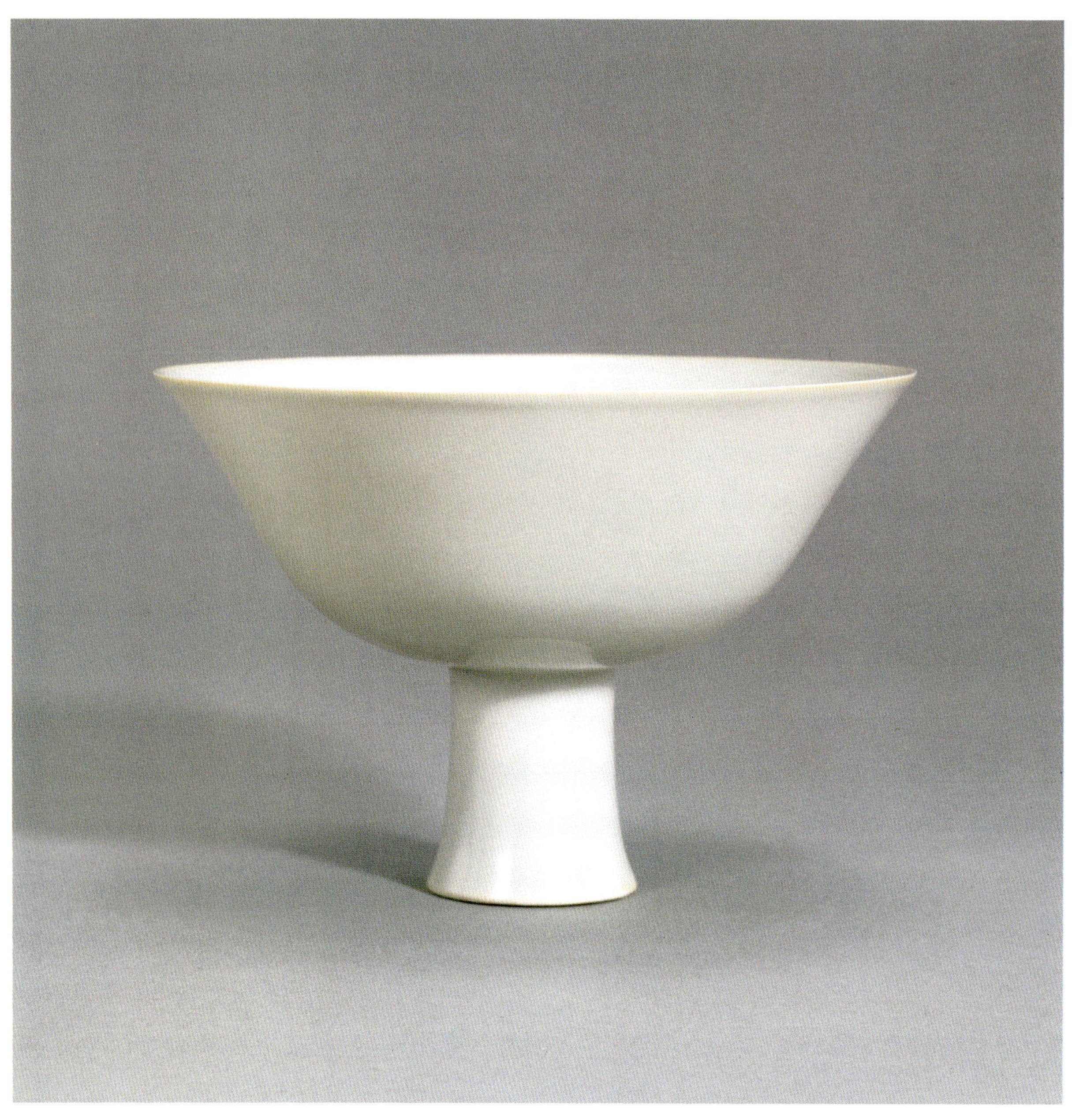

Stem cup, Ming dynasty,
Yongle period (1403–24), no. 15

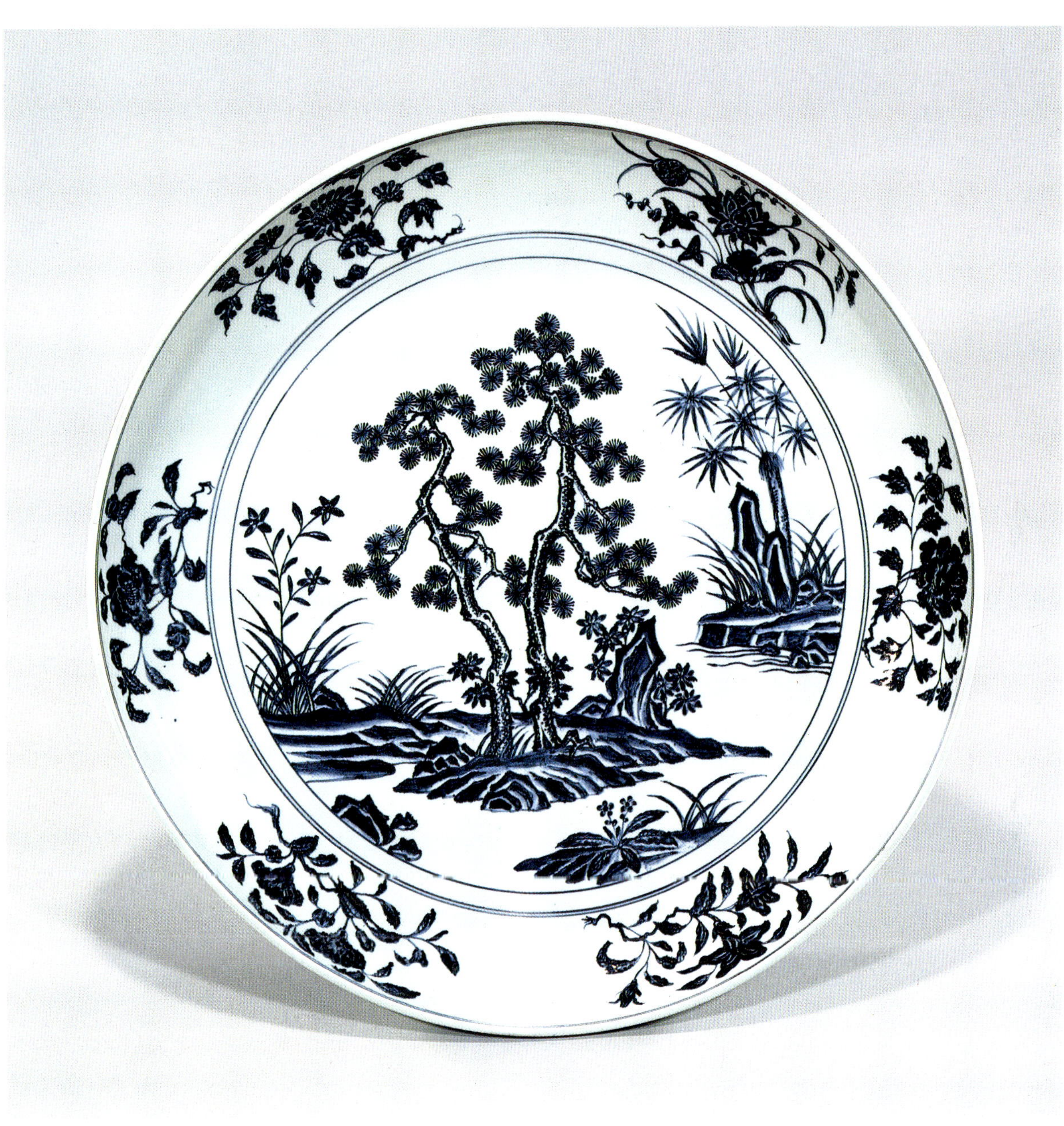

Large platter, Ming dynasty,
early 15th century, no. 18

period a native manganese-bearing cobalt began to be added to the imported ore. The boldly shaped *guan* jar (no. 21), with its sinuous three-clawed dragon striding across the sky, shows off to perfection the vibrant drawing of this classic period, which may profitably be compared with that of the fourteenth-century jar (no. 10). A four-character mark appears on the shoulder; more usually a six-character mark is used and is written on the base, as on the conical bowl (no. 23). On this piece painted ranks of lotus petals around the sides supplement the lotus-flower form.

Many new designs were produced during this period. The small dish (no. 24) shows one that continued through many subsequent reigns; in the center is a spray of flowering pomegranate which is surrounded by four fruits. It no doubt formed part of a palace service. The type is better known in its more sumptuous form with an added yellow enamel ground (as in the Hongzhi-period example, no. 36); blue-and-white examples such as this are rare.

Very few wares were painted in underglaze copper-red at this time, probably because the technique was not regarded as sufficiently reliable, but plain white, as well as red- or blue-glazed porcelains, often with incised designs, were made for the court. The fine white dish (no. 20) has an elegant design of water plants in this style, which is also found in blue-and-white versions; this piece has the reign mark written on the side, below the rim.

This early fifteenth-century production approached perfection in so many spheres that the wares became classic models for porcelain makers of later centuries. During the mid-century years that followed, however, the factories had little patronage and production fell off. Until recently little was known of the wares of this so-called Interregnum, which undoubtedly saw a marked decline. Standards were restored, however, in the reign of Chenghua (1465–87), whose porcelains are noted for their outstanding refinement. Above all their innovative use of colored enamels has impressed connoisseurs—reflecting, it has been said, the taste of the young emperor's favorite, Lady Wan. These porcelains do indeed include wares of a marvelously feminine delicacy and charm. The blue-and-white wares of the reign are hardly less accomplished, and a study of marked examples reveals their original character, including a most elegant refinement in both paste and potting and a smooth and flawless glaze, which often has a slightly smoky tone. The painting of the so-called palace bowls of Chenghua also shows a lighter and more delicate touch than any seen previously, and a style of economically drawn outlines filled in with a paler, flowing wash was favored. Simple scrolls of lily, hibiscus, and other exotic plants are often pictured. A rare and beautiful bowl (no. 32) displays a more traditional design, painted with an unusually fine brush, of dragons writhing vigorously over a sea of waves.

Sixteenth-Century Wares

By the sixteenth century, Ming porcelain began to appeal to a broader clientele; markets in eastern and western Asia and also in Europe showed a great appetite for blue-and-white. Production was redoubled to meet demand, and the quality of the output of both export pieces and those made for the court inevitably declined as resources in both skill and materials were stretched to the limit. Blue-and-white of this period nevertheless continues to display a characteristic Ming exuberance in form and design, and enameled decoration played an ever-growing part.

The blue-and-white produced during the long reign of Jiajing (1522–66) is famous both for its large size and variety and for the deep and brilliant purplish blue of its well-refined pigment. The style of painting commonly preferred was one of drawn outlines filled in with a full brush, a technique lending itself to production on a large scale. Decoration covered a much-expanded range of subjects. Flower and plant designs maintained their well-established role as main themes and in borders, but human figures and animals appeared more frequently and in greater

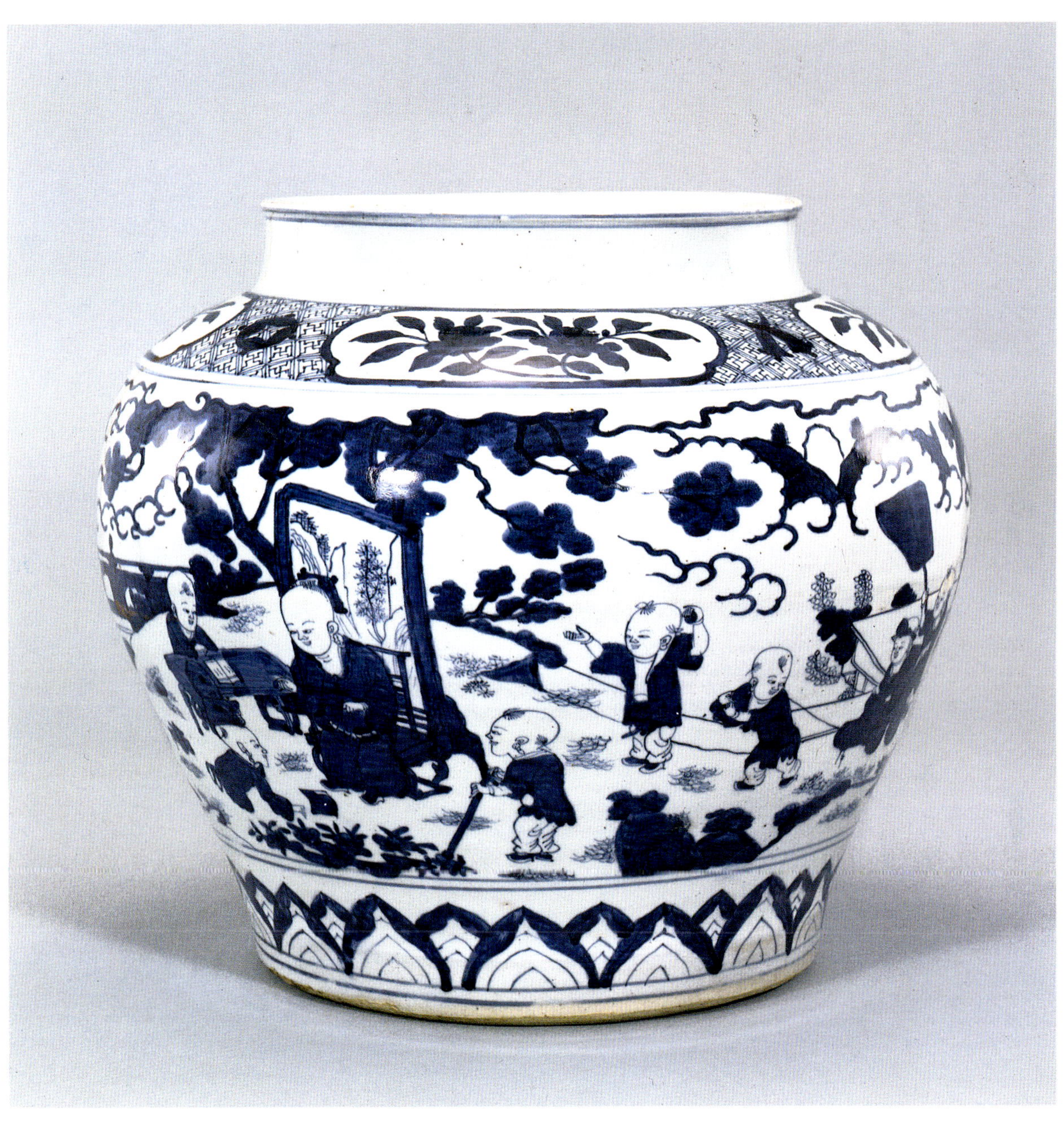

Large jar, Ming dynasty,
Jiajing period (1522–66), no. 48

variety, often in scenes from literature, legend, or art, as on the fine jar (no. 48) encircled by a long "scroll painting" of children playing in a garden. The emperor was a keen adherent of Daoism, and scenes incorporating Daoist deities or immortals were also popular. Indeed on closer examination much of the decoration of the later Ming wares is seen to be of a symbolic or emblematic character, appealing to common beliefs. The bowl (no. 45) with a powerful five-clawed dragon reserved in white on a blue ground, along with a floral scroll, is a more traditional piece, its style a deliberate throwback to the early fifteenth century.

The short reign of Longqing (1567–72) produced wares very much in the style of Jiajing. Covered boxes in many shapes (nos. 59, 60), serving a variety of purposes, are among the range of fine blue-and-white products suitably mirroring the luxury that surrounded the Ming court. In the reign of Wanli (1573–1619), however, this tendency extended even further. From this time are found many items made to stand on the scholar's desk: a brush with a porcelain handle (no. 73), a box to contain brushes (no. 75), and a brush rest in the form of three "dragon" peaks (no. 76). "Imperial" five-clawed dragons continued to decorate many of the other imposing wares of this reign, not all of them perhaps made for the court. In style the Wanli wares are generally distinguished by such features as a somewhat grayer and at times silvery toned blue and finer detail in the drawing of the designs, although standards were variable and at times even careless. This might be seen as reflecting the declining fortunes of the imperial house itself, which was increasingly unable to deal effectively with the country's problems, whether economic, social, or military.

Early Seventeenth-Century Wares

A feature of later sixteenth-century blue-and-white is the greatly increased output of wares intended for export to Japan, to the Middle East, and eventually to Europe. Some of these wares reflect foreign tastes, and the Portuguese, who carried much of this trade, might well have influenced the design of the so-called carrack or *kraak* porcelains, as they were called by the Dutch.[16] The dish (no. 78) with a many-paneled border and birds on a riverbank is typical. Thinly made and on occasion finely painted, if rather crowded in style, these wares were shipped westward until the end of the dynasty in quantity by the Dutch, who had seized control of the trade.

The more stoutly made basin (no. 80), which is finely decorated with a large basket of flowers, represents a somewhat different style. It was evidently intended for Japan and is dated by its reign mark of the Tianqi period (1620–27). By long tradition the Japanese had obtained much porcelain from China and in late Ming times they once again became a major client, as the flourishing of the tea ceremony created a demand for ceramic vessels that were both original in design and made to a special taste. The important group of such pieces included in the Idemitsu collection show a variety of pleasing forms and styles and are for the most part types quite unfamiliar in the West until recently.[17] First of these to appear were the *kosometsuke* (old blue-and-white) wares, a rather large class, often somewhat coarse in material and potting, with a glaze susceptible to chipped edges and sometimes found with grit from the kiln still adhering to the underside. Typical are the numerous sets of small dishes in elaborate shapes, such as those of animals or plants. As a whole they are characterized by decoration of unusual spontaneity and freedom, and they display painted subjects that, although mainly Chinese in inspiration, were clearly much to the Japanese liking. Other favored shapes were those of teapots and bowls for *sencha* tea, as well as water jars for use in the traditional ceremony. An octagonal water jar (no. 83) with painting of a vine winding over a trellis is a particularly fine example; in shape or design, such a piece has no counterpart in Chinese domestic taste. Quite un-Chinese in shape

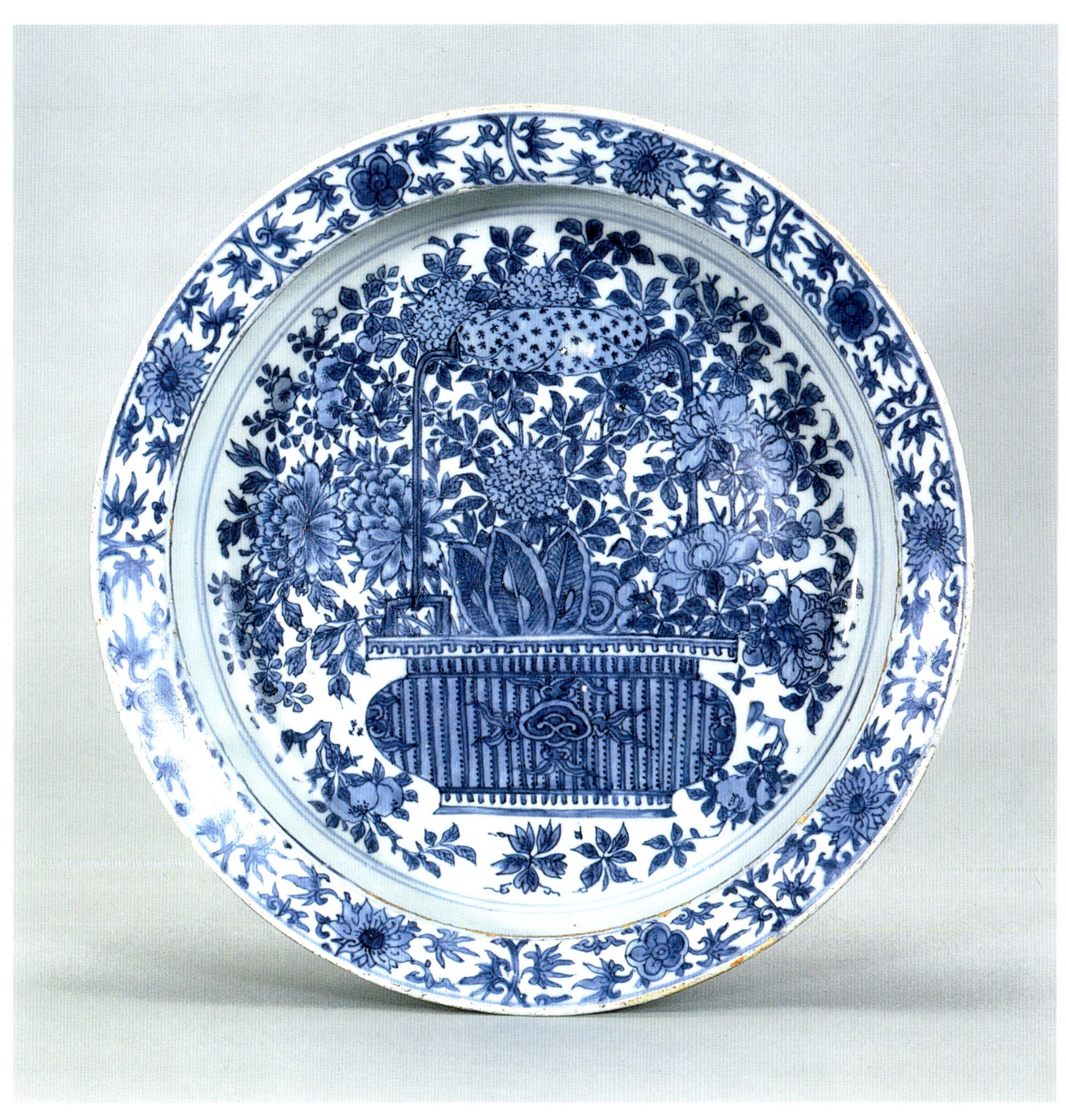

Basin, Ming dynasty,
Tianqi period (1620–27), no. 80

also is the two-handled bowl or dish (no. 81), which depicts a figure riding a mule and pointing to a literary inscription; this might otherwise have been made in Japanese Oribe ware.

Much in demand were incense burners and incense boxes for ceremonial use, writing-brush holders for the desk (no. 84), and flower vases. A celebrated example of the latter (no. 82) was ordered to be made in the shape of a rare Longquan celadon vase of a form, known as *kinuta* in Japan, where examples had been treasured since Song-dynasty times. This blue-and-white version is known by the Japanese term *takasago,* for the resemblance of its painted figures to characters in a Noh drama.

A final significant group of late Ming blue-and-white wares made for Japan appear to date mainly from the reign of Chongzhen (1628–44), or even later, and are if anything even more un-Chinese in character. They are known as *shonzui* wares, on account of an inscription appearing on some pieces, and were at one time thought to have been made in China by a visiting Japanese potter of that name. The inscription, which appears on the high-footed dish (no. 86), now seems more likely to have a Chinese than a Japanese meaning, but this remains to be conclusively determined. *Shonzui*-type porcelain is of superior quality and glazing and generally is painted in a rich violet-toned cobalt. The dish offers a finely painted landscape with figures on the inside, but especially characteristic of the type are the borders of roundels and diaper patterns that decorate the outside. The low-sided water jar (no. 87) painted with delightful flowering trees and birds is another rare and distinguished example of this intriguing late Ming porcelain.

John Ayers is former Keeper of the Far Eastern Department, Victoria and Albert Museum, London.

Notes

1. The most comprehensive study of the wares of this period is by Margaret Medley, *Yuan Porcelain and Stoneware* (London: Faber and Faber, 1974). Cobalt-oxide pigment might first have been imported into South China primarily for medicinal purposes, and its most probable source was Iran. The introduction of cobalt blue is discussed on pp. 32–35.

2. Medley, *Yuan Porcelain and Stoneware,* op. cit., chap. 3 and pl. 24.

3. John Alexander Pope, *Fourteenth-Century Blue-and-White: A Group of Chinese Porcelains in Topkapu Sarayi Muzesi, Istanbul* (Washington: Freer Gallery of Art, 1952; rev. ed. 1970). There is now a complete illustrated catalogue of the collection, *Chinese Ceramics in the Topkapi Saray Museum, Istanbul* by Regina Krahl, edited by John Ayers (London: Sotheby's Publications, 1986), see vol. 2, *Yuan and Ming Dynasty Porcelains.*

4. John Alexander Pope, *Chinese Porcelains from the Ardebil Shrine* (Washington: Freer Gallery of Art, 1956; rev. ed. 1981).

5. See Leandro and Cecilia Locsin, *Oriental Ceramics Discovered in the Philippines* (Rutland, Vermont, and Tokyo: C. E. Tuttle Co., 1967) and the summary article by John Addis, "Chinese Porcelain Found in the Philippines," *Transactions of the Oriental Ceramic Society,* vol. 37 (1967–69), pp. 17–36; also the exhibition catalogue *Oriental Trade Ceramics in Southeast Asia, 10th to 16th Century* by John Guy (Melbourne: National Gallery of Victoria, 1980) and its bibliography.

6. John Ayers, "Buddhist Porcelain Figures of the Yuan Dynasty," *Victoria & Albert Museum Year Book* (London, 1969) pp. 97–109.

7. Yu Yaofu, "Yuandai qinghua mudan tagai ciping," *Wenwu,* no. 1 (1981), p. 83.

8. *Sinan haeja yumul* (Sinan Seacoast Cultural Relics), exhibition catalogue (Seoul: National Museum of Korea, 1977); John Ayers, "The Discovery of a Yuan Ship at Sinan, Southwest of Korea: A First Report," *Oriental Art,* n. s. 24, no. 1 (1978), pp. 79–85; Tokyo National Museum, *The Sunken Treasures off the Sinan Coast,* exhibition catalogue (Tokyo, 1983).

9. Medley, *Yuan Porcelain and Stoneware,* op. cit., pp. 25–26.

10. John Addis, *Chinese Ceramics from Datable Tombs* (London and New York: Sotheby Parke Bernet, 1978), no. 26, p. 38.

11. John Addis, "A Group of Underglaze Red," *Transactions of the Oriental Ceramic Society,* vol. 31 (1957–59), pp. 15–37, and "A Postscript," 1964–66, pp. 89–102; but see also Medley, *Yuan Porcelain and Stoneware,* op. cit., pp. 46–47.

12. *Sekai tōji zenshū* (Ceramic Art of the World), vol. 14, *Ming Dynasty* (Tokyo: Shōgakukan, 1976), pls. 173–75.

13. John Addis, *Chinese Ceramics from Datable Tombs,* op. cit., pls. 37 d, e, and 39 g–j.

14. Osaka Museum of Oriental Ceramics, *Blue & White Wares in the Yuan Dynasty; 14th Century Ching-te Chen Wares,* exhibition catalogue (Osaka, 1985), fig. 51.

15. Compare the very similar dishes and other wares of this period illustrated and discussed in the catalogue of the Topkapi Saray Museum, Istanbul, vol. 2, op. cit., especially nos. 595–96. For Ming wares in general see Pope on the Ardebil collection and Sir Harry Garner, *Oriental Blue and White* (London: Praeger, 1954; 3rd ed., 1970).

16. A recent review of export blue-and-white of this period is provided by Regina Krahl in *Chinese Ceramics in the Topkapi Saray Museum, Istanbul,* op. cit., vol. 2, pp. 595–605.

17. A variety of these Japanese taste wares are described and discussed in *Chinese Ceramics from Japanese Collections* (New York: Asia Society, 1977), the catalogue of an exhibition arranged by Henry Trubner at the Seattle Art Museum.

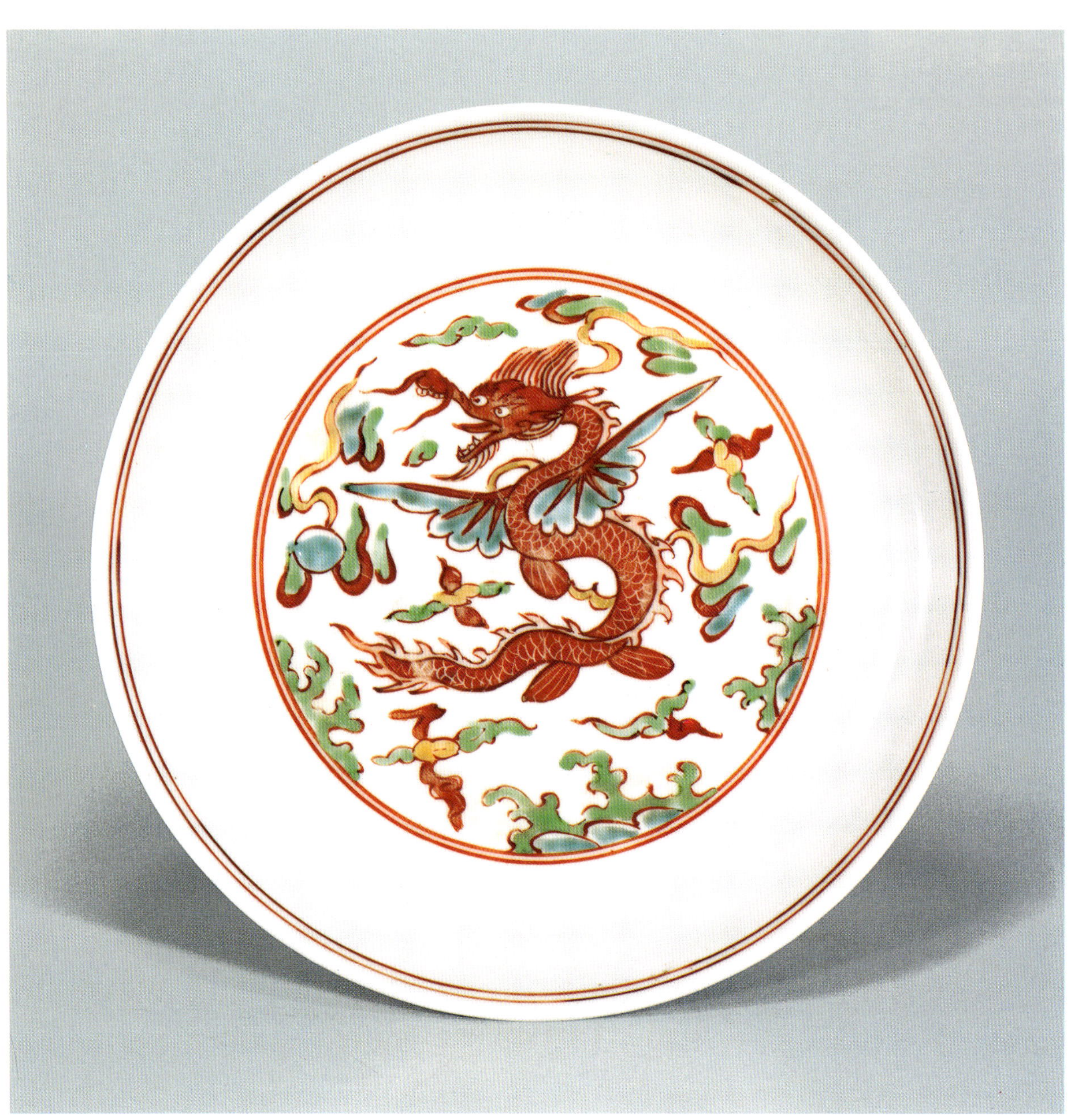

Dish, Ming dynasty, dated 1541?, no. 47

Ming Enamel-Decorated and Polychrome Ceramics

HENRY TRUBNER

The wealth of enameled Ming porcelains contained in the collection of the Idemitsu Museum of Arts provides a comprehensive overview of the development of porcelains decorated with colored enamels. The earliest extant examples of enamels applied to a porcelain body, usually in combination with underglaze blue, can be traced to the early part of the fifteenth century in China. But true polychrome or *wucai* (five-color) porcelain was not fully developed until the Jiajing period (1522–66). Polychrome enameled wares did not attain their full maturity until the sixteenth century, when they flourished during the Jiajing, Longqing (1567–72), and Wanli (1573–1619) reigns.

The weakness of Kublai Khan's successors and the breakup of the powerful Mongol rule led to the ultimate fall of the Yuan dynasty. Following a period of widespread uprisings, the Mongols were overthrown by a Chinese rebel leader, Zhu Yuanzhang, who captured the Mongol capital of Dadu in 1368 and established the native Ming dynasty, with its capital at Nanjing. The accession of Hongwu, the reign title by which Zhu Yuanzhang is commonly known, marked not only the establishment of a new dynasty but a new era for the ceramic industry.

Kiln sites were widely distributed during the Song dynasty, but in the late thirteenth and early fourteenth centuries the Raozhou area in northern Jiangxi, notably Jingdezhen to the east of Raozhou city, became the primary location of the emerging porcelain industry. At the same time, the manufacture of porcelain moved from the preserve of privately owned craftsmen's kilns to that of highly industrialized ceramic centers.[1] Jingdezhen has remained the ceramic metropolis of China to the present day, partially as a result of the local abundance of the raw materials essential for the production of porcelain, notably kaolin, a fine, white porcelain clay.[2]

The ever-increasing output of ceramics produced at Jingdezhen until about 1368 was intended primarily to meet the demands of an expanding foreign trade, especially with Islamic countries of the Near East, as well as a smaller domestic market. But with the establishment of the Ming dynasty and unification of the country, the arts flourished as they had not since the Tang dynasty, some five hundred years earlier. All the arts, including ceramics, lacquerwork, silk weaving, and metalwork, benefited from new imperial patronage and the demand for luxury goods for the emperor and court. Except for a brief period of turmoil and civil strife that occurred between the death of Hongwu and the ascension of the Yongle emperor, the ceramic industry at Jingdezhen entered upon a period of growth and expansion. For at least a century imperial and courtly taste were to determine the development of the decorative arts.

Ming ceramics showed a marked departure from the simple forms and high-fired monochrome glazes of the primarily stoneware Song ceramics in favor of true porcelain with underglaze cobalt-blue and copper-red decoration, technical innovations first introduced early in the fourteenth century. It only remained for the potters of Jingdezhen to add the technique of painting the finest quality porcelain bodies in colored enamels, a significant advance in ceramic decorative style.

The various aspects of Ming enameled porcelains and polychrome wares illustrated by examples in the Idemitsu collection can be arranged according to the following principal types and subgroups.

1. The red-and-green family of overglaze enameled wares. As the name implies, red and green are the predominant colors, sometimes with the addition of yellow enamel (no. 47).
2. Green enameled wares, mostly shallow bowls and dishes, decorated with dragons in green, enameled on biscuit, wax-resisted (no. 34) or enameled over a white glaze (no. 33). There are also examples of red dragon bowls, enameled in overglaze iron-red (no. 38), relating this type to the red-and-green family. The *sancai* (three-color) wares, enameled on biscuit, are a variant of the technique used for the green dragon bowls (no. 39).
3. The *wucai* (five-color) wares, which were predominant in the sixteenth century. The term is a synonym for polychrome-decorated wares (not in any way limited to five colors). In the earliest examples the enamels were used without underglaze blue (no. 56), but in the fully developed style polychrome enamels were freely applied in combination with underglaze cobalt blue (nos. 63, 66). Sometimes gold-leaf designs were applied upon an iron-red ground, a technique that emerged around the middle of the sixteenth century. Porcelains decorated in the *kinrande* technique found a ready market in Japan, where they were eagerly sought by tea masters for use in the tea ceremony (nos. 51, 52).
4. The Ming export wares, comprising both blue-and-white and enameled wares. The latter include *shonzui*-type ware (no. 88), made for the Japanese market, and the boldly decorated Swatow porcelains produced at kilns in southeast China (nos. 89, 90). Swatow porcelains were widely exported to Southeast Asia and Japan.
5. The *fahua* group of wares, decorated in lead-fluxed glazes applied directly to a stoneware body (nos. 57, 58), and the blue-and-yellow wares, decorated in underglaze-blue and overglaze enamels, essentially a subgroup of blue-and-white porcelain. This group is limited to shallow dishes with decoration of floral-and-fruit sprays (nos. 36, 37).

Red-and-Green Wares

The application of colored enamels to a previously fired and glazed white porcelain body was one of the major technical innovations of Ming potters seeking new ways to decorate the porcelains produced at the Jingdezhen kilns. The earliest examples, decorated only in red and green enamels, were produced about the middle of the fifteenth century.

Enamel-decorated wares were fired twice. The first firing followed the application of the underglaze-blue painting (if any) and the white glaze and was done at a high temperature, about 1250 degrees centigrade, in order to fuse both the porcelain body and the glaze. A second firing at a somewhat lower temperature, about 850 to 900 degrees centigrade, followed the application of the colored lead-silicate enamels, a form of glass used like glaze. The lower temperature was sufficient to fuse the enamels to the glaze without disturbing the underlying glaze.

Colored enamels applied to a stoneware body had been employed in Cizhou wares of the late twelfth and thirteenth centuries,[3] but no clear connection can be established between the earlier Cizhou products, which are strictly a northern ware, and the later enameled wares of the Ming period, which are largely southern products from the Jingdezhen kilns. Nor is there any explanation for the hiatus between the first use of enamels and its reappearance some two hundred years later.

The red-and-green enameled wares soon became popular and occurred in a variety of forms during the Chenghua period (1465–87) and beyond. They were still widely prevalent during the sixteenth century, even when the elaborately decorated *wucai* polychrome wares flourished. The style is well illustrated by a shallow dish decorated on both the interior and exterior with red, green, and yellow enamels on a ground of white glaze (no. 47).[4] The design consists of winged dragons with fishlike bodies (*feiyu* or "flying fish-dragon"), primarily in red enamels, among clouds and waves, mostly in green with touches of yellow enamel. The decoration is bordered by double lines in red, which also surround the foot and interior of the rim. A four-character cyclical year mark in red enamel and enclosed within a double circle on the base can be read as either the seventeenth year of Chenghua (1481) or the twentieth year of Jiajing (1541). The later date is more likely correct, based on style (especially the presence of the winged dragons) and characteristics of the porcelain body, which lacks the refinement of the Chenghua wares and is more in keeping with the coarser, heavier bodies of Jiajing.

Green-Enameled and *Sancai* Wares

Ming green-enameled porcelain is confined mainly to bowls and dishes, ranging in date from the reign of Chenghua to the end of Zhengde (1506–21). A number of pieces perhaps originally intended for enameling have survived, and they clearly illustrate this unusual technique. A bowl with milky white glaze and incised dragons around the exterior (no. 35) is a good example. Here the dragon designs were incised in the porcelain body but were never enameled after the glaze was applied to the remainder of the piece. As a result the design burned orange in the firing, and waves, clouds, and streamers appear as finely incised designs under the glaze. A six-character Hongzhi (1488–1501) mark in underglaze blue within a double circle is seen on the base.[5] A second dragon bowl (no. 34) with a Hongzhi mark is decorated on both the exterior and interior with dragons among clouds and waves but with the design in green enamel over a white glaze instead of enamel on biscuit. The contours and scales of the dragon bodies were incised under the glaze. This bowl can be considered a later and simplified version of the enamel-on-biscuit technique.

Stylistically similar to this green-decorated dragon bowl is a red-enameled bowl (no. 38). The design of dragons among clouds and waves, disposed around the exterior and contained within a circular medallion on the interior, were again first incised in the biscuit. The bowl was then covered with a white glaze, and the dragon designs were subsequently painted in an overglaze iron-red enamel. The billowing waves below the dragons on the exterior were, in addition, painted in an overglaze-green enamel. The bowl, which has a four-character Zhengde mark in overglaze red within a double circle on the base, relates more properly to the red-and-green family, illustrated by the dragon bowl (no. 47).

A leys jar or waste vessel in the shape known as *zhadou* (no. 39), represents a type known in blue-and-white as well as green-and-yellow enamel decoration. The vessel belongs to the enamel-on-biscuit family of *sancai* wares and is a variant of the green-enamel-on-biscuit type. The design of the present example, with five-clawed dragons chasing flaming pearls on the body and neck of the vessel and with a band of false gadroons above the foot, was first incised in the biscuit. Green and yellow enamels were then applied directly to the biscuit body. The inside and underside of the foot were glazed white, and a four-character Zhengde mark in underglaze blue within a double circle is centered within the foot ring.

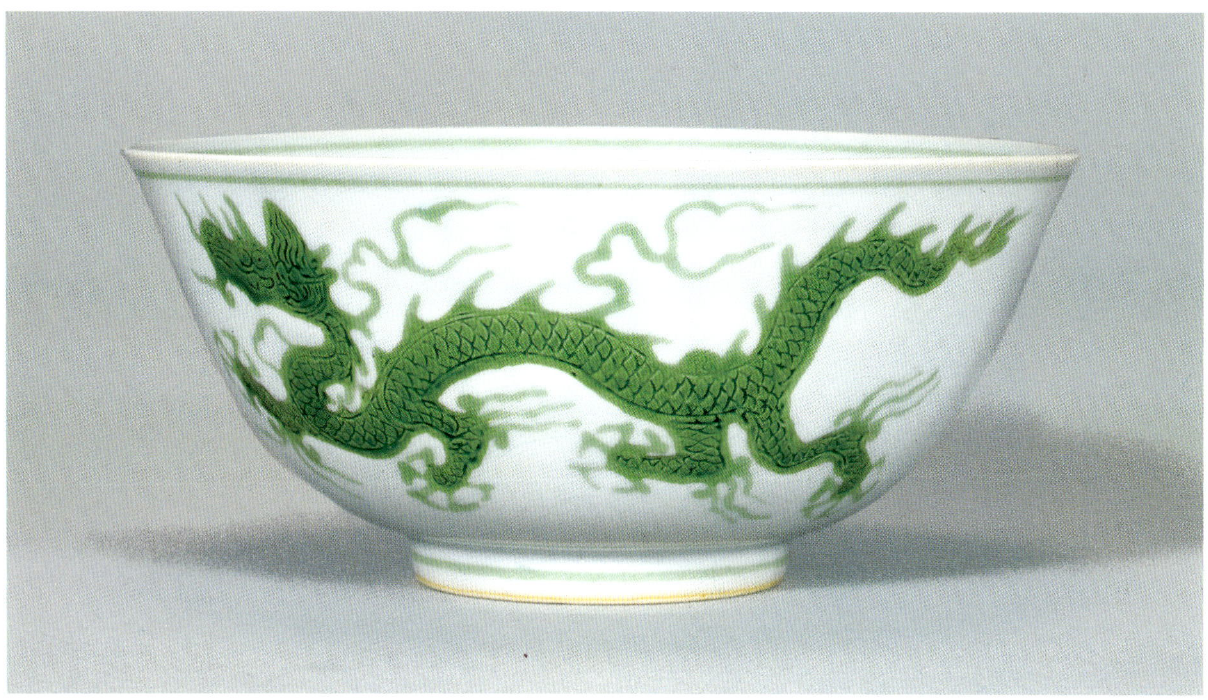

Bowl, Ming dynasty,
Hongzhi period (1488–1505), no. 34

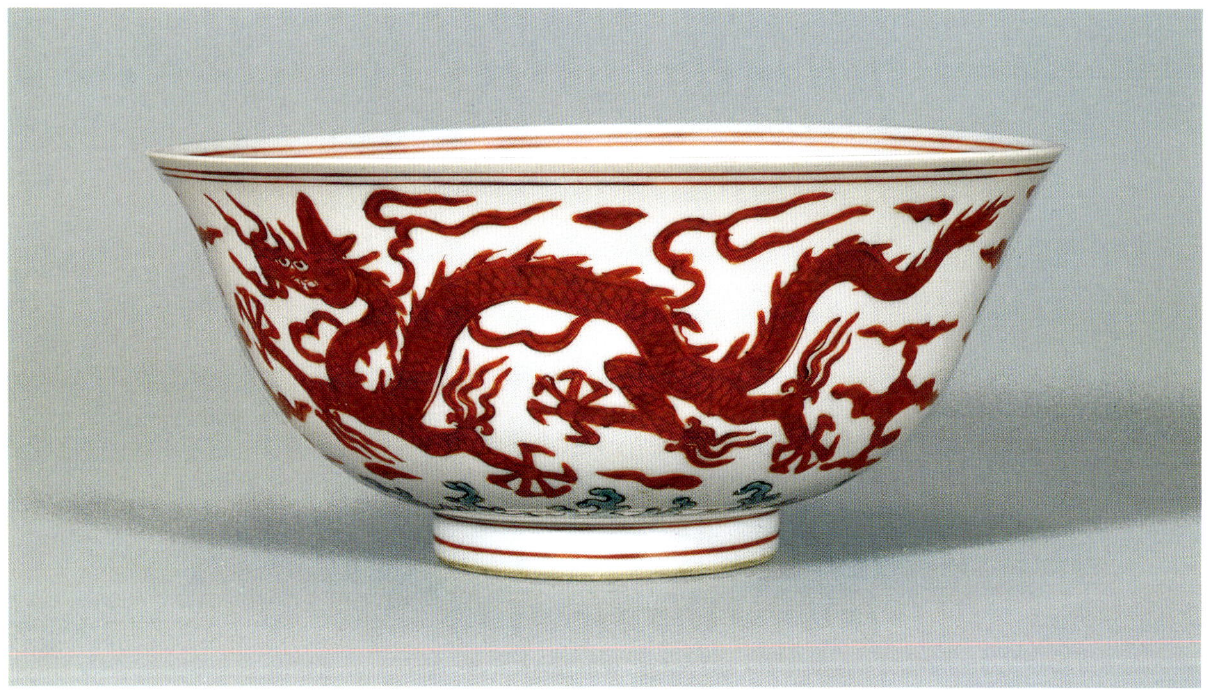

Bowl, Ming dynasty,
Zhengde period (1506–21), no. 38

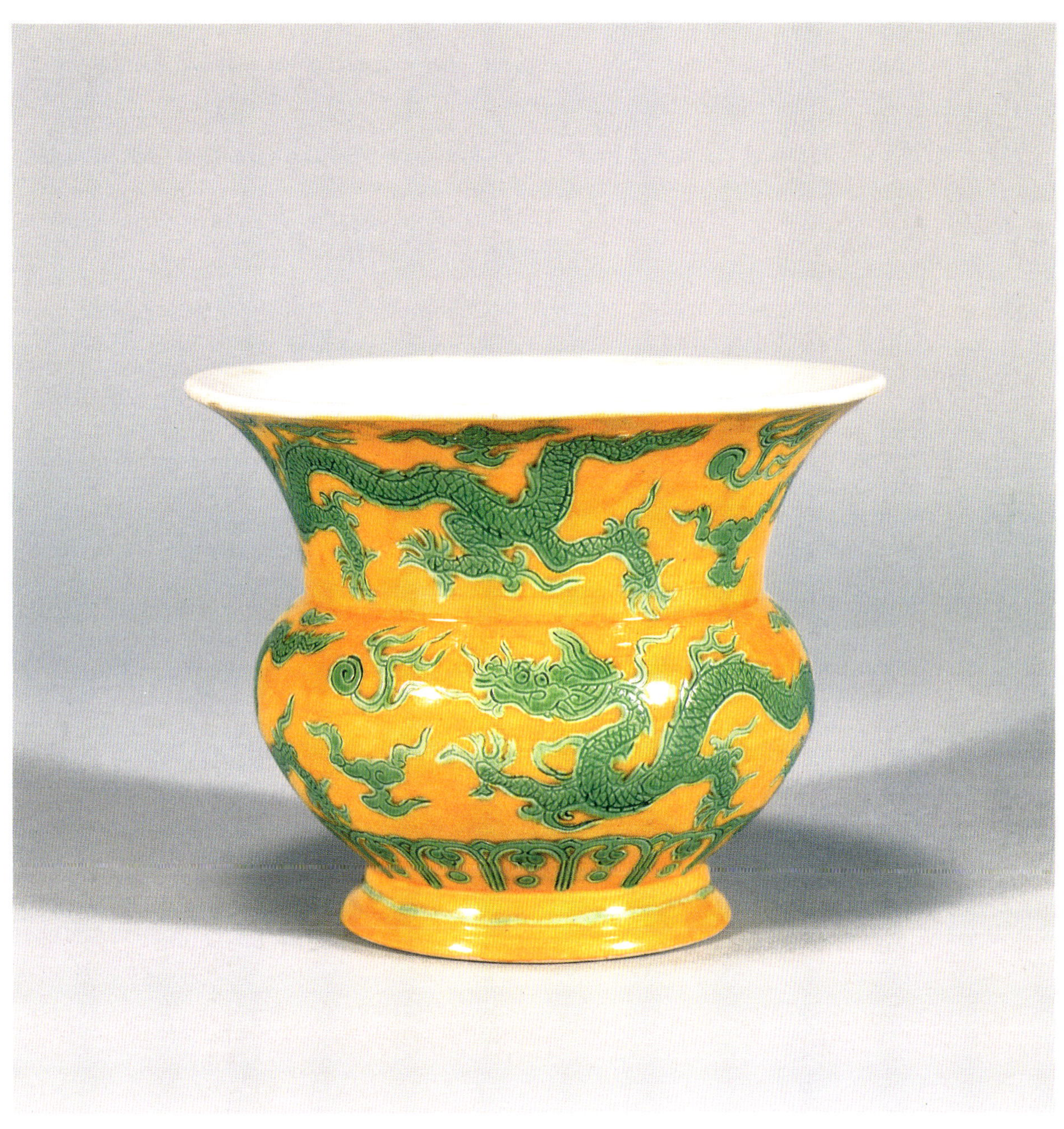

Zhadou, Ming dynasty,
Zhengde period (1506–21), no. 39

Wucai Wares

Colorful and elaborately decorated polychrome porcelains decorated in *wucai* (five-color) enamels flourished from the Jiajing through the Wanli periods. Developed from earlier red-and-green enameled wares, these wares were decorated in brilliant colors, primarily yellow, turquoise, aubergine, purple, and black. Red and black were used to outline the decoration on the glaze. Because the outlines were applied to a previously fired glaze, it was possible to make corrections in the contours and to wipe off existing outlines without disturbing the glaze. The *wucai* technique therefore offered potters more flexibility in ceramic decoration.

In the earliest *wucai,* overglaze enamels were applied without the use of underglaze blue. It is likely that this technique originated toward the end of the fifteenth century, during the Hongzhi period.[6] The principal colors used were red, green, yellow, and aubergine, as well as a turquoise enamel that took the place of underglaze blue. This technique was certainly established by the early sixteenth century and is well illustrated by several important examples (nos. 40, 52, 54–56). None of these has a reign mark, but they are no doubt products of the Jiajing period. By this time the traditional repertoire of dragons and clouds had lost ground to popular themes featuring figural and floral subjects; birds, especially phoenixes or peacocks; and aquatic settings with fish, waterfowl, and plants. The Jiajing decorative style exhibited a new vigor and freshness of motifs as well as technical innovations spurred by increased demand from the court and the expanding export trade. As a result of this growing output, a certain quality and refinement was sometimes lost but often compensated for by the exuberance and vitality of these porcelains. The jar and cover (no. 56), the covered box (no. 55), and the bowl with sages engaged in a game of chess and other pastimes (no. 40) are good examples of the growing interest in figural subjects.

A subgroup of Jiajing enameled wares made its appearance about the middle of the sixteenth century and is recognized by the predominant use of iron red, usually in combination with lesser amounts of green and yellow and limited areas of turquoise and black. Painting in underglaze blue might also be present. What distinguishes this group, however, is the application of gold-leaf designs upon the red ground, usually in the form of floral scrolls and arabesques (nos. 51–53). Bowls with red medallions and gilt decoration (no. 51) and footed ewers derived from a contemporary Chinese metal form (no. 52) were especially popular. Known as *kinrande* (gold-brocade design) in Japan, the method was highly esteemed by Japanese tea masters, who favored such wares for use in the tea ceremony; most *kinrande* porcelain was probably produced to fill their requirements. *Kinrande* ware also reached the Middle East but was largely unknown in Europe. The splendid jar with handles and panel decoration of peacocks amidst tree peonies, with mandarin ducks and lotus plants on the reverse side (no. 53), is an example of *kinrande* at its very best. Unusual in shape, the piece has no reign mark, but its ornamentation places it clearly in the Jiajing period.

The short-lived Longqing period (1567–72) produced relatively few ceramics compared to the vast output of the preceding Jiajing and the succeeding Wanli periods. Two splendid examples, blue-and-white boxes with covers, one rectangular and one round (nos. 59, 60), are typical of the porcelain products of this short reign, some decorated only in underglaze blue, others in *wucai* style in underglaze blue and overglaze enamels.[7] The Longqing wares continued to reflect the demands of the emperor and court for boldly decorated porcelains.

The Wanli period (1573–1619) saw the continuation of the decorative schemes developed in the Jiajing reign and the full maturity of the *wucai* polychrome style. Although the porcelains were lavishly and variously decorated with elaborate and richly colored designs in underglaze

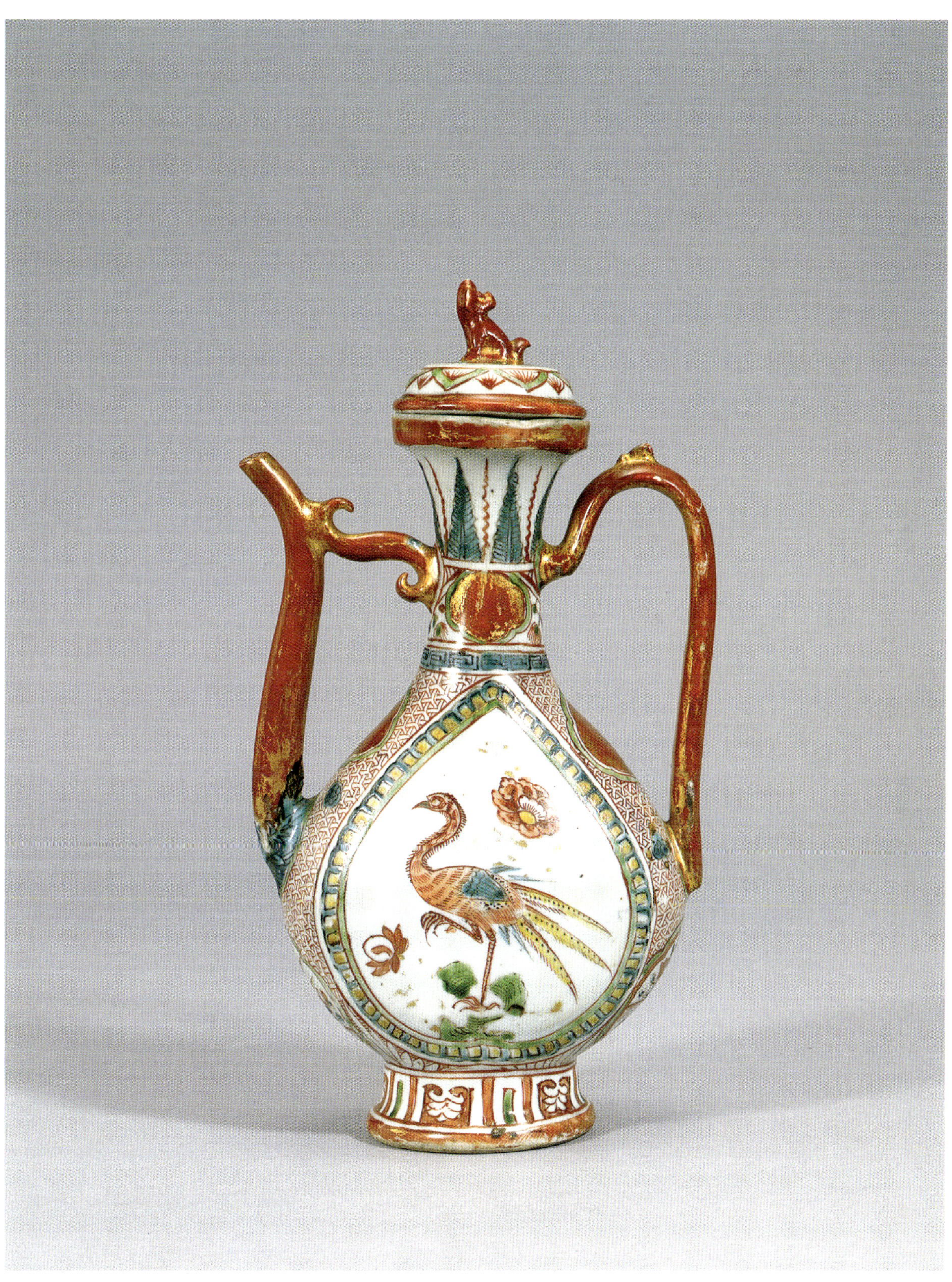

Ewer, Ming dynasty,
second half 16th century, no. 52

blue and overglaze enamels, the quality of the wares declined, notably toward the end of the sixteenth century. The Wanli court made ever larger and more frequent orders, and export trade continued to grow. The demands brought about by mass production soon depleted kaolin supplies at Jingdezhen and the short supply of imported cobalt. Potters came to rely more and more on existing processes and decorative styles, whose capacities they now pushed to their limits.

The Idemitsu collection possesses examples of Wanli porcelains decorated in the *wucai* technique that rank among the finest of their kind and illustrate the richness and variety of decorative motifs and designs prevalent at the time. Some are decorated with the traditional dragon-and-phoenix motif of pieces reserved for the personal use of the emperor and empress (nos. 62, 67); other designs clearly show a movement away from formal themes in a search for fresh sources of inspiration and new markets to replace waning imperial patronage.

In many instances *wucai*-decorated pieces have a counterpart in blue-and-white porcelain. Wanli underglaze blue was usually applied in broad washes and tends to be cloudy and more silvery than the brilliant luminous blue of the Jiajing era. The octagonal basin (no. 62), profusely decorated with imperial five-clawed dragons and clouds, has a parallel in the similarly decorated blue-and-white basin (no. 61). Such basins, some decorated with figures in landscape settings rather than the traditional dragon motif, were popular in the Wanli period[8] and reflect the opulence and splendor of the Wanli court.

A covered box of lobed shape, suggesting an open flower, and decorated in *wucai* style with figures in a setting of pine trees (no. 65), has a close parallel in a blue-and-white box with a similar design. Such boxes found a ready market in Japan, where they came to be used as water containers in the tea ceremony. Another box has a dome-shaped cover and is compartmented on the interior (no. 64). Richly decorated with designs of flowers in *wucai* enamels and underglaze blue, it is complemented by a similar box decorated in blue-and-white with formal dragon designs (no. 63). Covered boxes of this type, as well as rectangular and other shapes, were in demand throughout the Wanli period.

The splendid large fishbowl with decoration of mandarin ducks and lotus plants illustrates another favorite subject (no. 66). A new interest in designs of flowers and birds is seen in several pieces (nos. 68, 71, 72), and themes with figures, usually in garden or landscape settings, likewise enjoyed wide popularity (no. 69). Some of these designs were inspired by illustrated books of poems, dramas, legendary history, and anecdotes. Religious subjects, representing Shou Lao, the god of longevity, together with the emblems of immortality, were also introduced. The illustrated books were widely circulated, some as early as the Jiajing period, and thus provided a vast body of source material to inspire the artists who decorated the porcelains.

Of stylistic interest is a Wanli jar with a design of dragons in ogival panels, floral scrolls, and a stylized band of lappets around the shoulder incised under the glaze and decorated in green enamels on a yellow ground (no. 70). In appearance the jar, in contrast with prevailing Wanli *wucai*-enameled wares, relates more closely to the earlier Zhengde-period leys jar with green enameled dragons on yellow ground (no. 39). But whereas the Zhengde jar was enameled directly on the biscuit, the present Wanli example was enameled over a white glaze, the technique in vogue at the time and a modification of the earlier *sancai* method.

The pear-shaped vase with design of butterflies and flowers in underglaze-blue and overglaze enamels (no. 85) continues the *wucai* tradition, but its delicate and subdued design, with large areas of plain white glaze serving as the ground for the enameled decoration, clearly places it in a later period than Wanli. In its subtlety of decoration and restrained use of colors the vase anticipates the wares of the Transitional period (1620–83).[9] As its name implies, this period

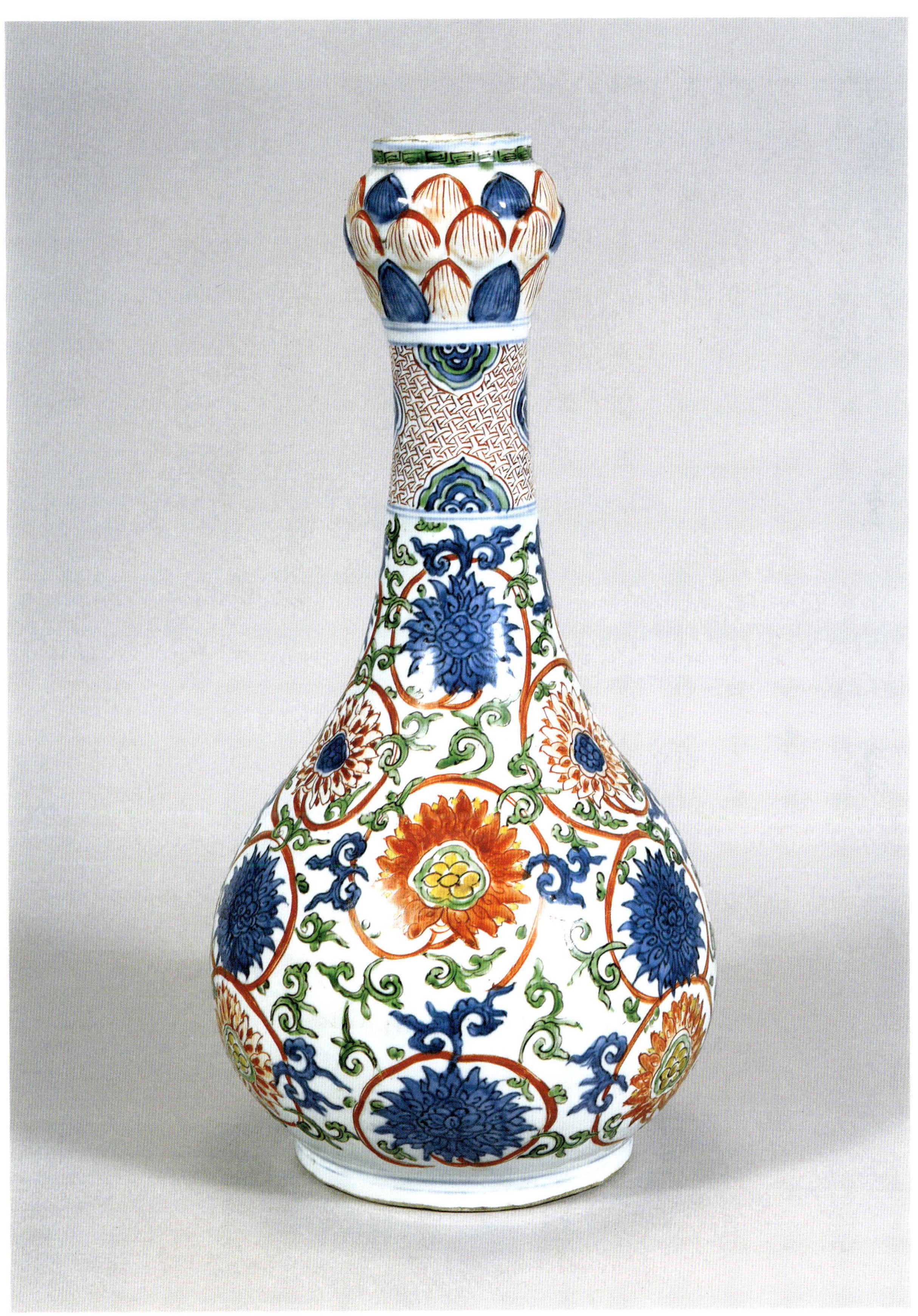

Garlic-headed bottle, Ming dynasty,
Wanli period (1573–1619), no. 72

covers the years when kiln production was not controlled by the imperial court, between the death of the Wanli emperor in 1620 and the arrival of the Qing Kangxi emperor's supervisor of ceramic production at Jingdezhen, Cang Yingxuan.

Ming Export Wares

Toward the end of the sixteenth century, the Chinese export trade began to expand significantly. As a result of the Wanli emperor's depleted financial resources, more and more money was diverted from official support of the Jingdezhen ceramic industry to fight numerous peasant uprisings and other domestic conflicts, which increasingly threatened the stability of the central government. At the time of the Wanli emperor's death, a marked increase in internal strife forced the total withdrawal of all imperial support of ceramic production in order to finance the Ming armies. The Jingdezhen potters therefore had to look elsewhere for patronage and for markets, which came to embrace Japan, Southeast Asia, the Middle East, and eventually Europe.

It was natural for the Japanese to fill the gap left by the suspension of imperial patronage of the ceramic industry. Many of the Jingdezhen products had in fact already found a ready market in Japan, notably the *kinrande* wares of the Jiajing period, the so-called *shonzui* ware, Tianqi-period (1620–27) enameled wares, as well as *kosometsuke,* a late Ming blue-and-white ware intended for export to Japan.

The dish with underglaze-blue and enameled decoration depicting a landscape within a central panel, surrounded by geometric patterns and a floral scroll around the rim (no. 88), is an example of colored *shonzui* ware made for the Japanese market. Most *shonzui* ware is decorated only in underglaze blue (no. 86), but there are instances of enameled porcelain of *shonzui* type. Contrary to the traditional theory that *shonzui* ware was produced by a Japanese potter who went to China to learn porcelain making, it is generally believed today that the ware was ordered in China by Japanese tea masters to serve as tea ceremony utensils.

Another distinctive group of Chinese export porcelain is known as Swatow ware, after the port city of Swatow, in Fujian province in southeast China, from where it was shipped. Developed in the course of the sixteenth century and produced at kilns in the extreme north of Guangdong, the ware was exported primarily to Southeast Asia and Japan. An important find of Swatow fragments recovered from Ichijō-in, a priest's residence at the Kōfuku-ji in Nara, documented extensive exports to Japan in the first half of the seventeenth century. The Ichijō-in was destroyed by fire in 1642; therefore, the Swatow fragments must have been imported prior to this date.

Swatow ware is most frequently decorated in polychrome enamels, but blue-and-white as well as slip-painted wares, the latter mostly on a light blue or light brown ground, were produced. Large plates and dishes as well as jars are the most common shapes, although bowls, and occasionally vases, also occur. Swatow porcelain is, as a rule, roughly made, especially the large dishes, and the foot ring and base are almost always splashed with glaze and covered with large amounts of grit from the bottom of the fire box, an indication that the potters were careless in placing the wares and firing the kiln. But these irregularities appealed to the Japanese and are among the hallmarks of Swatow porcelain that help in the identification of individual pieces.

Several magnificent examples of Swatow porcelain in the Idemitsu collection illustrate its distinguishing features. Decorated in red, green, and turquoise enamels, one of the dishes is decorated with a bold design of a fabulous animal (no. 89); the other depicts two figures and a horse in an outdoor setting (no. 90). The great freedom and spontaneity of the designs and the rough

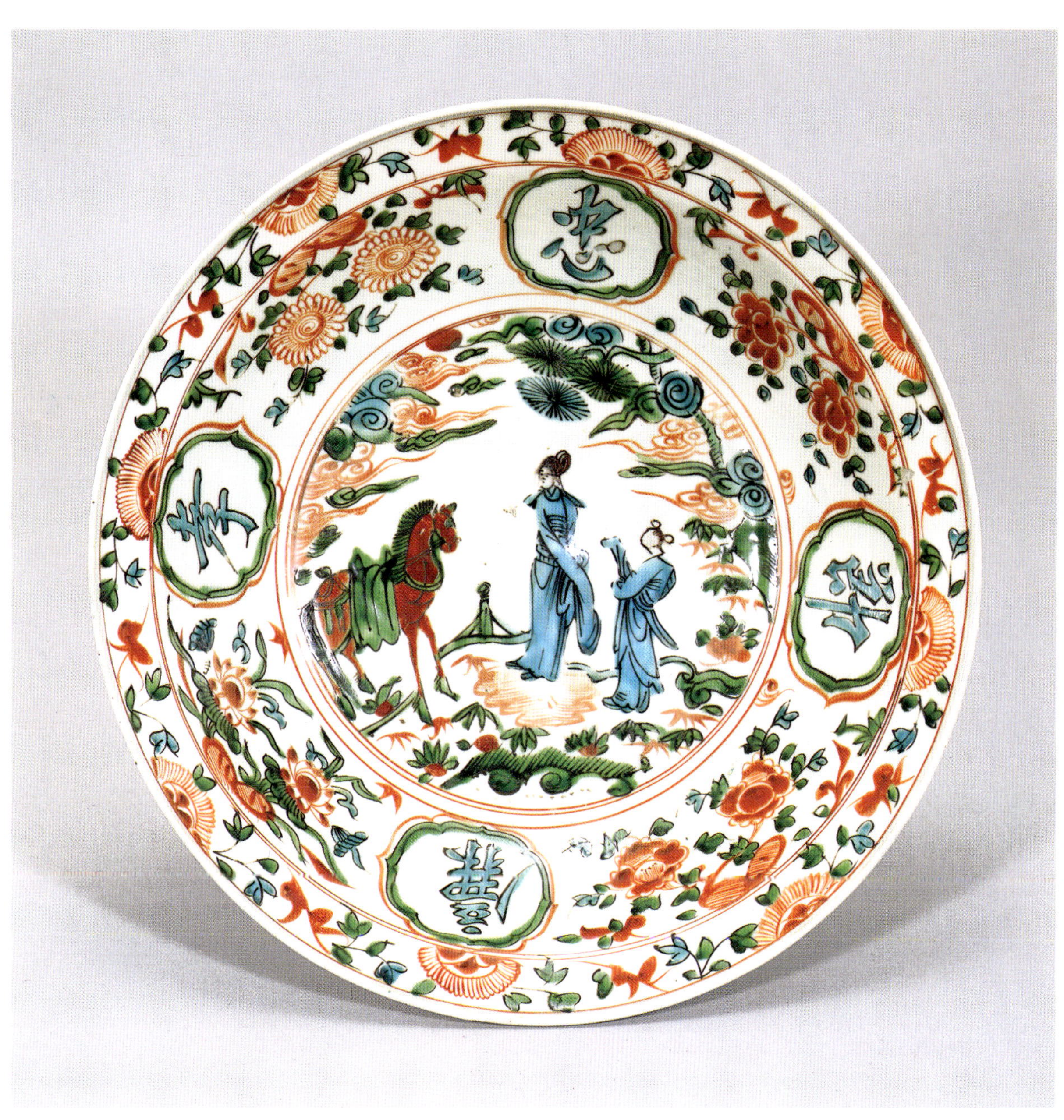

Large dish, Ming dynasty,
late 16th to first half 17th century, no. 90

potting and finish of Swatow porcelain contrast with the formal decoration of the more refined Jingdezhen porcelains.

Fahua and Blue-and-Yellow Wares

Two subgroups of Ming-dynasty polychrome decoration must also be mentioned. One is the so-called *fahua* wares, a group distinguished by the use of lead-fluxed glazes applied directly to the stoneware body without the intermediate transparent glaze associated with enameled wares. The second group, in a sense a subgroup of blue-and-white porcelain, consists of pieces decorated in underglaze blue with a yellow enamel applied to the white ground in a second firing, resulting in a design in blue on a yellow ground.

Deep cobalt blue, turquoise, and aubergine are the principal *fahua* colors, and these were used in combination with limited amounts of white, brown, or yellow. Popular decorative themes included figures in landscape settings, some probably of Daoist or literary derivation, as well as bands and floral compositions. The most commonly found *fahua* shapes are large *guan* jars, a variety of vases, and large garden seats. *Fahua* bodies often show imperfections and are generally of inferior quality when compared with other wares of the period.

The *fahua* group is represented in the Idemitsu collection by two characteristic examples: a large jar of *guan* type decorated with mounted figures (no. 57) and a pair of vases with elephant-head handles (no. 58). One of the distinguishing features of *fahua*-type ware, besides the application of colored glazes directly to the stoneware body, is the use of thin threads of trailed slip to outline the decoration, with details indicated by incised lines. When the colored glazes were applied within the lines of trailed slip, the latter served to separate the different glaze colors, in much the same way that enamel pastes are prevented from running when placed within the separate cells of cloisonné metalwork. The Idemitsu *guan* jar and the pair of vases are given a Jiajing date, the period when this ware flourished, although some *fahua* pieces might have been made somewhat earlier, around the end of the fifteenth century.

The second subgroup of Ming polychrome wares consists of the blue-and-yellow wares. This category is restricted to a series of shallow dishes, produced for the Ming court from Xuande through successive Ming reigns and revived in the early reigns of the Qing dynasty. Although dishes decorated in underglaze-blue and overglaze-yellow enamels are the most frequent, the same design also occurs in plain underglaze blue without the addition of the yellow enamel,[10] in white reserved on a blue ground,[11] and in a coffee-brown enamel on white ground.[12]

The two Idemitsu blue-and-yellow examples (nos. 36, 37) date from the Hongzhi and Zhengde reigns respectively. The designs of the various dishes in this Ming group follow a common pattern. The center is usually decorated with a floral spray in the form of two large flowers and a bud; four large flower and fruiting sprays are displayed around the cavetto. Floral sprays or scrolls decorate the outside. The reign mark is written in underglaze blue within a double circle on the base, or if the base is left unglazed, as on some of the Xuande and Chenghua dishes, the underglaze-blue mark appears in a cartouche on the outside of the dish, below the rim.[13]

Once the design had been painted in underglaze blue and if the piece was not to be left in plain blue and white (or white on blue ground), a yellow enamel was applied in a second firing, leaving the design in blue on a yellow ground. This remained a popular method of decoration throughout the Ming period, from Xuande on. Subtle differences in the coloring of the underglaze-blue and the overglaze-yellow enamel are associated with certain Ming reigns, but without reference to the reign marks, which can never be trusted completely, it is difficult to differentiate between blue-and-yellow dishes of different reigns.

Ming polychromes, like the blue-and-white wares, illustrate the successive states of ceramic development during this period. Both wares led directly to the rise in the seventeenth century of Transitional-period porcelains and the subsequent growth of the Jingdezhen ceramic industry under the Qing rulers. We are very fortunate that the Idemitsu Museum of Arts is the custodian of such an outstanding and superb collection of Ming ceramics, which has no parallel in the West. It provides a rare opportunity for new and significant insights into the wares of this critical period in the history of Chinese ceramic development.

Henry Trubner is Senior Curator Emeritus, Seattle Art Museum.

Notes

1. Margaret Medley, *The Chinese Potter: A Practical History of Chinese Ceramics* (New York: Scribner's, 1976), p. 171.

2. The majority of high-fire Chinese glazes applied to porcelain and stoneware bodies fall into two groups: lime glazes and lime-alkali glazes. Only very few examples of the latter type are feldspathic. The role traditionally believed to have been played by feldspar in the production of Chinese porcelain and glazes was in fact, in South China, performed by potassium mica. Where feldspar does occur, it tends to operate only as a secondary flux to the potassium mica. Nigel Wood, "The Two International Conferences on Ancient Chinese Pottery and Porcelain," *Transactions of the Oriental Ceramic Society,* vol. 50 (1985–86), pp. 40–44.

3. Compare with a Yuan-dynasty bowl in the Seattle Art Museum, Trubner et al, *Asiatic Art in the Seattle Art Museum* (Seattle Art Museum, 1973), p. 57, col. pl. 136; pp. 178–79, pl. 136.

4. *Chinese Ceramics in the Idemitsu Collection* (Tokyo: Heibonsha, 1987), p. 300, no. 182 and col. pl. 182.

5. Similar unfinished pieces in various collections are known. See Medley, *The Chinese Potter,* op. cit., p. 210, fig. 156. For the finished green-enamel-on-biscuit type, see also fig. 157 and Medley, *Ming Polychrome Wares in the Percival David Foundation of Chinese Art* (London, 1966), pl. 9, nos. A725, A726 (not illustrated). See also the green enameled bowl in the Russell Tyson collection, the Art Institute of Chicago, and a dish with dragons in reserve but without the green enamel in the Avery Brundage collection, Suzanne G. Valenstein, *Ming Porcelains, A Retrospective* (New York: China Institute in America, 1970), p. 67, no. 39 and p. 58, no. 30.

6. Valenstein, *Ming Porcelains,* op. cit., p. 17.

7. Two square jars, one in the Idemitsu collection, the other in the Tokyo National Museum, are decorated in underglaze-blue and overglaze enamels with design of birds and flowers within ogival panels and dragons in horizontal bands. See *Chinese Ceramics in the Idemitsu Collection,* op. cit., p. 341, no. 710, pl. 710 and *Sekai tōji zenshū* (Ceramic Art of the World), vol. 14, *Ming Dynasty* (Tokyo: Shōgakukan, 1976), p. 97, pl. 101. See also the Longqing dish in *wucai* style with decoration of dragons chasing flaming pearls, p. 96, pl. 100.

8. *Sekai tōji zenshū,* op. cit., pp. 102–193, pls. 104–105.

9. Compare Stephen Little, *Chinese Ceramics of the Transitional Period: 1620–1683* (New York: China Institute in America, 1974), p. 41, no. 4 and p. 55, no. 15.

10. John Ayers, *Chinese Ceramics: The Koger Collection* (London and New York: Sotheby, 1985), pp. 94–95, pls. 70–71.

11. Soame Jenyns, *Ming Pottery and Porcelain* (London: Faber and Faber, 1953), pl. 60A.

12. *Sekai tōji zenshū,* op. cit., pp. 66–67, pls. 68–69.

13. Ibid., nos. 174, 638.

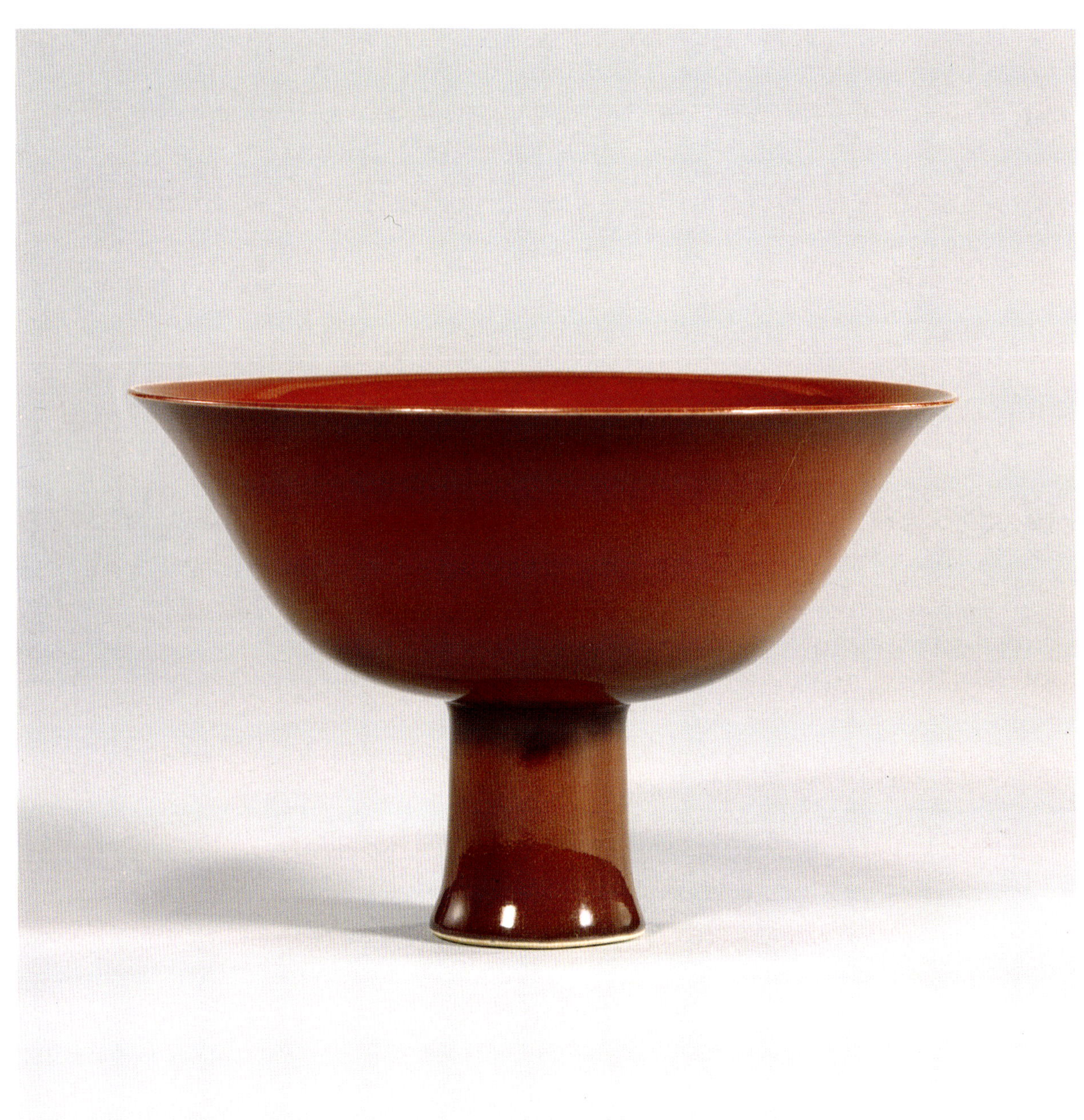

Stem cup, Ming dynasty,
Yongle period (1403–24), no. 16

Advances in Jingdezhen Research

TADANORI YUBA

Although Ming-dynasty ceramic wares have been abundantly studied from the points of view of aesthetics and connoisseurship, new approaches to ceramic research based on archaeological methodology and conducted from the standpoint of the function of ceramic objects as trade wares are ever increasing. Since the establishment of the People's Republic of China in 1949, excavations and scientific research conducted in China at ancient kiln sites have yielded a wealth of new material. This essay will focus on the kiln sites at Jingdezhen in Jiangxi province, which I visited in September of 1987, and discuss recent discoveries in Yuan- and Ming-dynasty porcelain.

Origins of Underglaze-Blue-Decorated Porcelain: New Material

New finds that I examined at Jingdezhen included both dated Yuan-dynasty porcelain and porcelain from datable Yuan tombs. Among these objects is an underglaze blue-and-red lidded jar, decorated with the *sishen* (Four Divine Animals), which was found in 1979 in a shop in Fengchengxian in Jiangxi province (fig. 1). Although this piece did not come from a controlled excavation, an inscription written on the jar indicates it was produced for a tomb located in Jingdezhen. There were actually four pieces so discovered: the lidded jar, an underglaze blue-and-red decorated model of a two-storied pavilion, and two sculptural figures of officials colored in copper-red glaze.[1] These new discoveries are especially noteworthy since both the jar and pavilion have Yuan-dynasty inscriptions corresponding to the year 1338. They thus predate by thirteen years the well-known pair of temple vases in the Percival David Foundation, which are inscribed with dates corresponding to 1351, and are extremely valuable in gaining a more complete understanding of the origins of underglaze-blue-decorated porcelain and its early development.

The Fengchengxian jar, only 22.5 centimeters high, consists of the body itself and a lid; except for one area the piece is in extremely fine condition. The body has a wide mouth, a short neck, and swelling shoulders, with the belly tapering to the base. The *sishen* or four divine animals (the Green Dragon, White Tiger, Black Tortoise, and Red Phoenix) were each molded and applied to the vessel and colored blue and red before glazing and firing. The dragon and tiger ascend upward from the belly to the shoulder, each forming one handle. The dragon is complete, but the tiger's head is now missing. The tortoise and the phoenix were applied in molded relief on opposite sides of the belly. The areas in between the animals were decorated with molded appliqués of scrolling arabesques. Lotus panels with raised outlines encircle the base. The underglaze-blue inscriptions written on the neck and shoulder respectively read: *Da Yuan zhiyuan wuyin liu yue* renyin *ji zhi* (Made on the auspicious day of *renyin* in the sixth month of the *wuyin* year of the Zhiyuan reign of the great Yuan), a date corresponding to 1338, and *Liu Dashi Zhai Ling shi yong* (To be used for Mistress Ling of the household of Ambassador Liu).

The lid itself is a distinctive form. Two pearl-beaded rings circle the periphery of the slightly domed top. The area enclosed by the inner ring contains the eight Buddhist emblems in

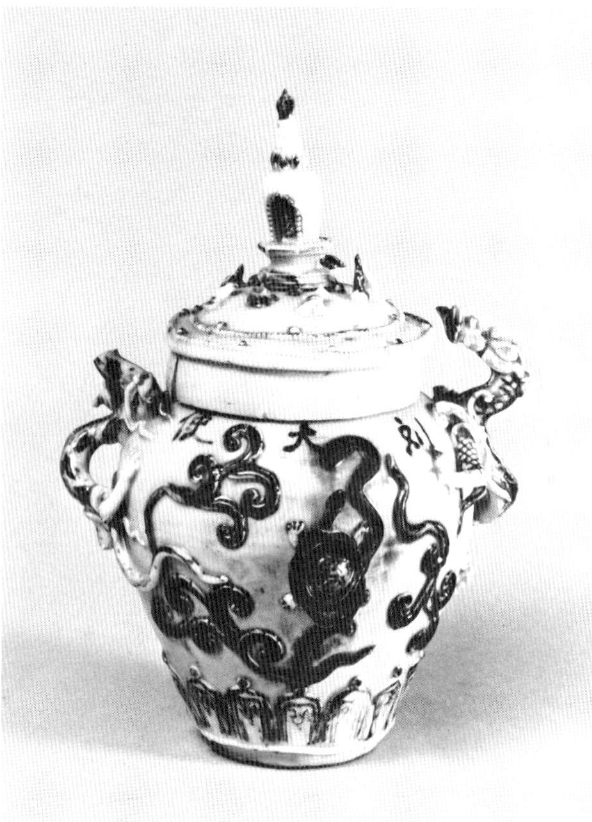

Fig. 1. Lidded jar with underglaze-blue-and-red decoration and the Four Divine Animals, Yuan dynasty, dated 1338, from Jiangxi province, h. 22.5 cm (8 7/8 in.)

molded appliqué. The knob surmounting the lid is in the shape of a stupa; a pearl-beaded band borders the opening to the stupa, and the hollow interior houses a Buddhist figure. The shape of this jar is unique, and its iconography, the form of the lid, and the inscriptions written on the neck and shoulder clearly indicate that it was produced for a religious purpose.

The David vases mentioned above, with inscriptions conveying wishes for the welfare and prosperity of the family and made for presentation to a Daoist temple, were also produced for religious use, but there is an essential stylistic difference in the manner in which the underglaze colors were applied to the jar and the vases. The David vases were decorated with high-grade cobalt blue to depict in exquisite fashion chrysanthemum scrolls, banana leaves, phoenix-and-floral scrolls, dragons and clouds, and waves. The cobalt itself was used as pigment for drawing the motifs, and its blue color, which shows clearly from beneath the bluish-tinged transparent glaze, is rich and vivid. The term *qinghua* (blue decoration, commonly rendered in English as blue-and-white or underglaze-blue-decorated ware) is used in reference to decoration in which cobalt is used to draw or paint motifs on the surface of white porcelain forms before firing. The David vases perfectly manifest this technique and can be regarded as typical underglaze-blue-decorated wares.

In the case of the Fengchengxian jar, on the other hand, the pigments applied to the appliqué designs of the Four Divine Animals, the lotus panels, the Eight Treasures, and so on, include vivid red, ash-brown, and grayish blue. The bluish color, not that typically seen in underglaze-blue-decorated ware, is close to colors produced by iron oxide, a phenomenon noted previously by a number of scholars. Such coloration as seen on this jar, in contrast to the brilliant blue produced from imported cobalt, is also characteristic of that produced when using impure domestic cobalt, suggesting that the cobalt used was of Chinese origin. The cobalt was not used to draw the motifs on the vessel surface but to provide a color coating for the molded and applied design, although a thin brush was employed to draw some details on the dragon and tiger. But for the most part the cobalt and copper were additions to images that had already been produced through molding and appliqué.

This writer was also able to examine an underglaze-blue-decorated *meiping* with peony design in the Jiangxi Municipal Museum, which was unearthed in Qiujiang city from a tomb datable to 1319 and is thus of an even earlier production date than the Fengchengxian porcelains.[2] Although the body is a common *meiping* shape, the vessel is quite distinctive: the knob surmounting the lid is in the form of a cylindrical nine-storied pagoda, a feature that allies the piece to the 1338 Fengchengxian jar with a stupa-shaped lid. The paste of the present piece is somewhat coarse, the transparent glaze grayish in color, and the quality inferior to that of standard underglaze-blue-decorated ware. Even so, the color of the glaze covering the elephant and lion heads on the shoulder of the vessel is quite attractive. The body is divided by two horizontal bands into three decorative sections containing a cloud collar, peony scroll, and banana leaves depicted in a well-organized composition. Radiating from the center of the lid are a series of veined leaves. The brownish color of these underglaze painted images suggests that the pigment used was iron oxide; examination of the surface with the naked eye reveals an appearance much different from that of typical underglaze cobalt-blue decorated porcelain.[3] This writer is thus of the opinion that cobalt might not have been used, despite the fact that Chinese scholars with whom I consulted stated that the color was the result of domestic Chinese cobalt. Scientific analysis of the piece would conclusively identify the pigment used.

The collection of forty-one Yuan-period underglaze-blue-decorated wares in the Topkapi Saray in Istanbul must be considered in assessing the porcelains recently recovered from Jingdezhen. Among the vessel types this writer examined in the Topkapi collection in the spring of 1986 were bottles, *guan* jars with pierced animal heads applied to the shoulders, *meiping*, pilgrim flasks, octagonal gourd-shaped bottles, and large plates, both shallow and deep. All of these pieces were intended for daily use; none are similar to the religious vessels from Fengchengxian. Moreover, the cobalt used to decorate the Topkapi porcelains produced a rich and strong blue color, and the decoration, which includes peony scrolls, wave patterns, the Eight Treasures, fish among water grasses, *qilin*, and horses against waves, was exquisitely rendered. Based on their shapes and designs, the Topkapi Saray objects, and also those porcelains in the Ardebil Shrine in Iran, appear to have been made within the second half of the fourteenth century, that is, consistent with the style of the David vases.

The newly discovered porcelains from China datable to 1319 and 1338 are significantly different from this style and alert us to both a stylistic and chronological gap between the Yuan underglaze-blue-decorated wares of the first half of the fourteenth century excavated in China and those of the latter half of the fourteenth preserved in collections of the Middle East. Our understanding of the blue-and-white wares prior to the David vase group is unfortunately still incomplete. The Chinese theory that the technique of underglaze-blue decoration was invented in China independent of outside influence during the Yuan dynasty cannot be easily dismissed. But elements of style, such as the geometrically organized compositions and meticulous designs present in the Topkapi porcelains, were in direct response to markets in Islamic countries of the Middle East and India.

Yuan Ceramics from the Gaoanxian Hoard

Jiaocang (storage pit, often translated as "hoard" in English), a form of underground storage, is a distinctive archaeological remain which differs from a tomb or other constructed edifice. A pit or hole, usually round in shape, was simply dug into the ground, and within it were placed such valuables as gold and silver ware, jewelry, and ceramics. Such hoards are believed to have been buried for safekeeping during times of warfare. One well-known Tang-dynasty example was discovered in Hejia village in Xi'an city, Shaanxi province. About one thousand pieces of gold and silver ware, medicinal products, and Chinese, Japanese, and Sassanian coins were found buried in two cisterns, most likely hidden by an aristocrat to protect his treasured possessions during the time of the Anlushan rebellion.[4] Storage pits have been discovered dating not only from the Tang but from the Song, Yuan, and Ming periods, and most have been discovered by accident.

The Gaoan hoard was discovered by chance in 1980 during construction work on telegraphic facilities.[5] The circular-shaped pit was 1.6 meters deep and 1.3 meters in diameter. During the years between 1351 and 1361 repeated bureaucratic infighting occurred in the district of Gaoan, simultaneous with the turmoil of the final stages of the Yuan dynasty, and this hoard might have been buried by a bureaucrat who was fleeing the chaos. As many as 239 fourteenth-century ceramics were recovered from the pit, including nineteen pieces of underglaze-blue and four of underglaze-red-decorated porcelain, forty-two pieces of white ware including *qingbai* (bluish-white) ware, 168 pieces of celadon, and in addition, three Jun ware bowls and one turquoise-glazed *meiping*. Needless to say, these ceramics, in themselves magnificent treasures, are important material for the study of the ceramic art of the Yuan period. They are rigorously safeguarded in the Gaoanxian Museum and have only recently been made accessible to foreign scholars.

Among the underglaze-blue-decorated wares in the museum's collection are *meiping*, large jars, a jar with pierced animal-head handles on the shoulder, stem cups, and a *gu*-shaped vase. All are typical Yuan-dynasty blue-and-white ware. The vessel surfaces have a somewhat bluish cast and the vividly rendered underglaze designs, which include peony scrolls, dragons, and lotus, are a marvelous blue color. A large jar decorated with dragon-and-peony decoration (fig. 2) has a lotus-leaf-shaped lid with a design of veined leaves and fish painted in underglaze blue. A jar in the Idemitsu collection with a scene of figures on horseback is similar in shape and also has a lotus-leaf-shaped lid with veined leaves depicted on the top surface.[6] That the Idemitsu jar and lid were intended to go together despite their dissimilar decoration is supported by the Gaoan find. A lidded *meiping* from the hoard has a decorative scheme like that of the dragon jar described above, the body circled by bands containing dragons and scrolling peony; comparable types are in the Topkapi Saray and the Ataka collection.[7] Unlike the large jar and *meiping*, an underglaze-blue-decorated stem cup from the Gaoan hoard has a muddy blue design and is somewhat inferior in quality (fig. 3).

A wide-mouthed jar from the Gaoan storage pit decorated in underglaze copper-red is a magnificent object and without precedent (fig. 4). The body of this impressive jar swells from below the short neck. A band of lotus panels decorates the shoulder, and on the belly are four quatrefoil panels in which phoenixes intertwine with scrolling flowers, all in a clear, bright copper red. Another example of underglaze copper-red decorated ware from the Gaoan hoard is a spouted pouring bowl with a goose-and-reed design in which the bird, with leafy vine held in its beak, is depicted on the bottom interior.

Among the white porcelains of the Gaoan hoard are cups, stem cups (fig. 5), deep bowls, bent-waisted bowls, pear-shaped bottles, and ewers. These include white wares of typical *shufu*

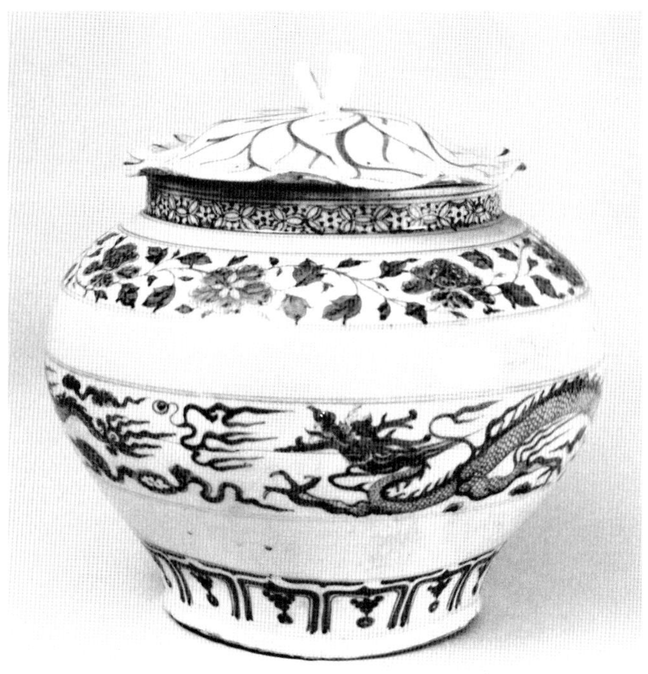

Fig. 2. *Guan* jar decorated in underglaze blue, Yuan dynasty, excavated in Gaoanxian, Jiangxi province, h. 36 cm (14 1/8 in.)

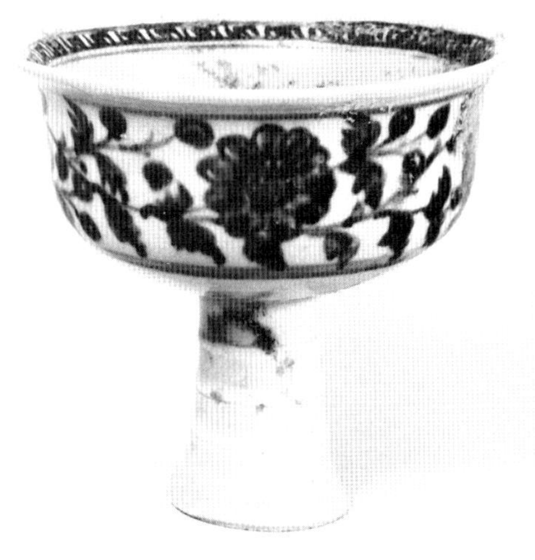

Fig. 3. Stem cup decorated in underglaze blue, Yuan dynasty, excavated in Gaoanxian, Jiangxi province, h. 9.5 cm (3 3/4 in.)

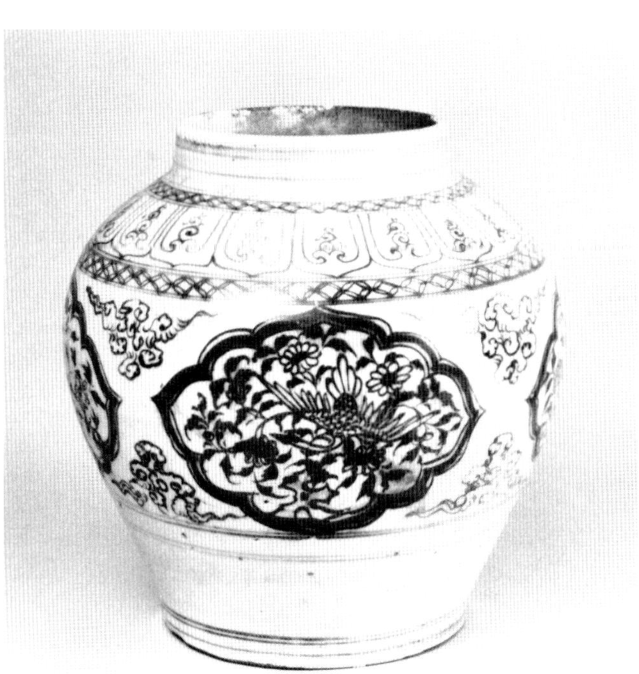

Fig. 4. Jar decorated in underglaze red, Yuan dynasty, excavated in Gaoanxian, Jiangxi province, h. 24.8 cm (9 3/4 in.)

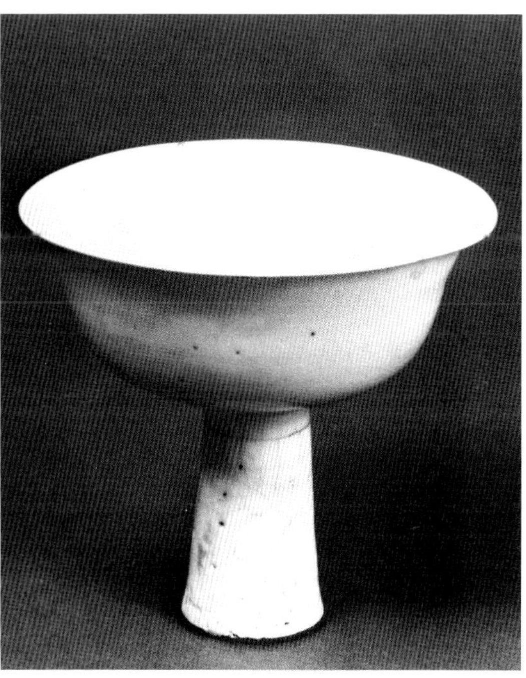

Fig. 5. White monochrome stem cup, Shufu type, Yuan dynasty, excavated at Gaoanxian, Jiangxi province, h. 12.2 cm (4 7/8 in.)

type, such as white porcelain stem cups whose inner surfaces were molded with dragon-and-cloud designs, and other wares of lesser quality. One pear-shaped bottle was decorated in gold foil with a dragon extending across the neck and body of the vessel; except for portions of the head and body of the dragon, the gold has almost completely flaked off. The use of gold foil for decorating white wares is known from several examples from Ding kiln sites and other kilns of the Northern Song period. However, this is the only example of a Yuan-period *shufu*-type porcelain with such decoration.

In addition to white, underglaze-blue-decorated, and underglaze-red-decorated wares, large quantities of Longquan celadon were also discovered in the Gaoan storage pit: twenty-eight large plates, forty-seven large dishes, twenty-nine stem cups, and twenty-one basins, among others. All reveal workmanship that is typical of Yuan celadon produced at the Longquan kilns.

These Yuan-dynasty ceramic vessels excavated from Gaoanxian were undoubtedly buried at the same time and in all likelihood had been used in day-to-day life until the time of their interment; they were not heirlooms. Although the dates of manufacture for the ceramics might be somewhat different, collectively they are relics of the same period and thus form a very important group.

Very similar to the Gaoan hoard is the group of Yuan wares excavated at Baoding in Hebei province in 1964.[8] Like the Gaoan hoard, these objects, most likely buried for safekeeping, were discovered quite by accident. Eleven ceramics were found: two underglaze blue-and-red-decorated jars, two underglaze-blue-decorated *meiping* with dragon-and-wave designs, one underglaze-blue-decorated pear-shaped bottle, one white porcelain dish with molded dragon motif, one white porcelain cup with lotus motif, one monochrome blue spouted bowl decorated with gold foil, one monochrome blue dish and one monochrome blue cup, each with gold foil decoration, and one underglaze-blue-decorated octagonal ewer. Although the number of ceramics from the Baoding storage pit is less than that of Gaoan, the quality of the wares is far superior. No definitive evidence dates the Baoding hoard, but the porcelains are typical Yuan-period wares. Similarly, the Gaoan objects are impossible to date on the basis of dated material from the find. However, if we examine the underglaze-blue-decorated dragon jar (fig. 2) and *meiping*, we note that the designs are somewhat simplified in comparison to the David vases, which typify the mid fourteenth-century style. Furthermore, the underglaze-red-decorated jar (fig. 4) is of the type currently believed to be from the late Yuan to early Ming periods. In addition, the style of painting on the underglaze-blue stem cup with peony design (fig. 3) is somewhat loose and the quality of the cobalt not very high. Taking these factors into consideration, it is possible that the Gaoan objects are somewhat later in date than the mid-fourteenth century.

Early Ming Porcelains Excavated at the Imperial Kilns at Jingdezhen

In addition to the new finds of fourteenth-century Jingdezhen wares introduced above, there has been one more very significant find: the discovery of the early Ming Yuqichang or Imperial Vessel Factory. Beginning in the Tang period, the production of porcelain, mainly that of white ware, was carried out at Jingdezhen, and one of the greatest innovations in the history of Chinese ceramics, underglaze-blue-decorated ware, originated there during the Yuan dynasty. Such wares were exported and admired throughout the world, in the Middle East, Europe, and even America. In the latter part of the fourteenth century, during the Ming dynasty, a factory for the production of ceramics was established at Jingdezhen. Called the Yuqichang, this government-

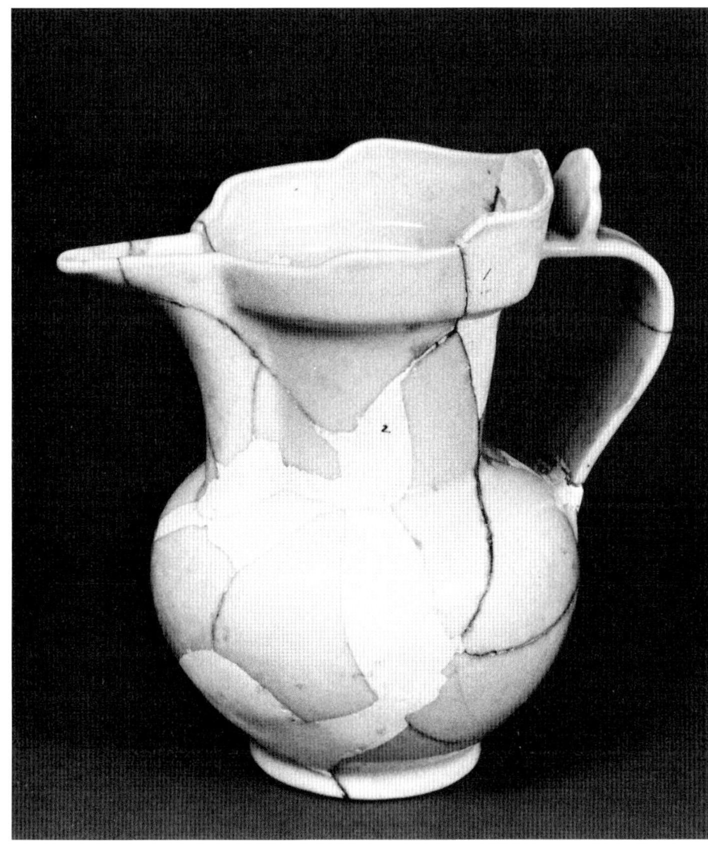

Fig. 6. White monochrome monk's cap jug, Ming dynasty, Yongle period, excavated from the imperial kilns at Jingdezhen, Jiangxi province, h. 19.2 cm (7 1/2 in.)

supervised workshop oversaw the production of porcelain, carried out research, originated new wares, and produced ceramics for the court's use. Tableware, decorative porcelain, and porcelain for ritual use by the emperor were all produced at the Yuqichang and transported to the imperial palace in the capital. The inscription of underglaze-blue reign marks, for example, *Da Ming Xuande nian zhi, Da Ming Chenghua nian zhi*, and *Da Ming Wanli nian zhi*, became obligatory on the porcelain of the Yuqichang. Opinions concerning the date of the Yuqichang's establishment are divided between the Hongwu, Yongle, and Xuande periods. A widely accepted theory posits that the Yuqichang was founded in the early Xuande period; however, this supposition is based entirely on literary sources of the Ming period and was formulated before the Ming-dynasty imperial kiln remains of the Yuqichang were discovered.[9]

During repair work and construction in November of 1982 at Zhushanlu, the main street of the city of Jingdezhen, porcelain shards from the official Xuande kilns were uncovered. Spurred on by this find, an excavation was carried out, principally by Liu Xinyuan and Bai Kun of the Jingdezhen Institute of Ceramics. The remains discovered are without doubt those of the Yuqichang, which according to literary sources, was established on Zhushan (Pearl Hill). A Chinese report on the excavation identifies the remains as those of a Xuande-period *se yao* (overglaze-enamel kiln) and describes an enormous quantity of shards of imperially marked white porcelain, underglaze-blue-decorated, underglaze-red-decorated, and enameled wares.[10]

The investigation of these shards has been enthusiastically conducted under the direction of Liu Xinyuan at the research laboratory at Jingdezhen. There, vessels have been reconstructed

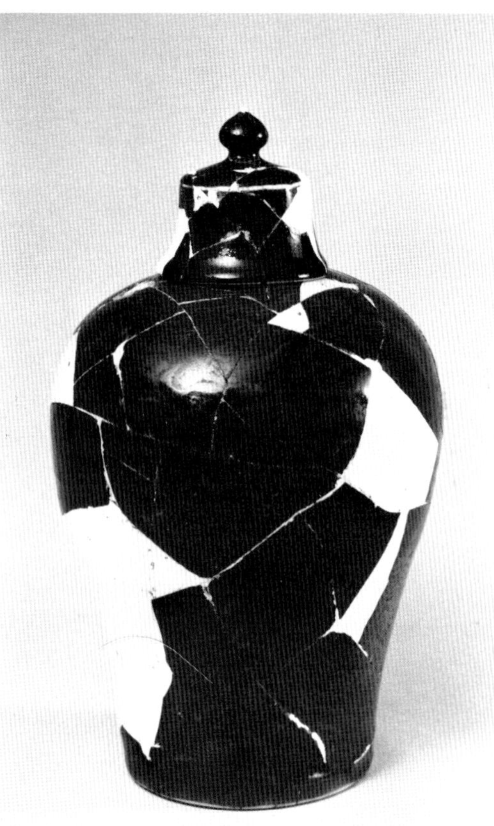

Fig. 7. Red monochrome *meiping*, Ming dynasty, Xuande period, excavated at the imperial kilns in Jingdezhen, Jiangxi province, h. 38.5 cm (15 1/8 in.)

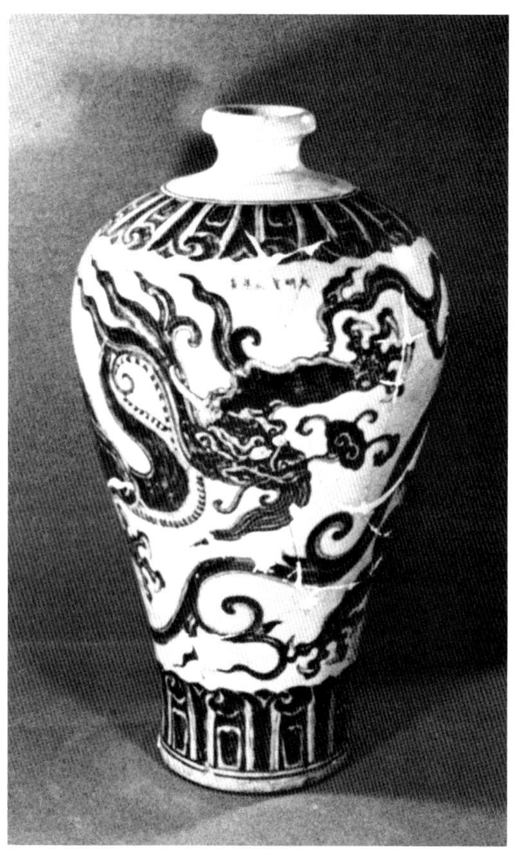

Fig. 8. *Meiping* decorated in underglaze blue, Ming dynasty, Xuande period, six-character Xuande reign mark, excavated from the imperial kilns in Jingdezhen, Jiangxi province

from the excavated shards: Yongle-period stem cups, monk's cap jugs (fig. 6), large jars, a large Xuande-period plate with peony decoration in white reserve against a blue ground, and underglaze-red-decorated stem cups. The quantity of shards recovered is beyond imagination; those that cannot be pieced together are simply piled into a bamboo basket.

The only kiln remains to be confirmed are those of a *se yao*, possibly its stoking hole or a vent. Bricks were found arranged in a semicircle, in front of which were the remnants of a wall where the flues and chimney would have been. Five holes were constructed in the wall. The remains are about two meters wide, and if reconstructed, the kiln would be three to five meters long, generally somewhat smaller than kilns for firing white or biscuit wares.

Shards were discovered in nine different places, although what these areas were has not been fully reported. They might have been parts of kilns, storage areas for wares, or refuse piles where defective wares were thrown; they were most likely the latter. As stated above, the Yuqichang supervised the production of ceramics, and imperfectly fired wares, marred for example by pinholes, were apparently broken and discarded. The lower portion of a Xuande-period monochrome-red-glazed vase with a dragon-and-wave design incised beneath the glaze (fig. 7), examined by the author, had blackened during firing, and for this reason was most probably consigned to the refuse heap.

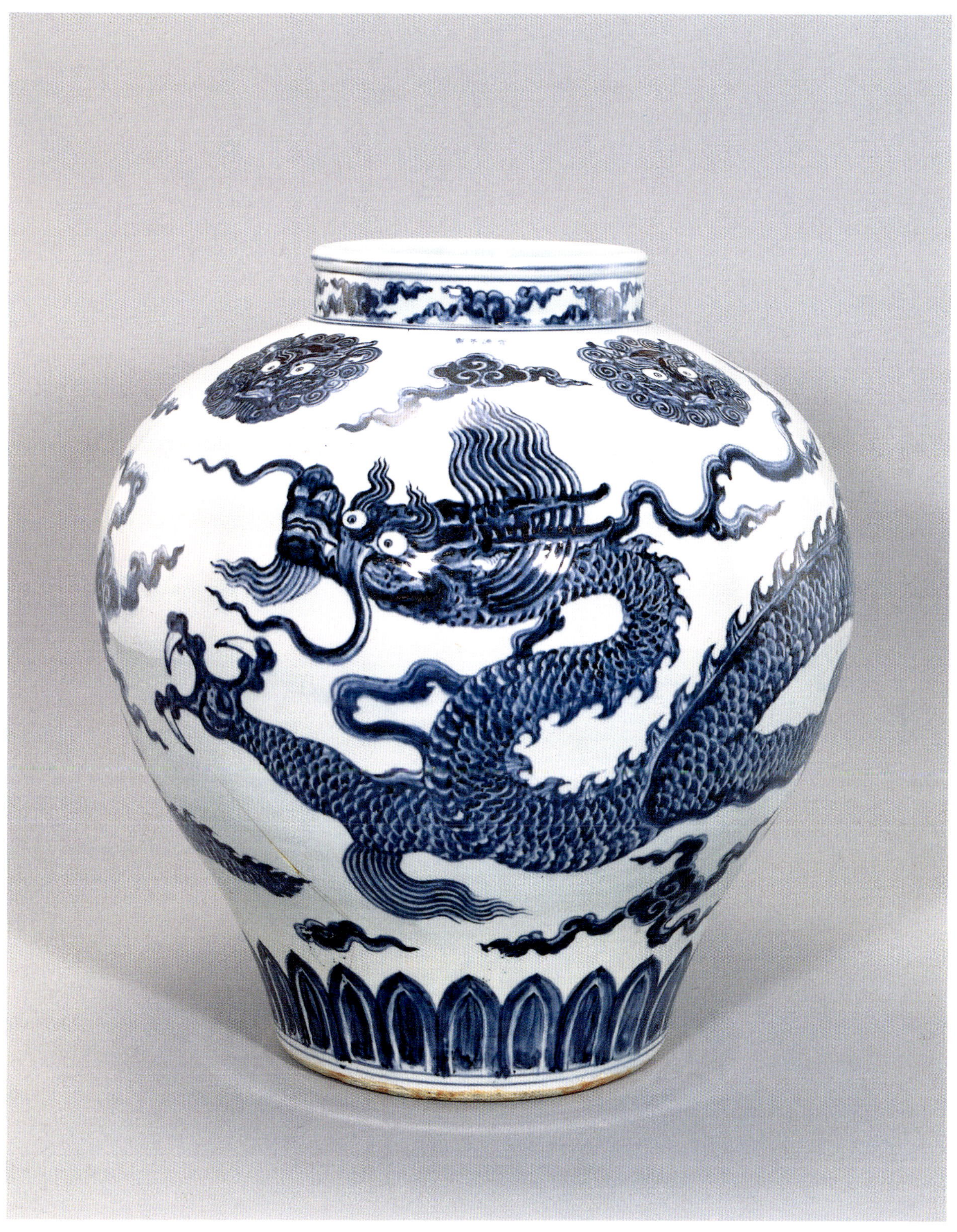

Large *guan* jar, Ming dynasty,
Xuande period (1426–35), no. 21

A number of white porcelain stem cups with Yongle-period reign marks were excavated. The bowls have thin walls, deep sides, and high feet, and incised in seal script under the glaze on the interior bottoms of the bowls are reign marks reading *Yongle nian zhi.* Stem cups with such Yongle reign marks can be seen in a number of museums throughout the world, including the Idemitsu Museum of Arts (see nos. 15 and 16). Until now the authenticity of these Yongle stem cups has been questioned, but the excavated examples support their attribution.

Also excavated from the Yongle levels at Zhushan were white porcelain monk's cap jugs, platters and bowls, and other shapes incised with designs of fungus, peony scrolls, loquats, pomegranates, and other plants. This method of decoration is a major hallmark of the Yongle period. A noteworthy feature of the reported finds is that over 95 percent of the Yongle-period porcelain was white ware, whereas monochrome-red glazed ware and underglaze-red and underglaze-blue-decorated wares were completely absent. This suggests that Ming-dynasty ceramic specialists might be in error in attributing unmarked early Ming blue-and-white porcelain to the Yongle period.

Many different varieties of glaze colors appeared on the wares from the Xuande levels. According to the excavation report, examples were found of monochrome white, monochrome red, monochrome blue, celadons, and brownish-glazed wares, as well as underglaze-blue-decorated wares and underglaze-red-decorated wares. Among these, monochrome-red-glazed and underglaze-blue-decorated porcelains were the most numerous, in sharp contrast to the high percentage of white ware of the Yongle period.

The most prevalent shapes among the monochrome-red-glazed vessels were small dishes and bowls. The widest range of shapes occurred in the underglaze-blue-decorated wares, with numerous examples of large-sized vessels. The shapes include large plates and jars, small vases and jars, brush holders, candlestands, monk's cap jugs, and pilgrim flasks. Many are types similar to the underglaze-blue-decorated wares of the early Ming dynasty found today in museums in Japan, Europe, and America. Examples of unmarked Xuande-period underglaze-blue-decorated vessels as well as pieces with the *Da Ming Xuande nian zhi* reign mark were recovered. Noteworthy among the marked wares are a *meiping* with dragon decoration (fig. 8) and a large jar with dragon decoration. The *meiping* is similar in decor to the large jar with dragon design and Xuande mark in the Idemitsu Museum (see no. 21). The vessels differ in that the dragon on the Idemitsu piece has three-clawed feet, whereas that of the *meiping* has four; the Idemitsu piece has a four-character reign mark (*Xuande nian zhi*), the excavated *meiping* a six-character mark (*Da Ming Xuande nian zhi*).

Examples and variants of certain types, hitherto unknown among the wares of the Xuande period, were discovered. Until now, underglaze-blue-decorated plates with grape designs and without reign marks (see no. 19) have been considered products of the Yongle period. However, a foliate plate with grape design found at the imperial kilns bears a Xuande-period mark. Attributions of this type of early Ming porcelain must now be reconsidered. Variants were found among underglaze-blue and red-glazed wares, wares with underglaze blue against a yellow enamel ground, and white porcelain with underglaze-brown painting. Numerous shards from the Chenghua, Hongzhi, and Zhengde periods, including overglaze-enamel wares of the Chenghua period, were also recovered. Findings such as these and continued research on the kiln remains will eventually form a clearer picture of early Ming imperial porcelain production at Jingdezhen.

Tadanori Yuba is Curator of Chinese Art, Idemitsu Museum of Arts, Tokyo.
Translation by Joseph Seubert.

Notes

1. The Fengchengxian material is published in *Wenwu,* no. 11 (1981).

2. This piece was previously known outside China primarily through a small black-and-white reproduction, which appeared in *Wenwu,* no. 1 (1981).

3. The author examined the *meiping* in the company of Kato Takuo, a potter.

4. *Kaogu,* no. 1 (1972).

5. *Wenwu,* no. 4 (1982).

6. See *Chinese Ceramics in the Idemitsu Collection* (Tokyo: Heibonsha, 1987), no. 143.

7. For the Topkapi piece, see Regina Krahl, *Chinese Ceramics in the Topkapi Saray Museum*, vol. 2, *Yuan and Ming Dynasty Porcelains* (London: Sotheby's Publications, 1986), pl. 578, TKS 15/1366, and for the Ataka piece see *Sekai tōji zenshū* (Ceramic Art of the World), vol. 13, *Liao, Jin and Yuan* (Tokyo: Shōgakukan, 1981), pl. 58.

8. *Wenwu,* no. 2 (1965).

9. For a summary of these theories see Feng Xianming, et al., *Zhongguo taoci shi* (Beijing: Wenwu Press, 1982), pp. 360–65.

10. A report on the discovery and excavation of the imperial kilns was compiled by Bai Kun and others and appeared in *Zhongguo taoci,* no. 7 (1982).

Catalogue

of the Exhibition

MARY ANN ROGERS

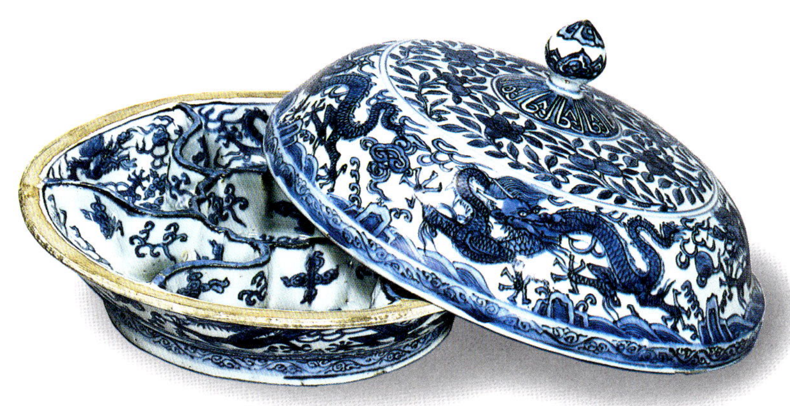

Strongly potted, this jar has a broad short neck, low sloping shoulders, and a full, rounded belly. The sturdy foot and recessed base are unglazed, revealing a coarse body burned buff in firing. The interior is covered with a deep brownish black glaze and the exterior with a creamy white slip. A dragon-and-cloud design was painted in chocolate-brown slip around the upper two-thirds of the vessel between horizontal bands, with details scratched through to the light-colored slip below. The exterior was then completely covered with a thin, colorless glaze, which suffered some imperfections during firing and is minutely crackled throughout. The location of three lumpy patches of kiln grit adhering to the glaze suggests the manner in which the vessel was supported in the kiln during firing.

The single decorative zone is inhabited by a horned and bearded dragon lumbering through a sky of flat, motionless clouds. His slender tongue leaps out at a bizarre flaming pearl from a disproportionately large reptilian head; the thin neck loops to a stiff horizontal body, which stretches around the belly of the jar and is kept aloft on giant four-clawed feet. The flat application of dark slip and the blunt edges of the motifs leave no trace of the brush, which contributes to the unusual flavor of the design. Aside from the more-or-less descriptive rendering of the face, head, and horns of the ungainly beast, the remaining incised details appear as casual linear ramblings or capricious scribbles; note especially the interiors of the clouds.

Despite a wide qualitative range and some variety in composition and motifs manifested by extant examples of this distinctive group, of which such storage jars form the majority, stylistic, technical, and physical features held in common suggest production at a single or small group of closely related kilns in northern China.[1] The vitality of kilns specializing in slip-decorated stonewares—known collectively as Cizhou or Cizhou-type wares—remained strong during the course of the Yuan dynasty, and their products were very popular both at home and abroad. Although examples related to the present piece have been discovered as far north as Beijing and Mongolia and as far south as the Philippines, a dragon-and-cloud jar recovered from the Sinan shipwreck, which is datable to around 1323, provides the most important evidence for dating.[2]

1. For a discussion of the Idemitsu jar and related examples see Yutaka Mino, *Freedom of Clay and Brush Through Seven Centuries in Northern China: Tz'u-Chou Type Wares 960–1600 A.D.* (Bloomington, Ind.: Indiana University Press, 1980), p. 206.

2. Wooden shipping tags with ink-written dates corresponding to 1323 were attached to several bundles of coins found among the extensive remains of the Chinese cargo ship discovered in waters off the Sinan coast of Korea in 1976. The dragon-and-cloud jar is illustrated in the catalogue of the special exhibition of the Sinan material held at the National Museum of Korea in Seoul, *Sinan haeja yumul* (Sinan Seacoast Cultural Relics) (Seoul, 1977), no. 221.

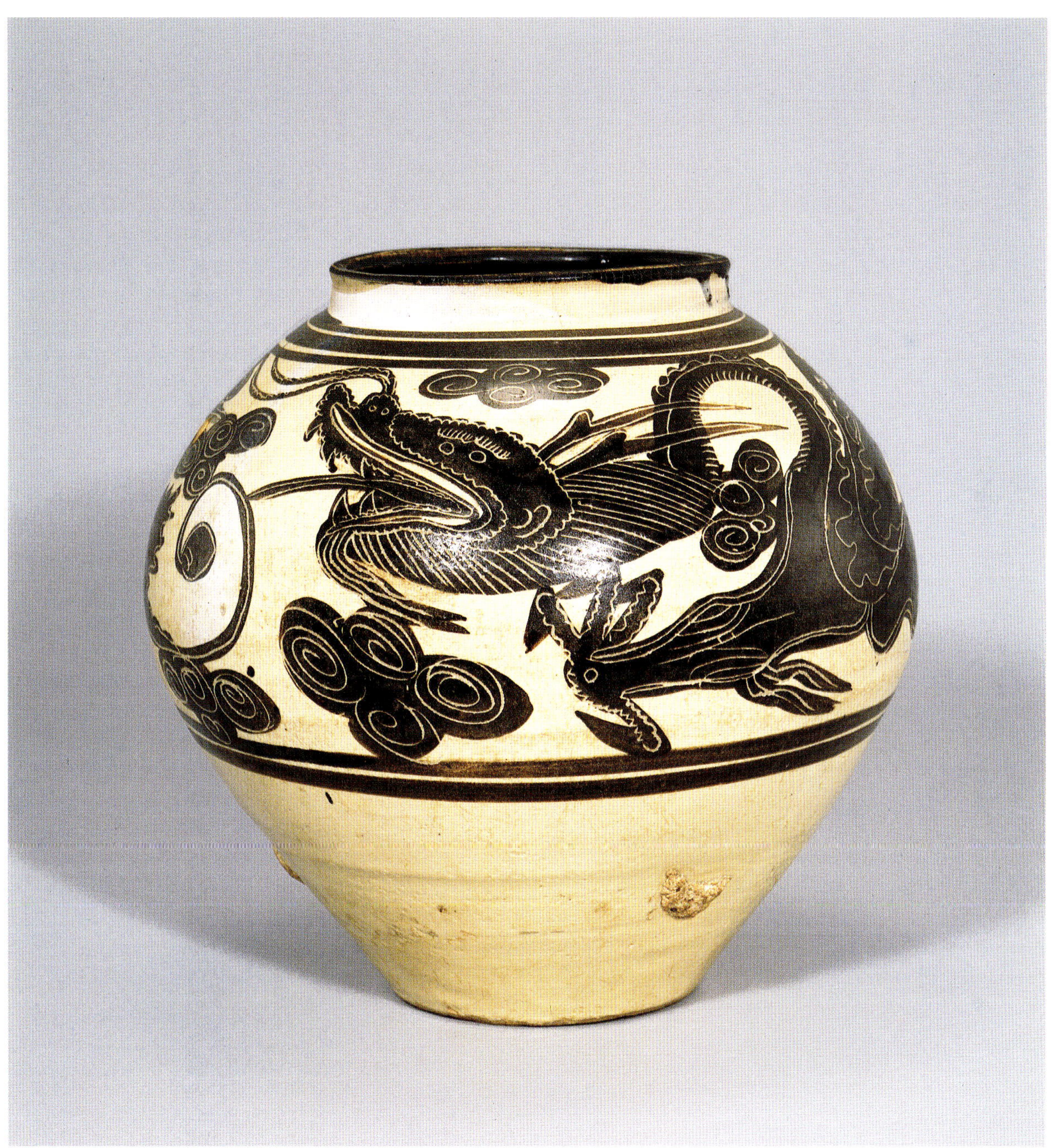

1

JAR

Cizhou-type ware, slip-decorated stoneware with dragon-and-cloud design

Yuan dynasty, early 14th century

H. 26.1 cm (10 1/2 in.)

This *meiping* flows up and outward from its gently everted foot through a swelling body to a short cylindrical neck with a thickened mouth rim. The dense, off-white clay body is visible on the somewhat roughly glazed recessed base and has burned a deep orange color on the sturdy, unglazed foot rim. The pale sea-green celadon glaze has a softly lustrous surface, high opacity, and a network of widely spaced vertical crackles; dark spots decorate the surface. The mossy, greenish brown tonality of these dots differs from the rust-brown color more usual in such decoration. Also remarkable are minuscule areas that fired pinkish to bright red, a color range produced by copper when fired under the reducing conditions necessary to produce the celadon-green glaze.[1] The color spots were applied with a brush, apparently before glazing, in a carefully calculated arrangement, although the visual impression is one of pigment flung against the surface; the term *tobi seiji*, literally "flying celadon," is used for such wares in Japan, where they have long been admired.

Given the usual translation of the word *meiping* as "prunus vase," the function of the vessel is often understood as that of a flower vase, but the name is of comparatively recent origin.[2] Even today many *meiping* are equipped with covers or are designed to receive stoppers; it is likely that most if not all were intended to hold liquids. Although the increased frequency with which *meiping* appear among Longquan wares from the early Yuan onward suggests influence from Jingdezhen, the shape of the Idemitsu piece is closely related to Korean celadon *meiping* in vogue during the thirteenth century in both China and Japan.[3]

Some indication of the great popularity of Longquan celadons in Japan during the early fourteenth century is provided by the sheer number, nearly ten thousand, recovered from the wreck of the Sinan ship, whose major port of call was to have been Japan. It carried Longquan celadon *meiping* with full-blown upper body sections and sturdy feet similar to the present example. Although several types of Longquan wares with applied spots were also recovered from the ship, the *meiping* appears not to have been among them. The combination of this type of decoration with the *meiping* form is in fact highly unusual, if not unique, a circumstance suggesting that the Idemitsu piece might have been specially ordered.

1. A spouted celadon bowl in the Cleveland Museum of Art was scientifically tested, and its distinctive reddish-colored decorative spots shown to contain copper.

2. *Chinese Porcelain: The S. C. Ko Tianminlou Collection* (Hong Kong: Hong Kong Museum of Art, 1987), pt. 2, pp. 35–36, notes that the term does not predate the Qing dynasty and that in the *Yinliuzhai shuo ci* of the Qing period the term is explained as having been adopted for the shape because the mouth was as small as slender plum branches.

3. See Feng Xianming, "Persian and Korean Ceramics Unearthed in China," *Orientations* (May 1986), pp. 47–53. Seven Korean celadons from the Sinan shipwreck have been published: three in the 1977 Sinan exhibition catalogue, *Sinan haeja yumul*, (nos. 1, 2, and 3) and four additional pieces in the 1985 publication of the same title and published by the Ministry of Culture and Information of Korea, vol. 3, pl. 1 (nos. 2 and 3) and pl. 2 (nos. 4 and 5). It is believed that these Korean wares, which included a *meiping*, were acquired in China for resale in Japan.

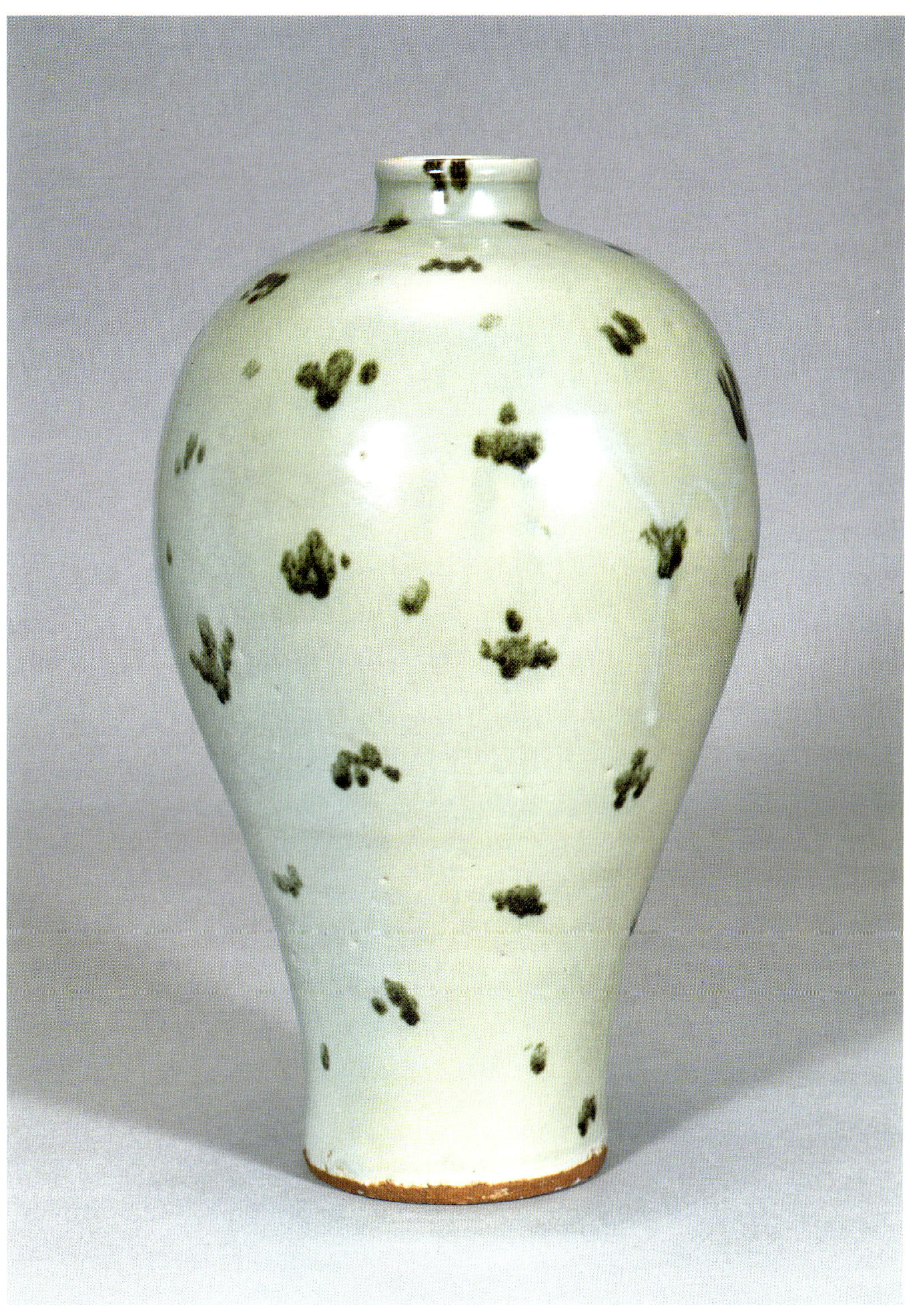

2

MEIPING

Longquan ware, celadon with applied spots

Yuan dynasty, late 13th–early 14th century

H. 36.7 cm (14½ in.)

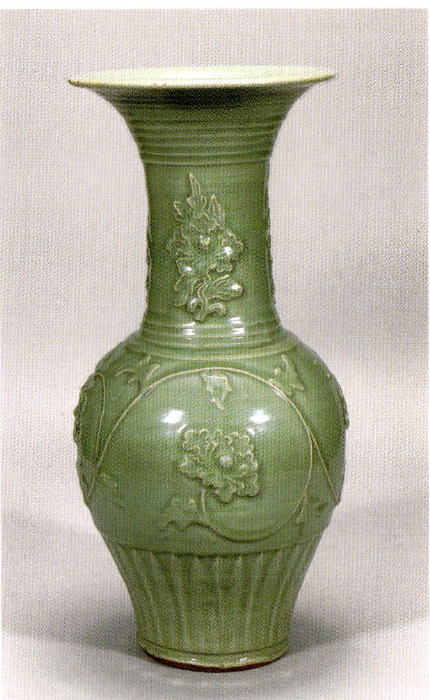

3

BALUSTER VASE

Longquan ware, celadon with applied and carved floral decoration

Yuan dynasty, late 13th–early 14th century

H. 45.8 cm (18 in.)

A trumpet-shaped neck with flaring mouth springs from the ovoid body, which rises from a somewhat splayed foot. The white porcelaneous clay has burned brick red on the thick, unglazed foot rim. The deeply recessed base was formed by inserting a shallow saucer-shaped disk over the open body. Four molded peony blossoms and small leaves were applied to the body along the slip-trailed scrolling stem. Molded peony blossoms framed by leaves were placed upright on the neck, bordered by carved horizontal rings above and below, with pointed petals carved around the foot. The glaze is thick, opaque, and lustrous.

The baluster shape was developed during the late thirteenth century by potters at the Longquan kilns in Zhejiang province. They produced it in great quantity during the Yuan period, and the form remained almost exclusively their preserve until well into the Ming dynasty. The attractive shape, with its visually engaging profile, perfectly accorded with the Yuan-period taste for strong, arresting forms, which explains in part the popularity of the type in China and abroad. The decorative scheme seen here so suited the baluster vase's distinctive form that it became a standard one for the vessel.[1] The rings enhance the splaying of the neck, and the upright peonies stress its height; the curving scroll emphasizes the fullness of the body, and the vertical petals reinforce its upward thrust from the base.

Noteworthy here is the exceptional clarity of the molding and the suppleness of the blossoms, whose multilayered petals undulate and overlap in a sumptuously organic fashion. The white clay, visible where the glaze has pulled back from the highest protrusions of the relief design, creates bright highlights against the deeper green of the surrounding glaze. The glaze's depth and luminosity are the result of unmelted quartz and clay particles and tiny air and gas pockets trapped within the glaze. Methods based on more thorough pulverization of materials and higher firing temperatures produced the majority of contemporaneous celadon glazes, which exhibit a quite different character. But the present example is proof of a continuing ability to produce a rich, subtle jadelike glaze not unlike that which catapulted the Longquan wares to fame during the Southern Song period.

1. The earliest datable example of celadon appliqué-peony decoration occurs on a *lian* incense burner excavated with a stone tablet dated to 1265 from the base of a pagoda in Shaoxingxian in northern Zhejiang province (*Wenwu*, no. 4, 1980, p. 3, fig. 2). A date corresponding to 1309 on a Jun *ding*-shaped incense burner provides evidence for an early fourteenth-century date for the peony-decorated Longquan baluster vase excavated with it (*Wenwu*, no. 5, 1977, p. 76, fig. 3). See Yutaka Mino and Katherine Tsiang, *Ice and Green Clouds, Traditions of Chinese Celadon* (Bloomington, Ind.: Indiana University Press, 1986), p. 200. A similarly shaped vase with only the carved rings as decoration was illustrated among the finds from a Yuan-dynasty tomb at Yuanyichang in Dongxi, Jianyang, Sichuan province (*Wenwu*, no. 2, 1987, p. 72, fig. 4), which, given the late Song character of the accompanying celadons, might date from quite early in the Yuan period. The Sinan material included three baluster vases with applied relief, two with peony design (*Sinan haeja yumul*, 1977, col. pl. 10, and 1985, vol. 3, pl. 13, no. 19), and one with the far rarer applied chrysanthemum (*Sinan haeja yumul*, 1985, vol. 3, pl. 14, no. 20). The scant number suggests that this decorative idiom was becoming obsolete by the second decade of the fourteenth century.

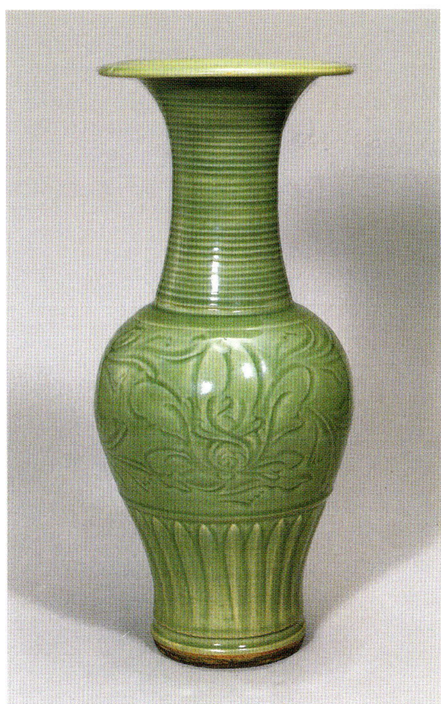

4

BALUSTER VASE

Longquan ware, celadon with carved floral decoration

Yuan dynasty, 14th century

H. 46.5 cm (18 3/8 in.)

This baluster vase has a trumpet-shaped neck with a strongly everted rim and a swelling body that tapers downward, contracting above the foot. The stepped foot encloses a deeply recessed base, which was formed by covering the open base of the body with a disk-shaped piece of clay. The pale gray porcelaneous body has burned a golden brown on the exposed foot and is covered by a bubbly yet transparent green glaze with a yellowish tone.

The strongly carved decoration consists of parallel horizontal grooves circling the neck, slender lotus petals above a deep horizontal channel around the foot, and within the central body zone, large peony blossoms on the front and back with leaves intermingling at the sides, giving an impression of a continuous scroll. The floral design was produced with a carving tool held at an oblique angle to slice away the background, leaving each petal and leaf slightly raised in an animated and varied low relief.

The more assertive character of this vase, in comparison to the previous example (no. 3), is due to slight but effective adjustments in form: the everted mouth flares more insistently, the break between neck and body is accented by the expansive shoulders, and the constriction at the base is more pronounced. The strength of the shape coupled with a vigorously carved design and a bright transparent glaze of a distinctly yellow tone account for its more up-to-date appearance and indicate a clear break with the late Song aesthetic that influenced the former piece. Vases similar to the present example in both shape and carved decoration have been discovered in Yuan-dynasty archaeological contexts alongside the peony-relief type; the pagoda find of 1309 included a pair, and several were aboard the 1323 Sinan ship.[1] Although the two types were produced simultaneously for some time, technical and aesthetic features suggest a somewhat later entry into the Longquan repertoire for the present type. A close parallel in shape is the well-known vase in the Percival David Foundation dated to 1327. Carved decoration, rather than appliqué, continued as the major decorative mode during the fifteenth century, although by that time the character of both the baluster shape and its carved decoration had changed significantly.[2]

1. See *Wenwu,* no. 5 (1977), p. 76, fig. 2, for the 1309 pair and *Sinan haeja yumul* (Seoul: National Museum of Korea, 1977), no. 312, for a group of five carved baluster vases.

2. See Margaret Medley, *Illustrated Catalogue of Celadon Wares* (London: School of Oriental and African Studies, 1977), no. 81, pl. 8, for the Percival David Foundation's 1327 vase; for baluster vases with carved decoration, dated by inscription to 1432 and 1454, see nos. 98–99, pl. 10.

A relatively broad neck curves outward to a thickened lip rim on this *meiping*. The descent of the body from the shoulder is rather steep, and despite the gradual taper to the everted foot, the shape appears relatively straight. The casually trimmed foot ring has an irregular rusty discoloration and the scraped-out base is roughly glazed, exposing areas of the dense white body. The slumping that occurred at the juncture of the neck and shoulder probably resulted from an excessively high firing temperature. The decoration is carved in three horizontal registers separated by undecorated narrow bands: two fluently carved and naturalistic lotus sprays on the neck, a dragon bobbing in and out of waves in the main body zone, and upright lotus panels containing trefoil elements surrounding the base. The pale, greenish blue tinted glaze is bright, clear, and smooth.

The *meiping*, whose origins can be traced to the Tang period, was established as a major form during the Song dynasty and remained so well into the Ming.[1] In this early fourteenth-century manifestation the elegance and weightless grace of the classic Song shape were sacrificed for an appearance of greater stability, provided by the straighter sides and wider base. Contributing to the earthbound appearance is the horizontal division of the body which, though not unprecedented, became a compositional standard during the Yuan period.

The distinctive color of the glaze was achieved by adding a small amount of iron oxide to a compound prepared from the remarkably pure "China stone," available in the region of the Jingdezhen kilns, and by firing in a reduction atmosphere. The origin and early development of this *yingqing* (shadow blue) glaze occurred at Jingdezhen during the second half of the tenth century; from the beginning of the eleventh century[2] until well into the Yuan period, *yingqing*-glazed porcelain, often decorated with incised, carved, or molded designs, was the staple product of the kilns and was widely distributed throughout China and abroad. Given the traditional technique of the carved design and the use of a *yingqing* glaze, and considering the technical and decorative innovations of the Yuan dynasty, this *meiping* is a conservative vessel. Yet its decorative scheme, which is shared by a number of other *meiping* and *guan* jars archaeologically datable to the early fourteenth century, provided a springboard from which the decorators of underglaze-painted porcelains launched their creations.[3]

1. A white-ware *meiping* of northern manufacture with stopper-lid, in the Shaanxi Provincial Museum in Xian, is dated to the Tang dynasty; another without lid also with a Tang attribution is in the Shanghai Museum of Art.

2. The origin and development of *yingqing*-glazed wares are discussed by Mary Ann Rogers in "The Ceramic Jade of Jao," a paper presented at the International Symposium on Chinese Ceramics, sponsored by the Oriental Ceramic Society of the Philippines, Manila, 1983.

3. One of a pair of similar dragon-decorated *meiping* discovered from a tomb with date corresponding to 1325 in Wannianxian, Jiangxi province, is illustrated in *Chinese Ceramics from Datable Tombs* (London and New York: Sotheby Parke Bernet, 1978), no. 26, p. 38. Another of this group from the Sinan shipwreck of 1323 is illustrated in *Sinan haeja yumul* (Seoul: National Museum of Korea, 1977), no. 150, also a similarly decorated *guan* jar, no. 164.

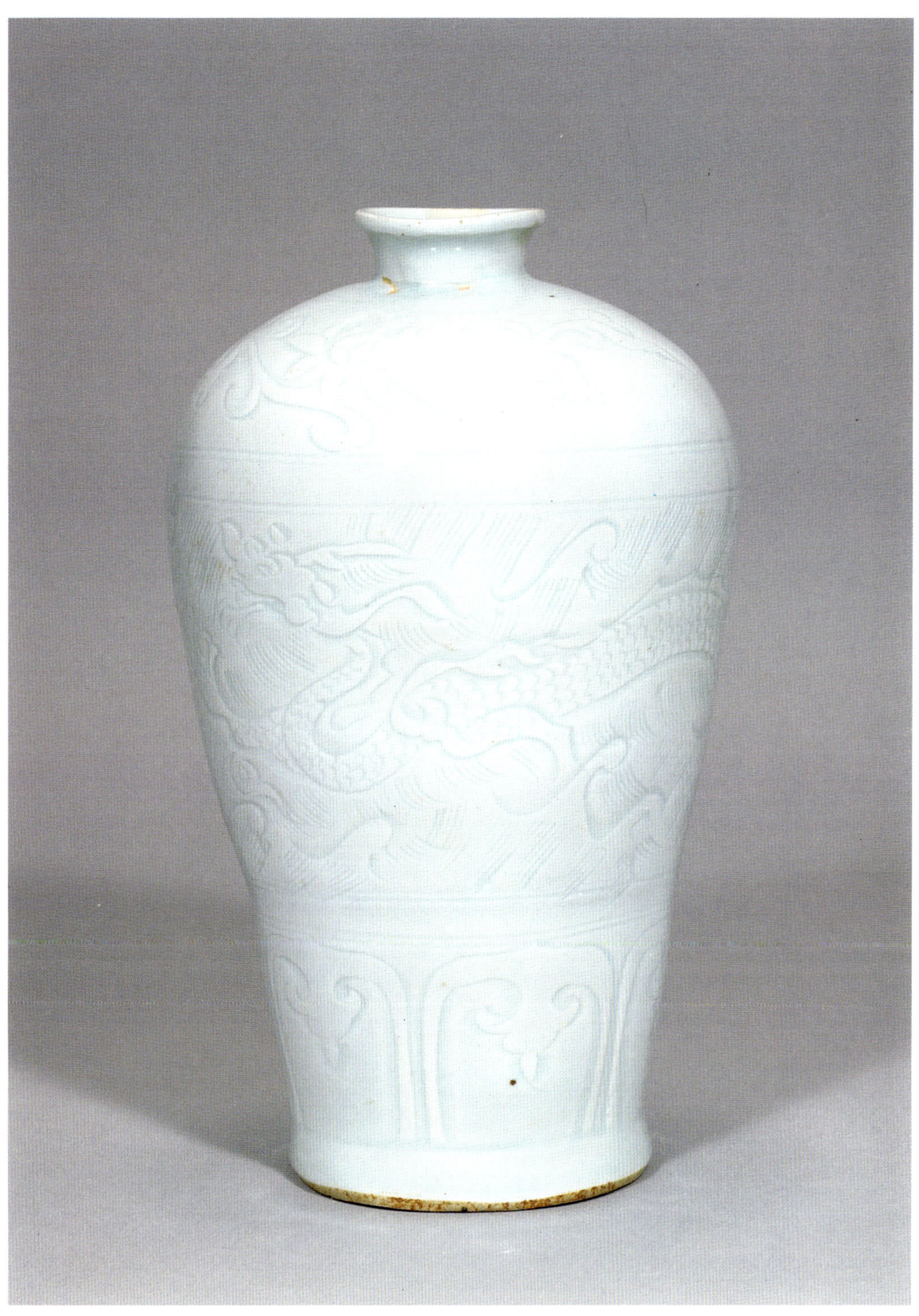

5

MEIPING

Jingdezhen ware, *yingqing*-glazed porcelain with carved dragon design

Yuan dynasty, early 14th century

H. 26.3 cm (10 3/8 in.)

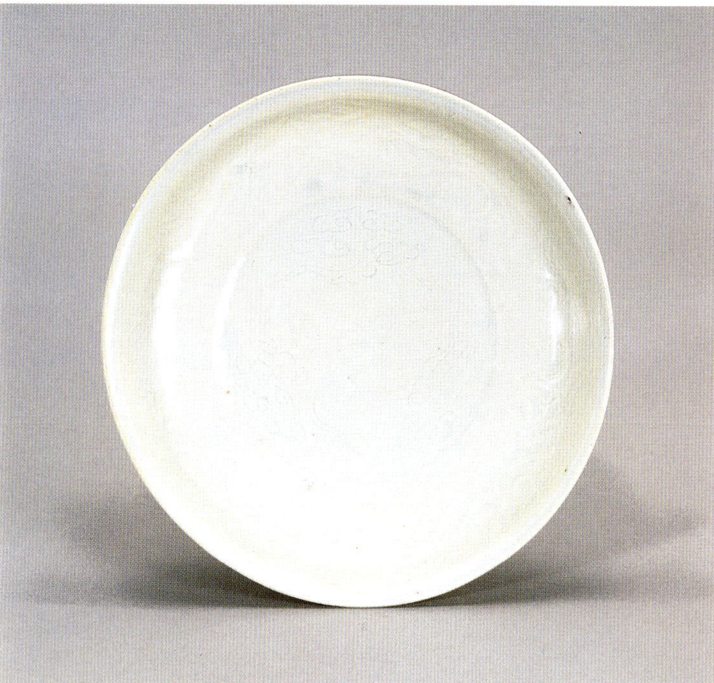

6

SHALLOW DISH

Jingdezhen ware, monochrome white porcelain with molded and incised phoenix-and-cloud design

Yuan dynasty, mid 14th century

D. 19 cm (7 1/2 in.)

Gently curving translucent walls, an everted mouth rim, and a wide base distinguish this shallow dish. The thick, opaque glaze with a greenish tinge and pearly luster covers the entire piece save for the foot rim, the interior of the narrow, wedge-shaped foot, and the convex base, which in firing turned a mottled reddish buff color flecked with iron stains. Two finely detailed phoenix and fungus-shaped clouds are molded on the cavetto in low relief; the three clouds in the central field are incised.

The monochrome white wares produced at Jingdezhen during the fourteenth century display a notable array of glaze tonalities and varying degrees of brightness and translucency. The relative opacity and low reflectivity of the glaze on this example are due, in comparison to the standard *yingqing* glaze, to a low ash content, which increased the viscosity necessary for the high temperatures—between 1280 and 1300 degrees centigrade—at which such pieces are believed to have been fired. This modification in glaze constitution appears to have been prompted during the Yuan period by new production methods devised for heavier and thicker-walled vessels. Even so, the Idemitsu piece is quite thin and light in weight.

Technical, physical, and decorative similarities to the dish in the Percival David Foundation with inscribed date corresponding to 1328 extend to the warping of the pieces and the iron spitouts in the glazes.[1] A noteworthy and perhaps significant difference between the two occurs in the interior central-field decoration, where the David dish has a molded design in technical congruency with the molded decor of the cavetto. The techniques of molding and incising had traditionally been quite separate at Jingdezhen; usually one or the other was used exclusively on a given piece. Their combination in the decoration of a single ceramic, as in this example, can be viewed as an innovative step and allies the Idemitsu dish with a number of similarly decorated pieces produced during the later fourteenth century (see no. 13).

The distinctive triple-cloud group is related to later fourteenth-century ceramic design, as exemplified in the shards from the Hongwu palace site in Nanjing,[2] and appears not infrequently in underglaze-blue-decorated wares of the fifteenth century. The Idemitsu dish, therefore, might postdate that in the David Foundation and was possibly produced toward the middle of the fourteenth century.

1. The 1328 dish is illustrated and discussed by Margaret Medley in "A T'ien-Shun Saucer," *Archives of Asian Art*, vol. 21, (1967–68), pp. 67–69.

2. The porcelains excavated at the site of the late fourteenth-century palace built by the first emperor of the Ming dynasty, Zhu Yuanzhang, during the Hongwu period (1368–98), was reported in *Wenwu*, no. 8 (1976), pp. 71–77. See fig. 7, p. 75, for a dish shard with molded dragon cavetto and three clouds painted in underglaze blue on the interior bottom, and pl. 1 for an overglaze-red enamel dish shard with five-clawed dragon on the cavetto and two clouds in what remains of the bottom interior.

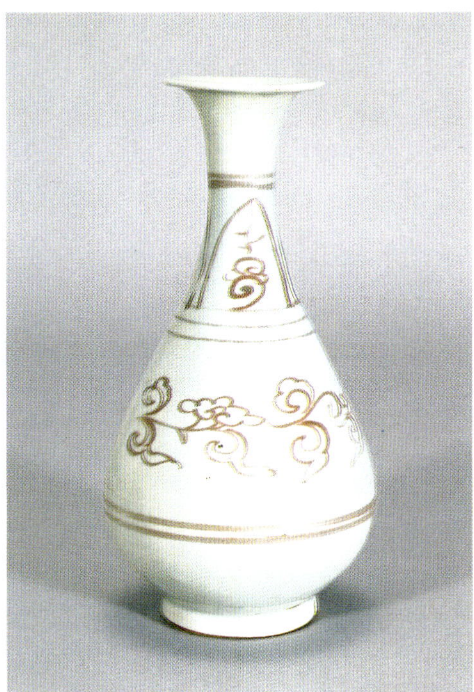

7

YUHUCHUN BOTTLE

Jingdezhen ware, underglaze-red-decorated porcelain with fungus design

Yuan dynasty, mid 14th century

H. 23.6 cm (9 1/4 in.)

This bottle has a pear-shaped body, slender neck, flaring mouth, and slightly splayed foot. The unglazed foot ring is strongly cut and has burned a rusty buff color in firing. The thickly applied glaze on the recessed base and steep interior wall of the foot has parted in areas, exposing the white body, which exhibits some discoloration. The two horizontal registers of decoration are painted in a warm copper-red beneath a bright, smooth glaze of slight grayish tonality.

Yuhuchun, the term by which this shape is known, means literally "jade-vessel spring" and is also the title of a Yuan-dynasty play in which a beautiful heroine composes a poem with the same name. How the title came to be associated with the ceramic form is not clear, nor even when the practice began, but at some point figural scenes or themes derived from that drama might have played an important role in the decoration of such bottles.[1]

The *yuhuchun* bottle became a standard shape at Jingdezhen during the Yuan dynasty and was produced with designs that might be incised, carved, appliquéd, or painted either in underglaze cobalt or, as here, with underglaze copper oxide. In the decoration of underglaze-red vessels the copper solution was applied either directly to the unfired clay body or to a base coat of clear glaze covered by a final single layer of glaze before firing in an atmosphere that included a reduction period within a range of 1250 to 1280 degrees centigrade.[2]

The term "spare style" aptly describes this design's scant number of motifs, their simple disposition, and the economical brushwork. The rapidly brushed images possess an air of practiced spontaneity, like that of a calligrapher producing by rote a passage of "running-script" style; a number of copper-decorated vessels are in fact ornamented with lines of calligraphy. Inscriptions written in underglaze red occur on some of the earliest datable underglaze copper-red decorated vessels of the Yuan, including a four-lobed flat dish from the Sinan shipwreck of 1323 with a couplet written on the interior.[3] The same ship carried a number of *yingqing*-glazed bottles with spare incised designs remarkably similar in style to the painted design of the present piece. This suggests that the carved and painted *yuhuchun* are almost contemporaneous, or at least that the spare carved style was translated into underglaze painting soon thereafter.

1. Kikutaro Saito in "Mid 14th-Century Yuan-Dynasty Blue-and-White and the Yuan Drama," pt. 2, *Kobijutsu*, no. 19 (October 1967), also notes the relationship between the title of the play and the name of the vessel.

2. *Jingdezhen taoci*, no. 2 (1984), p. 21.

3. See *Sinan haeja yumul*, vol. 3 (Seoul: Ministry of Culture and Information of Korea, 1985), pl. 73, no. 94 a and b.

This pear-shaped bottle has a narrow neck, flaring mouth, and slightly everted foot enclosing a glazed, recessed base. The dense body has burned buff on the beveled foot ring. The multibanded decoration was painted with underglaze blue of a slightly gray tonality. The relatively bright glaze has a bluish tinge.

The horizontal banding of the design is typical of late Yuan-dynasty composition, as are a majority of the motifs: the lotus panels ringing the base and shoulder, the banana leaves on the neck, the various filler patterns in the narrow divider bands, and the simplified leaf-shaped elements ringing the foot. The decoration of the interior of the mouth, here a classic scroll, is also typical of *yuhuchun* bottles of this period.

Most captivating and original is the figural scene that unfolds within the central body register. Daoist lore, a fertile source of inspiration for both the Yuan dramatist and painter, provided the porcelain decorator with his theme. The immortal Lu Dongpin, a late eighth-century scholar whose repeated failure in the examinations led to his conversion to Daoism, appears in a fungus-rich garden and enveloped in the clouds that declare his true ethereal nature.[1] Pictured in his scholar's cape and robe and carrying the magical sword by which he overcomes malevolence and makes himself invisible, Lu is joined by the wondrous deer capable of finding the elusive fungus of immortality and by a rabbit whose fabled ancestor pounds the elixir of immortality on the moon. The importance of this immortal and of Daoism in general in Yuan society makes his image a natural choice for the decoration of this popular ware.

The casualness of the drawing, the grayish tonality of the underglaze blue, and the simple forms of such elements as the fungus and lone chrysanthemum flower relate the work to examples, usually less ambitious in design, found in Southeast Asia. However, a bottle similar to the Idemitsu piece in all respects save for its dragon-and-cloud decoration in the main body zone, belonging to the Cultural Bureau of Guangdong province, and another depicting an early Han-dynasty military scene as its main subject, in the Hunan Provincial Museum, are evidence of the popularity of such bottles within China itself.[2] Whatever the intended market, such figural themes provided opportunities for early essays in narrative composition and continued to occupy the potters of Jingdezhen for many centuries thereafter.

1. The theme of this bottle was identified by Kikutaro Saito in "Mid Yuan Blue-and-White and the Yuan Drama," pt. 1, *Kobijutsu*, no. 18 (July 1967), pp. 34–35.

2. The piece in Guangdong is illustrated in *Jingdezhen taoci*, no. 2 (1984), p. 55, and the Hunan bottle in *Wenwu*, no. 9 (1976), figs. 1–2 and pl. 9.

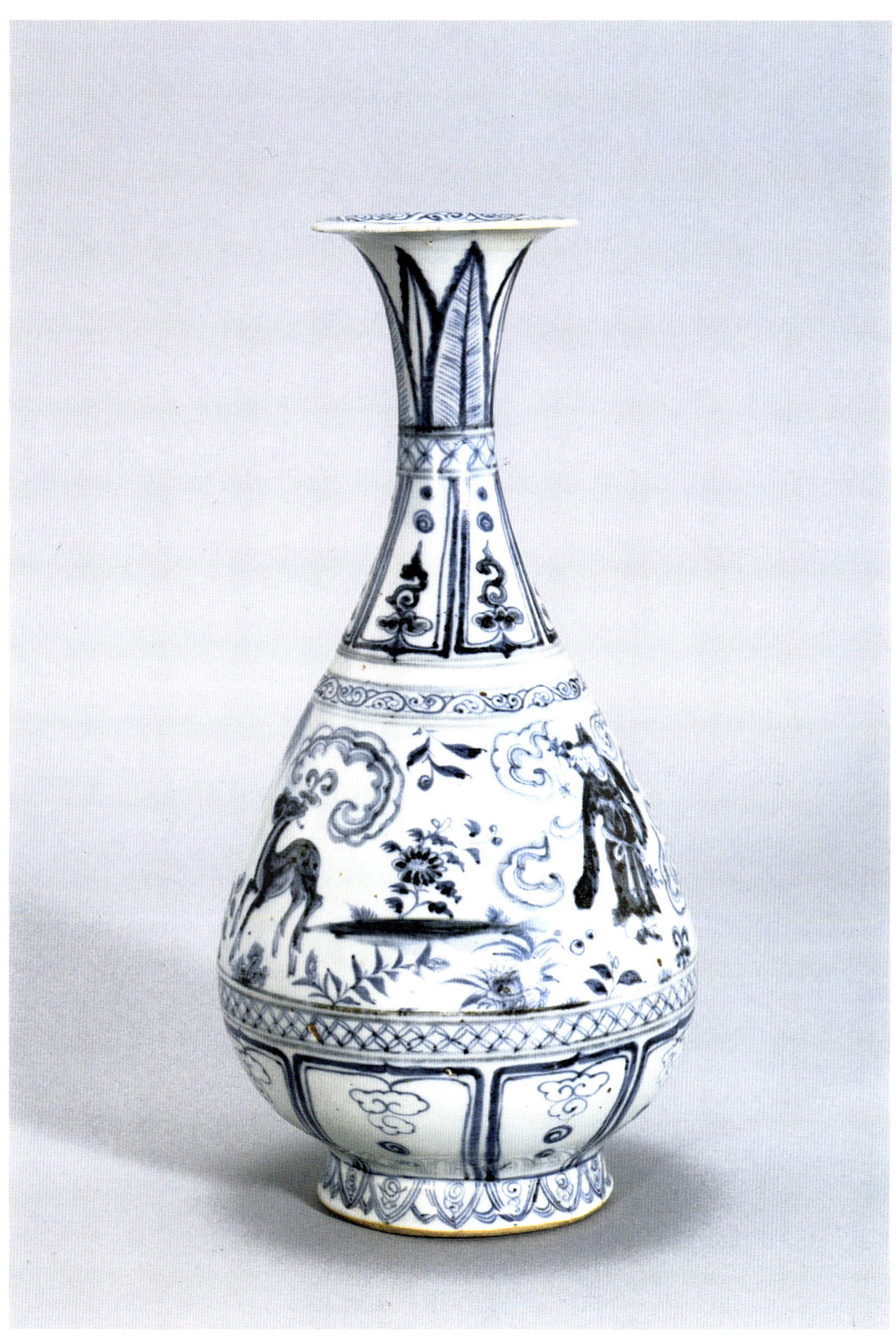

8

YUHUCHUN BOTTLE

Jingdezhen ware, underglaze-blue-decorated porcelain with scene of Lu Dongpin

Yuan dynasty, mid 14th century

H. 30.5 cm (12 in.)

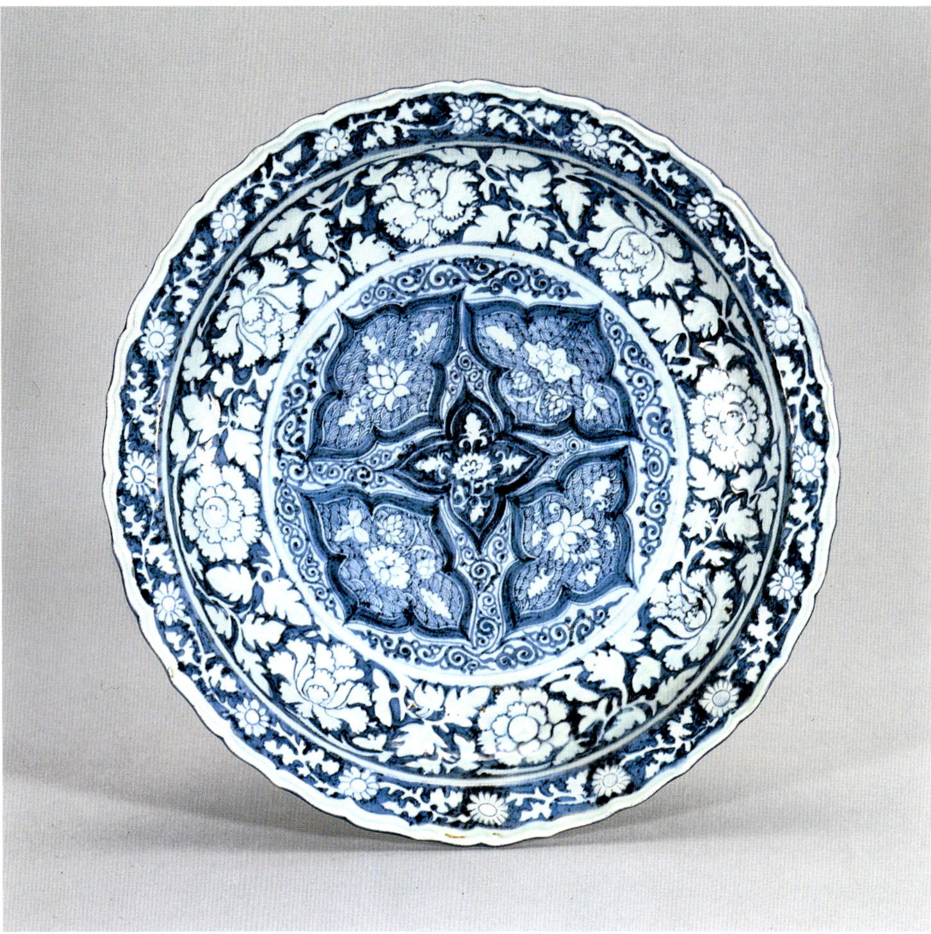

9

LARGE FOLIATE-RIMMED DISH

Jingdezhen ware, porcelain decorated with white-reserve floral design against blue ground

Yuan dynasty, mid 14th century

D. 45.3 cm (17 7/8 in.)

This large dish has a rounded cavetto, a flattened mouth rim with a thickened bracket-foliate edge, and a narrow foot surrounding an unglazed, buff-colored base, where a faded ink inscription, possibly in Arabic, is written. The predominantly white-reserve design is painted in the interior bottom and combined with molding in the cavetto and on the mouth rim. The cobalt is rich in color, and its application ranges from thin to so thick that the pigment has risen to the surface of the glaze, forming metalliclike patches, a phenomenon known as the "heaped-and-piled" effect. The bright glaze has a bluish tinge.

The central four-pointed medallion, which contains a formally arranged flower and leaves in white against blue, establishes quadrants into which elongated quatrefoil panels heavily outlined in blue are placed against a knobbed-scroll ground. Within these quatrefoil frames, lotus blossoms and attendant foliage spring from slender stems across concentric arc-shaped waves. This central zone, already a varied and complex mixture of forms, is framed by the molded peony scroll of the cavetto. These flowers, seen alternately from side and frontal views, are further demarcated by blue lines, a treatment repeated in the molded chrysanthemum scroll on the flattened rim. The foliation of the rim is soft and vague but nevertheless enhances the ornate floral character of the piece.

This dish and others with white-reserve designs against a blue ground constitute a group that, even though sharing a horror vacui and the same vocabulary of motifs, is tremendously diverse. No two are quite alike. What sets them apart artistically from standard blue-on-white porcelains is their independence, by and large, from a painterly aesthetic. Although the large size of the dish was determined by the dining requirements of Islamic patrons, none of the motifs was devised specifically for that lucrative market. However, the copious ornament marshaled to fully consume the dish's surface was a response to an aesthetic quite alien to indigenous, traditional Chinese taste, yet one that Chinese potters perfectly embraced in the creation of this dazzling style.

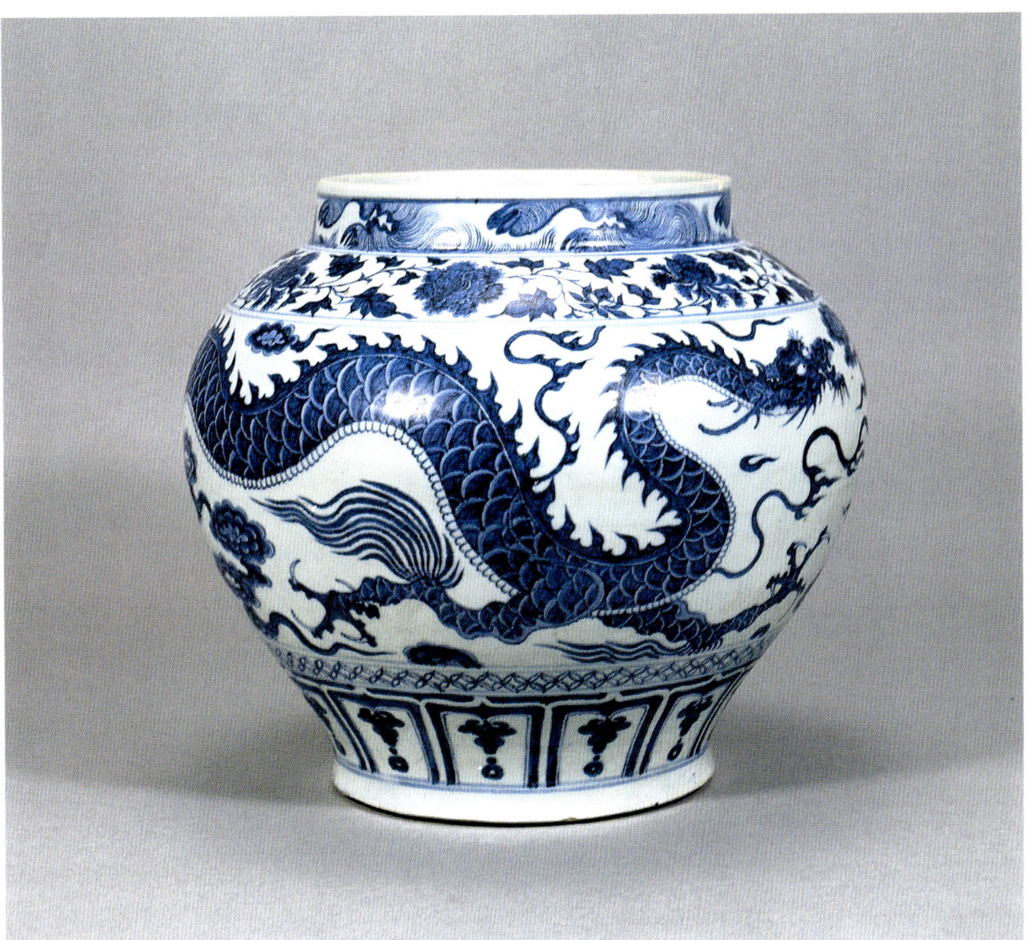

10

LARGE JAR

Jingdezhen ware, underglaze-blue-decorated porcelain with dragon design

Yuan dynasty, mid 14th century

H. 30.3 cm (12 in.)

The wide neck of this large jar slants gently inward to a thickened, round lip rim and its body swells from a strongly everted foot. The foot is beveled on the exterior and slides into the slightly recessed unglazed base, which is a warm buff color. The cobalt blue of the underglaze decoration is deep and rich in tone. The lusterless glaze surface resulted either from long and intimate contact with alkaline sand or earth during burial or from too diligent a cleansing after the piece was found at an undisclosed site in the Philippines.

The main body provides the field for a mighty, four-clawed dragon, who charges energetically across a cloud-dotted sky. The head of the dragon is compact, tense, and alert, his scaly body and limbs muscular and agile, and his fiery eyes and jagged, bristling spine expressive of the vehemence of the beast. A change of mood is created by the lush peony scroll undulating across the shoulder, but the dominant theme is restated by waves cresting vigorously on the neck. A linked-coin band frames the base of the main composition; its horizontal orientation balances the vertical lotus panels above the foot.

The sensitive and well-controlled application of cobalt-blue pigment to produce fully descriptive yet intensely expressive forms is a characteristic shared by a small number of extremely high-quality late Yuan underglaze-blue-decorated vessels with the dragon as the central theme, including the pair of temple vases in the Percival David Foundation dated by inscription to 1351.[1] Some agree that the striking stylistic similarity between these stunning pieces makes it possible to conclude that they were produced by the same consumately skilled artist. The great visual strength and attractiveness of this extraordinarily handsome jar derive from its fine potting, its well-balanced shape, the effectiveness of its composition, and a superb underglaze-blue painting—truly a stunning example of Yuan-dynasty blue-and-white porcelain at its very finest.

1. *Oriental Ceramics*, vol. 6, *Percival David Foundation of Chinese Art* (Tokyo: Kodansha, 1982), pl. 25. For a discussion of the Idemitsu jar and its relationship to the David vases, see Tadanori Yuba, "Sometsuke ryūmon tsubo," *Kokka*, no. 1911, pp. 19–24.

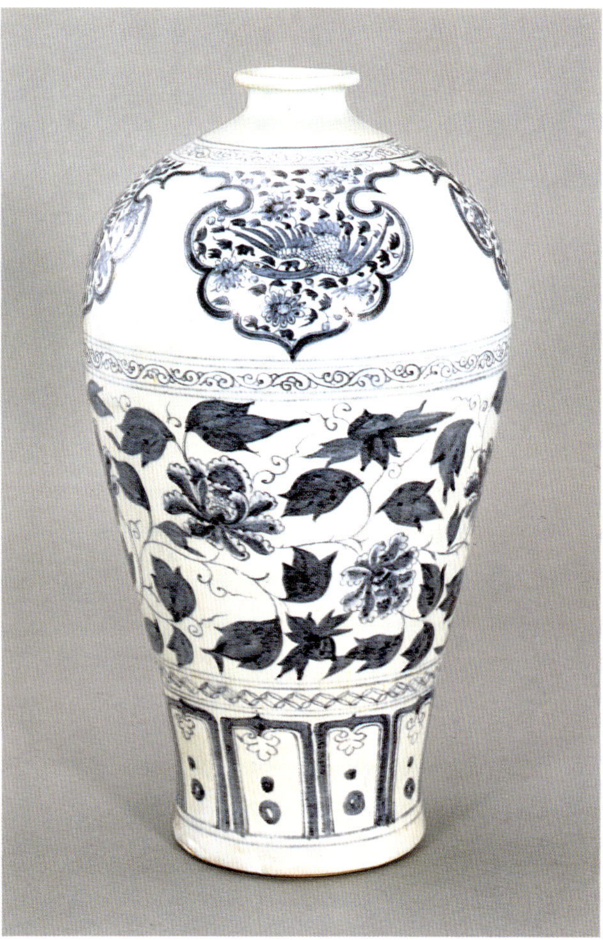

11

MEIPING

Jingdezhen ware, underglaze-blue-decorated porcelain with peony design

Yuan dynasty, third quarter 14th century

H. 39 cm (15 3/8 in.)

This *meiping* has sloping shoulders, a gently everted foot, and a short neck, which flares abruptly to a thickened lip rim. The broad foot ring surrounds a recessed base; both have burned salmon red in firing. The deep blue pigment of the decoration has a granular texture and the bluish-tinged glaze a soft luster. One side of the vessel is heavily crazed and discolored.

A number of motifs recurrent in late Yuan underglaze-painted ceramics are here arranged according to a standard compositional formula. The shoulder is symmetrically draped with a four-pointed cloud collar, so-called because of its resemblance to the decorative garb popular in princely circles during the Yuan period. A leafy peony scroll twines around the body, and a ring of upright lotus panels encircles the base. These major zones are bordered by narrow geometric bands: classic scrolls above and a linked-coin band below. Each of the four cloud-collar lappets contains a single goose set against a floral ground consisting of peony, chrysanthemum, or five-petaled flowers. In the central zone the well-articulated petals of the peony blossoms, with their dark interiors, white outer rims, and firm outlines, appear lush and buoyant; the surrounding large leaves, though applied with relatively even and flat strokes of blue, twist and turn, adding a rhythmic vitality to the decoration.

The thin stems of the peony scroll sprout delicate, scrolling tendrils, a very rare embellishment repeated on a nearly identical *meiping* in the Metropolitan Museum of Art in New York.[1] The two pieces share similarly discolored, crackled, bluish white glazes. It is tempting to suggest that they were not only painted by the same decorator but even produced in the same firing.

1. Suzanne G. Valenstein, *A Handbook of Chinese Ceramics* (New York: Metropolitan Museum of Art, 1975), pl. 73. This uncommon decorative device is also exhibited by a large jar with tendrils issuing from a central peony scroll in the Topkapi Saray Museum, illustrated by Regina Krahl in *Chinese Ceramics in the Topkapi Saray Museum, Istanbul*, vol. 2, *Yuan and Ming Dynasty Porcelains* (London: Sotheby's Publications, 1986), pl. 587, TKS 15/7800.

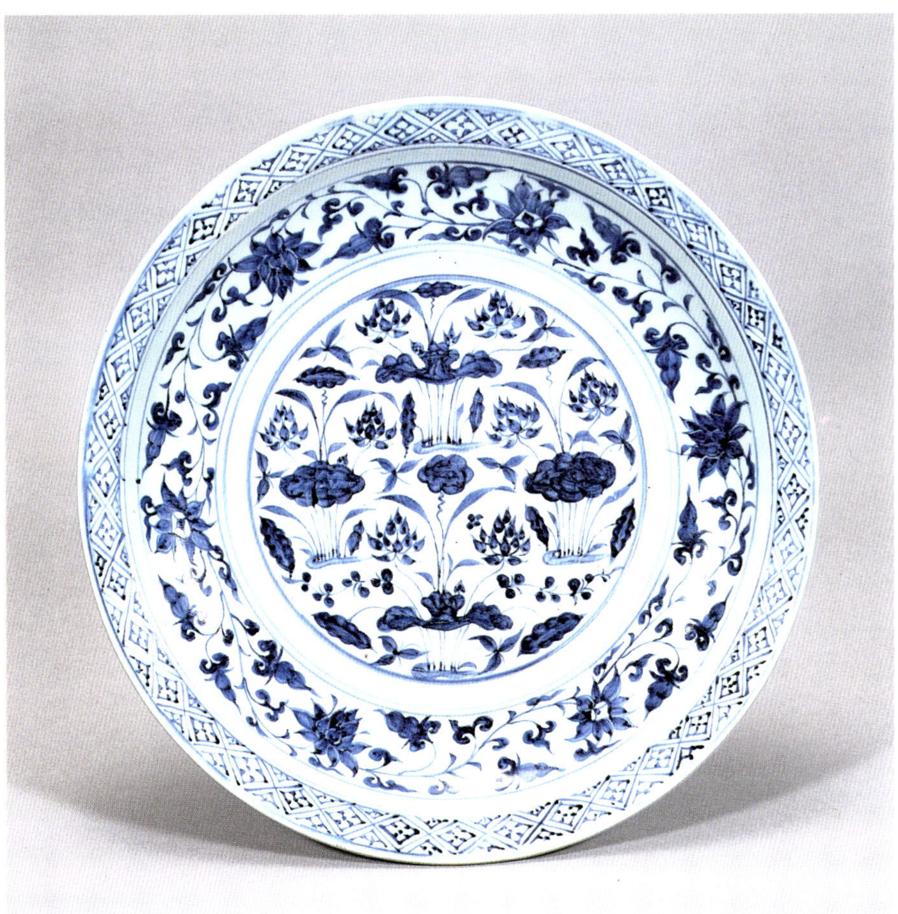

12

LARGE DISH

Jingdezhen ware, underglaze-blue-decorated porcelain with lotus-pond design

Yuan dynasty, third quarter 14th century

D. 40.1 cm (15 3/4 in.)

A flat, circular bottom, wide, rounded cavetto, and flattened mouth rim with thickened edge define this dish. The interior of the foot slants toward the unglazed base, which is remarkably white and free of discoloration. The underglaze cobalt is intense in color and richly "heaped-and-piled" to form a predominantly floral design under the bright, smooth glaze.

The diamond-diaper border on the mouth and the spiky-leafed lotus wreath repeated in the cavetto and on the reverse were often-used patterns in porcelain decoration of the Yuan period. Here they are combined with a carefully contrived scene of a lotus pond. The opened flowers and spreading leaves of the four separate plants are symmetrically and rigidly arranged, as are the plant groups stationed in relation to one another. Subjecting a scene, which had been so naturalistically portrayed in painting and in previous ceramic decor, to such rigorous control emphasized the planar surface of the porcelain field and created an orderly structure yet retained the lively ornamental quality so much in vogue during the late Yuan period. The tightly organized arrangement and the regularity of this design suggest a date somewhat later than that of the mid fourteenth-century David vases. Similar examples found at the Tughlag Palace in Delhi, the Topkapi Saray in Istanbul, and the Ardebil Shrine in Tehran are evidence of the wide distribution and appreciation of such late Yuan ceramics.

This strongly potted bowl has steep curving sides, a slightly everted mouth, and a high, beveled foot with the inner wall slanting to the base. The dense white body revealed on the unglazed foot rim and recessed base is marked with large iron flecks. A band of ten lotus panels is neatly incised on the exterior above the foot beneath a thin cobalt-blue glaze, and marks left by a paring tool are visible beneath the glaze. The cavetto is molded with a design of two five-clawed dragons among clouds and the bottom incised with a single cloud cluster under a warm copper-red glaze. The darker patches appear as though additional pigment or glaze was brushed over the initial coating.

The combination of two contrasting glaze colors on a single porcelain vessel is quite extraordinary and occurs on a very small number of extant pieces of the early Ming period .[1] The colors vary, including reds, blues, browns, and white, but all examples exhibit both strong potting and molded dragon-and-cloud cavetto decoration with incised cloud interiors. During the excavation of the remains of the Nanjing palace of the Hongwu emperor, a shard consisting of the intact foot, base, and portions of the lower wall of a bowl was discovered.[2] The interior has a molded dragon design in the cavetto and an incised cloud cluster on the bottom under a *jiqing* (sky-clearing blue) glaze, and the exterior has incised lotus panels above the foot beneath a *jiang* (soya bean) glaze. The body and construction of the bowl are consistent with those of other examples, supporting a later fourteenth-century date during the Hongwu period for the entire group.[3]

This evidence of experimentation and innovation in porcelain during the earliest decades of the Ming dynasty is especially intriguing. Not only are the two-color schemes novel, but the nature of the colors themselves suggests a pioneering attitude. The location of the kilns established by Zhu Yuanzhang at Zhushan (Pearl Hill) in Jingdezhen is reportedly known, and future excavations should shed more light on this fascinating group.

1. For example, a bowl with brownish black interior, and white exterior in the Yamato Bunkakan near Nara in Japan, illustrated in *Exhibition of Blue and White Wares in the Yuan Dynasty; 14th Century Ching-te Chen Wares* (Osaka: Museum of Oriental Ceramics, 1985), pl. 51; a stem cup and a dish, each with blue interior and brown exterior, and a dish with blue interior and brown exterior in the British Museum, *Oriental Ceramics*, vol. 5, *The British Museum, London* (Tokyo: Kodansha, 1981), pls. III and 30; a stem cup with blue interior and brown exterior in the Nelson Gallery, *Sekai tōji zenshū*, vol. 13, *Liao, Jin and Yuan* (Tokyo: Shōgakukan, 1981), pl. 238; and a bowl with red interior and blue exterior illustrated by Sherman Lee and Wai-kam Ho in *Chinese Art under the Mongols* (Cleveland: Cleveland Museum of Art, 1968), pl. 162. All of the above have molded dragon cavetto designs and incised clouds on the interiors.

2. *Wenwu*, no. 8 (1976), pl. 5:5. Good color reproductions of the shard are published in *Sekai tōji zenshū*, vol. 14, *Ming Dynasty* (Tokyo: Shōgakukan, 1976), pls. 173 (left) and 174 (left).

3. Wang Qingzheng, "Some Remarks on the Hongwu Ware Made in Jingdezhen in the Ming Dynasty," *Shanghai bowuguan jikan*, no. 4, special issue (September 1987), p. 293, includes the Idemitsu bowl in his discussion of the group, which he assigns, using the Nanjing shard as evidence, to the Hongwu period.

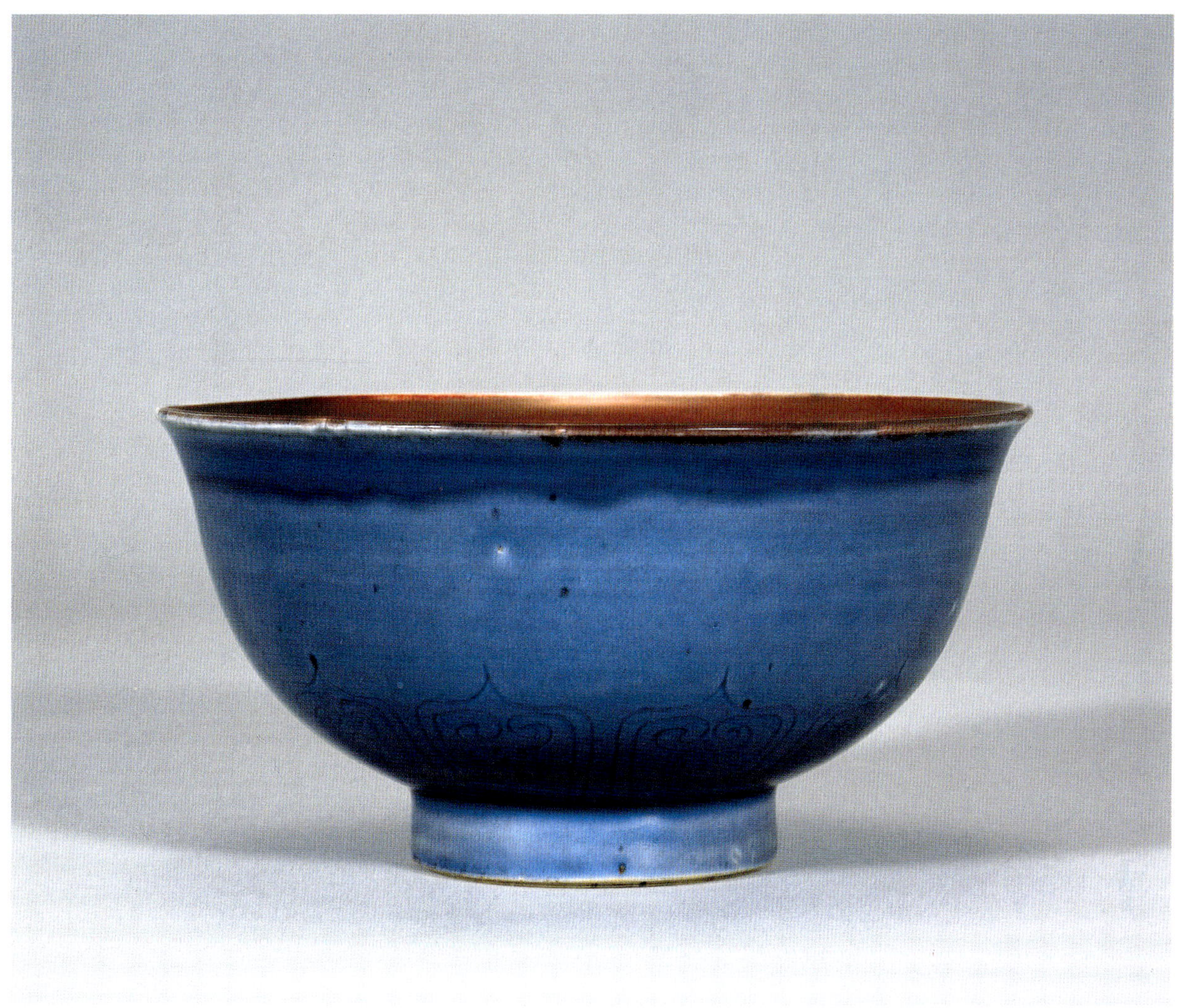

13

BOWL

Jingdezhen ware, red- and blue-glazed porcelain with molded and incised dragon-and-cloud design

Ming dynasty, Hongwu period (1368–98)

D. 19.5 cm (7 3/4 in.)

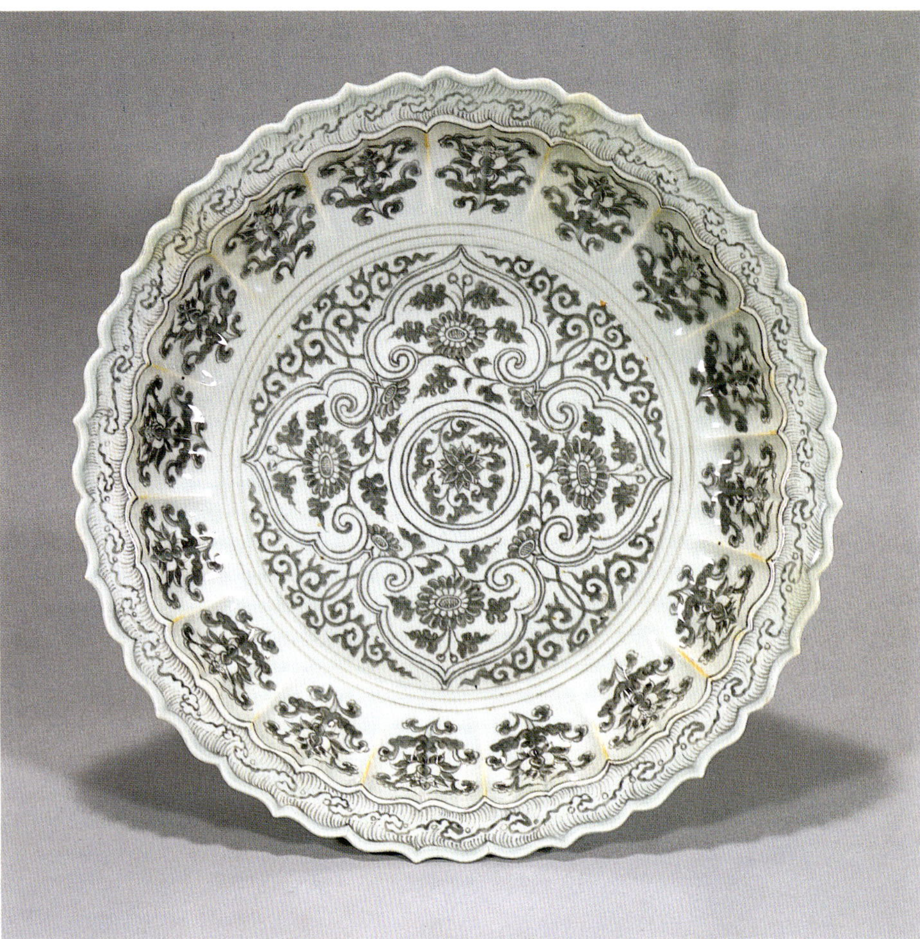

14

LARGE FOLIATE-RIMMED DISH

Jingdezhen ware, underglaze-red-decorated porcelain with floral design

Ming dynasty, Hongwu period (1368–98)

D. 46.5 cm (18 3/8 in.)

This large dish has a deep bracket-lobed cavetto and a slanted foliated rim. The narrow foot is neatly trimmed and the flat recessed base unglazed. The entire piece was swabbed with an iron wash before glazing, which accounts for the orange coloration visible beneath the glaze on the protruding edges. An attempt must have been made to scrape the dressing from the base before firing, since only portions of the base exhibit the orange color. The copper-oxide decoration has a warm grayish tone, and the glaze is thick and smooth with a bright sheen.

The bottom of the dish contains a symmetrically arranged cloud collar with four lappets radiating from a central circular medallion. A chrysanthemum scroll twines in and out of the four panels, with the leaf-framed blossoms precisely centered in each. Barbed scrolls stemming from paired vines anchored to the panels provide a background that is similarly regulated. The central medallion contains a flat, star-shaped lotus; the same flower appears in profile in the sixteen sections of the cavetto and on the reverse wall. A formal wave pattern appears on the flattened rim and on its underside.

Stylistic features of the underglaze-red-decorated group to which this piece belongs suggest a later fourteenth-century date of production. The absence of the type among late Yuan export wares is instructive, and moreover, the presence of such dishes in the palace museums in Beijing and Taipei supports the belief that these ceramics were Hongwu-period official or imperial wares. The underglaze-red-decorated shards discovered at the Hongwu palace site in Nanjing are further evidence of the imperial status of copper-decorated wares during the late fourteenth century.[1]

Such wares relate in style to a group of underglaze-blue-decorated porcelains of similar shape and design. The cobalt-painted wares exhibit the dull, grayish blue color of native Chinese ore, which potters were forced to use in the face of the Hongwu emperor's strictures against foreign trade. The shortage of high-quality imported cobalt might explain in part the increased use of copper oxide at that time. It is possible, however, that red carried a special significance for the Hongwu emperor: the character for his surname means cinnabar red.

1. *Sekai tōji zenshū*, vol. 14, *Ming Dynasty* (Tokyo: Shōgakukan, 1976), pl. 175.

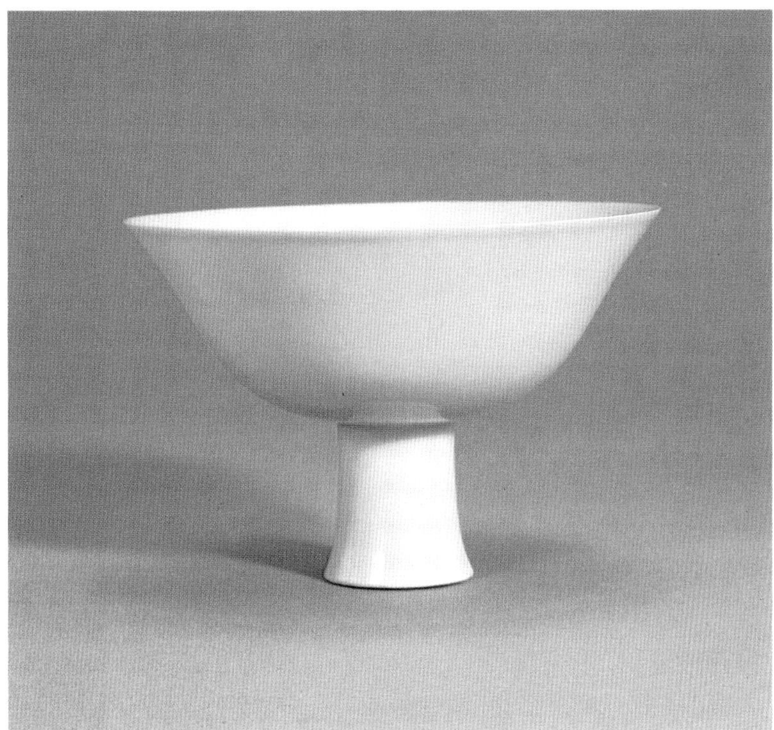

15

STEM CUP

Jingdezhen ware, monochrome white porcelain with molded dragon-and-cloud design

Ming dynasty, Yongle period (1403–24); Yongle four-character mark, *Yongle nian zhi*

H. 10.3 cm (4 in.), D. 15.4 cm (6 1/8 in.)

Moderately curved, this cup opens generously. The slightly splayed, high hollow foot was attached to the cup before glazing; the smooth white body is free of glaze at the foot rim and on a small margin on the inner stem. Two five-clawed dragons and clouds on the interior wall are visible only when the cup is held up to strong light. The intricate design was most likely mold-pressed. The cup's interior was then coated with glaze, before the entire piece was glazed and fired,[1] so that its outer walls could be pared to an extreme thinness. The four-character mark was carefully incised in large seal-script characters in two rows on the bottom of the cup. The extremely smooth glaze has a satiny sheen.

The conclusion that monochrome white porcelain was especially favored during the Yongle period is supported by evidence from the excavation of the early Ming imperial kiln area at Zhushan in Jingdezhen. More than 95 percent of the Yongle porcelain remains were white wares. Among them were fragments of fine white porcelain stem cups that were incised in seal-script with the same four-character reign mark as on the present piece.[2] This reign mark, which appears to be the earliest of Ming imperial marks, is written in a distinctive seal-script style for which the early Ming court calligrapher Shen Du (1357–1434) was widely known and highly esteemed.[3] Having received a court appointment on the basis of his calligraphic skills, Shen Du became the favorite calligrapher of the emperor, attending the monarch daily and even accompanying him on journeys between Nanjing and Beijing. Shen was thus the logical choice to produce a model for the porcelain marks.[4] Indeed, the high standards and great refinement of the wares made by the potters at the imperial kilns during the Yongle emperor's reign were due in no small part to imperial taste and involvement. The sublime elegance and grace of the Idemitsu stem cup, a superb example of the achievements of the era, rest in the perfect union of an exquisitely balanced form, a chaste porcelain body of great thinness, lightness, and translucency, an *anhua* (hidden decoration) of extreme delicacy and subtlety, and a mellow *tianbai* (sweet white) glaze.

1. This is the technique described for such Yongle wares by Geng Baochang in *Ming Qing ciqi jianding*, Ming vol. (Hong Kong: Zhonghua shuju, 1984), p. 33.

2. During this momentous discovery and excavation Yongle porcelain remains were recovered from beneath a Xuande-period imperial kiln, as well as nearby, on the north side of Zhushanlu. Bai Kun, et al., "Jingdezhen Ming Yongle Xuande yuchang yicun," *Zhongguo taoci*, no. 7 (1982), pp. 171–82. For the marked stem cups see p. 173.

3. For a biography of Shen Du see L. Carrington Goodrich, ed., *Dictionary of Ming Biography 1368–1644*, vol. 2 (New York and London: Columbia University Press, 1976), pp. 1191–92.

4. Mr. Liu Xinyuan of the Jingdezhen Ceramics Institute has also arrived at this conclusion, according to Cecilia Riely Lewis and Laura Barnes, whom the author wishes to thank for sharing information obtained during their recent visits to Jingdezhen.

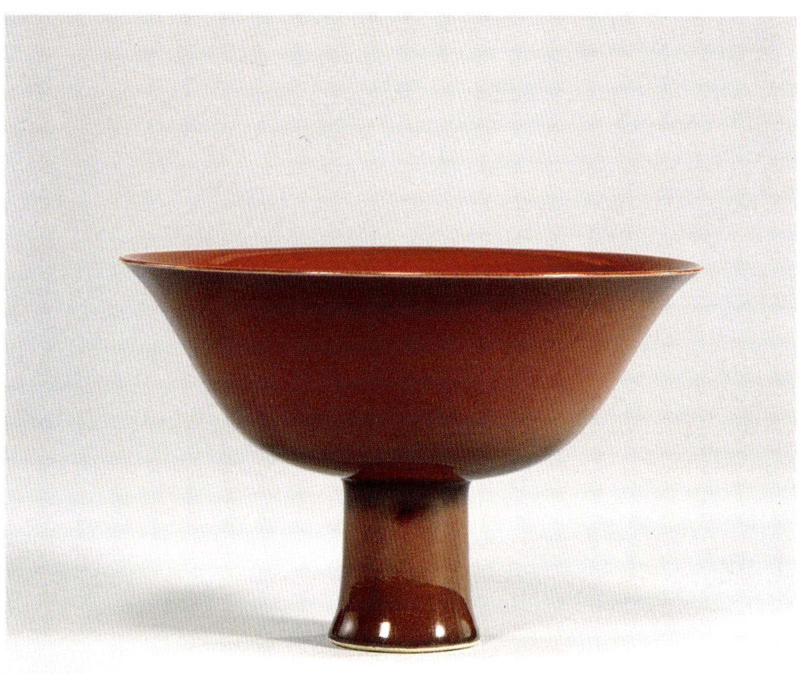

16

STEM CUP

Jingdezhen ware, monochrome red porcelain with molded dragon-and-cloud design

Ming dynasty, Yongle period (1403–24); Yongle four-character mark, *Yongle nian zhi*

H. 10.4 cm (4 1/8 in.), D. 16.2 cm (6 3/8 in.)

This stem cup has a wide bowl with a gently flaring mouth and a slightly everted hollow stem. A finely worked design of two five-clawed dragons and clouds is molded in the cavetto, and the four-character seal-script mark is incised on the bottom of the bowl. The interior of the stem and base of the bowl are covered with a transparent glaze of cool tonality. The color of the smooth glaze applied to the exterior and interior of the bowl was produced from copper oxide, which matured during firing to a deep warm red. The glaze thins at the mouth rim and was wiped neatly from the foot, exposing the pure white body; it is very finely crackled on the exterior and has a rich but subtle sheen. Even though enticingly misted in red, the decoration is easily visible. In shape, decoration, mark, sheer technical refinement, and exquisite beauty, this piece is indeed a most suitable and stunning mate for the monochrome white stem cup (no. 15).

The molded dragon-and-cloud cavetto decoration and copper-red glaze descend from such Hongwu-period wares as the bowl in no. 13, though here the Yongle reign mark replaces the incised clouds in the central field. The use of copper as a coloring agent for monochrome red glazes and underglaze-red painted decoration during the preceding decades of the later fourteenth century provided a solid technical foundation for the development of superior monochromes during the Yongle period. Red-glazed porcelains of the Yongle reign era are quite rare and much more so are those bearing a reign mark. *Xianhong* or "fresh red" vessels of this period, however, were noted as being most precious in the Qing-dynasty text *Jingdezhen taolu*. The present piece is an extraordinary example of what the author—or an earlier source from which he might have been quoting—must have had in mind.[1]

1. Lan Pu, *Jingdezhen taolu* (1815), chap. 5, p. 5 (Taiwan reprint, 1969, p. 169).

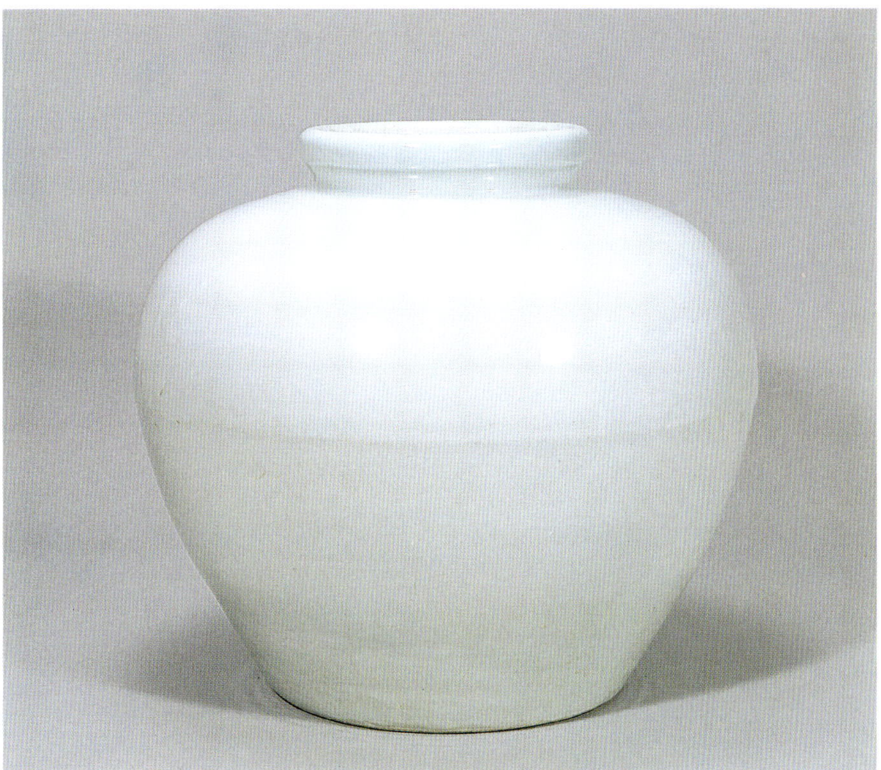

17

GUAN JAR

Jingdezhen ware, monochrome white porcelain

Ming dynasty, early 15th century

H. 42.1 cm (16 5/8 in.)

The swelling shoulders of this voluptuous jar rise from a wide base. The jar is surmounted by a strongly formed neck, joined to the body of the vessel at a sharp angle, with a wide, thickened mouth. The carefully cut, narrow foot surrounds a flat, unglazed, and recessed base, where the compact white porcelain body is revealed. The glaze has a bright luster and is quite smooth. Numerous small air bubbles are trapped within the glaze, but only a scattering of fine surface pores is visible. The glaze displays few imperfections or iron spitouts. The interior is fully glazed and only on the inner lip and neck, where the glaze has gathered thickly, is there a prominent bluish green cast.

Although the midsection join has not been entirely erased, the piece is otherwise extremely well crafted, with a sharpness, clarity, and distinction of form typical of the fine white wares of the early fifteenth century. The technical quality of this jar is made manifest by comparison with monochrome white wares of the later fourteenth century (see, for example, a *guan* jar with incised dragons from the 1389 tomb of Zhu Tan and an undecorated covered *guan* jar from the 1395 tomb of Tang Hou) and with those from the Yongle-period tombs of Song Sheng and his family.[1]

Guan jars with lotus-leaf-shaped covers are listed among the Yongle monochrome white porcelains excavated from Zhushan sites in Jingdezhen.[2] Although the present piece no longer has its cover and the excavated examples are not illustrated in the kiln report, the quality and character of the body and glaze of this piece compare well with the wares described there, suggesting a Yongle-period date of production.

1. The Zhu Tan and Song Sheng family tombs and ceramics are illustrated and discussed by John Addis in "Hung Wu and Yung Lo White," *Transactions of the Oriental Ceramic Society*, vol. 41 (1975–77), pp. 35–57, and *Chinese Ceramics from Datable Tombs* (London and New York: Sotheby Parke Bernet, 1978), pp. 58–65 and pl. 32h for the Zhu Tan tomb and jar, and pp. 85–128 and pls. 37a–37n and 39a–39t for the Song Sheng group. The Tang Hou vessel is illustrated in *Wenwu*, no. 2 (1977), p. 38, fig. 7.

2. *Zhongguo taoci*, no. 7 (1982), p. 173.

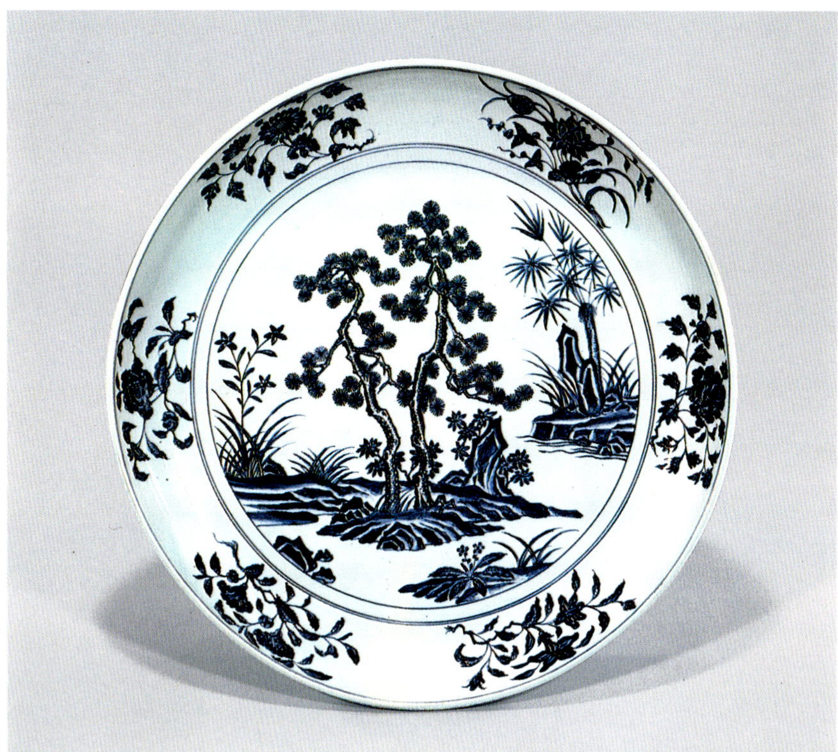

18

LARGE PLATTER

Jingdezhen ware, underglaze-blue-decorated porcelain with garden scene

Ming dynasty, early 15th century

D. 62.6 cm (24 5/8 in.)

The expansive flat inner field of this extravagantly large platter provides ample ground for a garden scene, painted in underglaze blue. Restraint governed the decoration of the cavetto and the similarly decorated exterior wall, where five blossoming branches and a single lotus bouquet are generously spaced against the white ground. The blue is vibrant and rich, and the motifs are clear and distinct beneath the luminous, smooth, colorless glaze.

Not only a decorative embellishment, the garden scene is a convincing picture. The forms are substantial, and the spatial relationships comparatively naturalistic. Depending on the particular form, the pigment was densely or thinly, darkly or lightly dabbed, brushed, smudged, stroked, lined, or stippled. Layered earthy mounds form a ground for the growth of primrose, grasses, lily, azalea, palm, and pine. The downswept evergreen branches are laden with thick clusters of prickly needles, and the gnarled roots, scaly bark, and twisted knots of the tree trunks convey strength and nobility. The careful placement of various outcroppings and of a few undulating lines at the foot of the far bank implies the receding plane of a pond or stream.

The similarity between such splendidly executed pictorial scenes as this and a number of early Ming paintings suggests the participation of professional painters, who were likely employed by the court and responsible if not for the actual execution of such decoration then for the compositional models.[1] The use of models and pattern books resulted in the standardization and repetition of design so evident in early Ming porcelain.[2]

Yongle-period underglaze-blue-decorated porcelain has not yet been reported from the excavations at Zhushan, although the excavators do date one find relevant to the present dish to the Xuande period.[3] A shard from a platter, it is decorated with clustered pine needles and spiky palm leaves not unlike those appearing in the upper right of the Idemitsu platter. Despite this evidence for a Xuande dating, the prevailing judgment that this piece and others of its kind are representative of a Yongle underglaze-blue decorative style might ultimately be supported by further archaeological evidence.

1. Note, for instance, the striking resemblance between two similarly decorated flasks with landscape and figural scenes in the Topkapi Saray Museum and the National Palace Museum in Taipei and the paintings of the early Ming court painter Li Cai, for example, *Jin Kao Riding a Carp* in the Shanghai Museum of Art. See *Porcelain of the National Palace Museum*, vol. 1, pl. 11, 11a–b (Hong Kong, 1963) and Regina Krahl, *Chinese Ceramics in the Topkapi Saray Museum, Istanbul*, vol. 2, *Yuan and Ming Dynasty Porcelains*, (London: Sotheby's Publications, 1986), pl. 612 and col. pl. p. 422, TKS 15/1403.

2. Large platters alike in size, design, and technique to the present piece are in the Ardebil Shrine collection (John A. Pope, *Chinese Porcelains from the Ardebil Shrine*, Washington: Freer Gallery of Art, 1956, pl. 42, 29.312) and in the Umezawa Kinenkan Museum in Tokyo (*Sekai tōji zenshū*, vol. 14, *Ming Dynasty*, Tokyo: Shōgakukan, 1976, pl. 12).

3. *Zhongguo taoci*, no. 7 (1982), pl. 24, fig. 30.

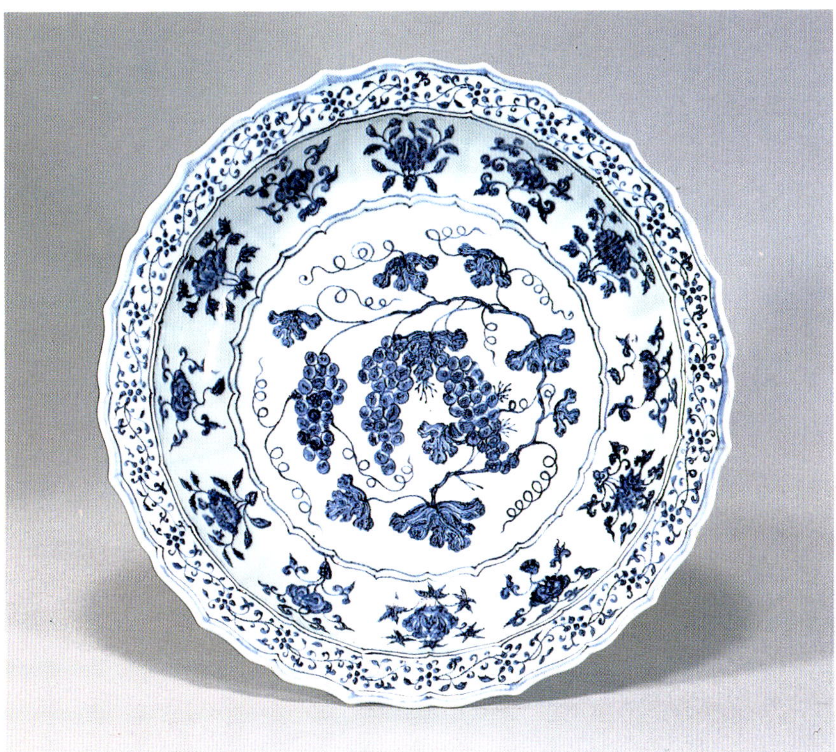

19

LARGE DISH

Jingdezhen ware, underglaze-blue-decorated porcelain with grapevine design

Ming dynasty, early 15th century, probably Xuande period (1426–35)

D. 43.5 cm (17 1/8 in.)

A flattened mouth rim raised at the edge of this dish is foliated to correspond with the twelve bracket lobes of the cavetto. The low, narrow foot encloses an unglazed, recessed base, which has fired to an ocherish color. Arabic, Persian, and Sanskrit inscriptions written in ink on the base, three discrete holes drilled into the base, like those found on ceramics in Near Eastern collections, and a single line inscription engraved on the exterior of the foot indicate a history in the Islamic world, where a number of similarly decorated "grape dishes" remain even today. Three bunches of grapes with leaves and delicate curling tendrils issue from a single vine in the central field. This is framed by paired underglaze-blue lines, which parallel and enhance the foliation at the base of the cavetto. Grapevines appeared as a motif in underglaze-blue designs as early as the fourteenth century, but they were usually only one of a number of elements drawn from nature and grouped in abundant decorative schemes popular during that period. Here the singular motif is presented as a carefully composed image or, in the words of John Pope, as a still life.[1]

In the cavetto six fungus sprays alternate with camellia, chrysanthemum, gardenia, hibiscus, lotus, and peony designs. The reverse is decorated with similar sprays, including pinks, morning glory, and mallow, each a formal presentation consisting of a central blossom or fungus symmetrically surrounded by leaves. A thin scrolling vine sprouting numerous small leaves and six-petaled star-shaped flowers forms a wreath upon the mouth rim.

The color varies from a thinly applied grayish blue to a densely heaped, deep inky color. In a number of areas cobalt particles are displaced and appear to flow in the glaze, resulting in blurred and indistinct images, a phenomenon termed *fanjing* (sailing blue). The particular character of this cobalt blue as well as the orange-peel texture and bluish tinge of the glaze are not inconsistent with those features found on well-known marked Xuande types. The discovery during the Zhushan excavations in Jingdezhen of an identically decorated dish bearing a Xuande reign mark provides an even more compelling reason for dating the Idemitsu dish to the Xuande period.[2]

1. John Alexander Pope, *Chinese Porcelains from the Ardebil Shrine* (Washington: Freer Gallery of Art, 1956), p. 94.

2. *Zhongguo taoci*, no. 7 (1982), pl. 24, fig. 27.

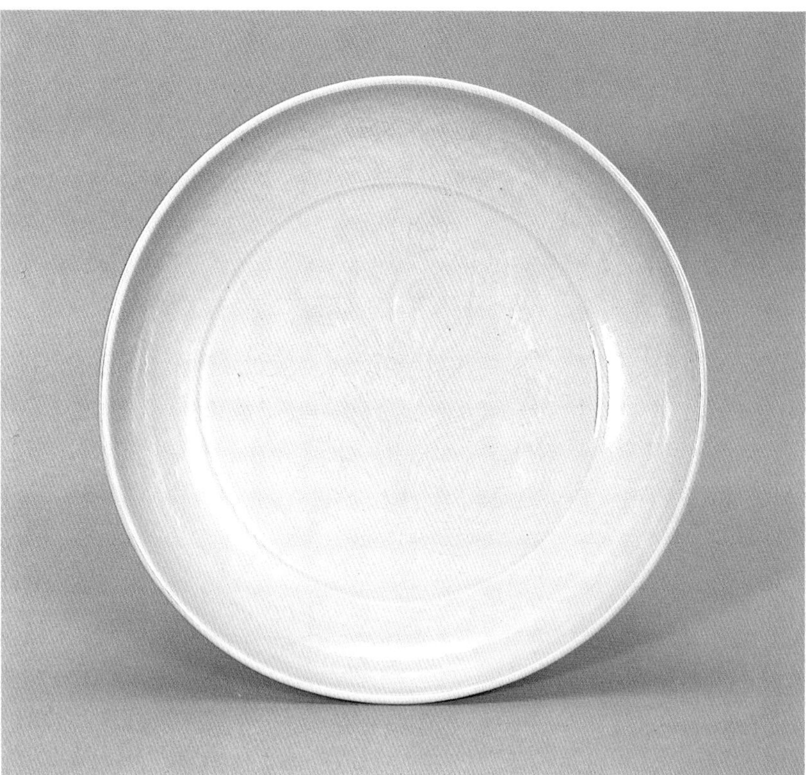

20

LARGE DISH

Jingdezhen ware, monochrome white porcelain with incised lotus-bouquet decoration

Ming dynasty, Xuande period (1426–35); Xuande six-character mark, *Da Ming Xuande nian zhi*

D. 33.7 cm (13 1/4 in.)

This large dish with sloping sides is supported on a low foot enclosing a broad, unglazed recessed base, which has burned a pale orange-buff and is heavily flecked with brown specks. Under the luminous greenish white glaze, which has a distinct orange-peel texture, a predominantly floral decoration was firmly and meticulously incised with a sharp pointed tool. The slender stems of lotus flowers and leaves, a lotus seedpod, and other aquatic plants are gathered in a bowed ribbon to form a large and handsome bouquet on the bottom of the dish. An undulating vine containing thirteen paired blossoms, including camellia, chrysanthemum, lotus, peony, gardenia, mallow, and what is perhaps pomegranate, decorates the cavetto, with a classic scroll placed beneath the mouth rim. A composite scroll of similar paired flowers is incised on the outer wall with a classic scroll above, a sectioned key fret below, and a single bowstring on the foot. The six-character reign mark is written in underglaze blue on the exterior below the rim and appears somewhat blurred and hazy.

Precedents for floral bouquets in ceramic decoration exist in twelfth- to thirteenth-century Cizhou-type and Northern celadon wares, but such designs did not become frequent until the Yuan-dynasty production of cobalt-painted porcelains. The arrangement found here, however, is consistent with the numerous underglaze-blue-painted lotus-bouquet dishes of the early fifteenth century and appears to be a pictorial innovation of that period. Also typical of the period is the inclusion of a number of different flowers in one continuous scroll, a case in which naturalism was sacrificed for the sake of decorative and symbolic variety. Although similar to the incised *anhua* (hidden decoration) of Yongle-period wares, here the lines are more strongly and deeply incised, and the distinct greenish tinge deepened where the glaze filled the incised recesses. The exquisite subtlety of the Yongle *anhua* style has been lost, but this design is far more easily read and enjoyed.

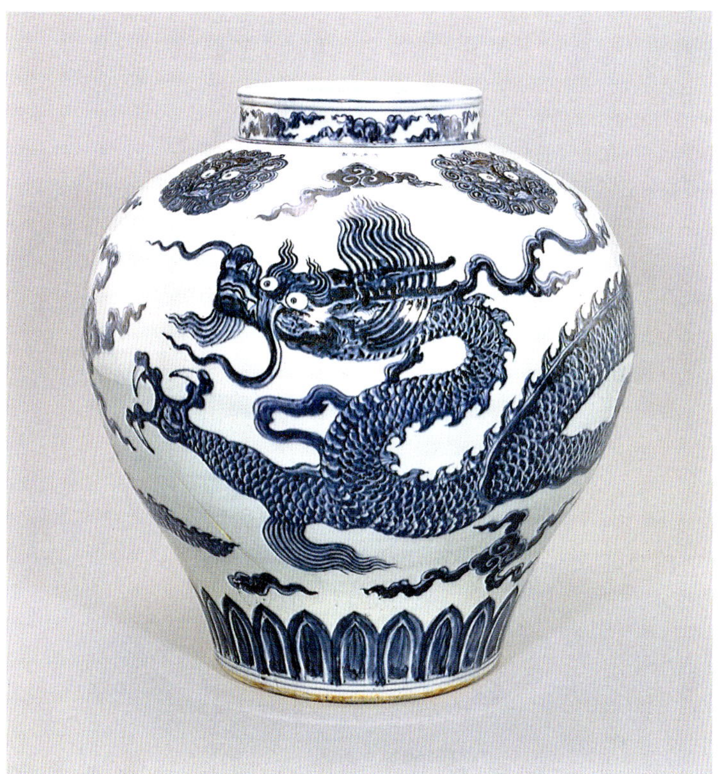

21

LARGE *GUAN* JAR

Jingdezhen ware, underglaze-blue-decorated porcelain with dragon design

Ming dynasty, Xuande period (1426–35); Xuande four-character mark, *Xuande nian zhi*

H. 52 cm (20 1/2 in.)

The swelling shoulders, cylindrical neck with thickened round lip, and relatively narrow base of this vessel are so well proportioned that it appears buoyant despite its colossal size. The broad, somewhat rounded foot and the flat recessed base are unglazed, revealing a dense white body with spots and patches of oxidized iron. The cavernous interior is neatly coated with a thick, bluish white glaze; the glaze on the exterior has a gentle luster and a light orange-peel texture. The cobalt pigment was applied in most areas with a heavily laden large brush. The color, though intense (especially where it has "heaped and piled"), is less bright and vibrant than usual in pre-Xuande wares, due to the mixing of native manganese-bearing ore with imported cobalt. In certain areas—the clouds around the neck, for example—a blurring of the painted images resulted from displaced cobalt particles. The four-character reign mark is neatly written in small *kaishu* script-style in one horizontal line on the body below the neck.

The majesty of the single striding three-clawed dragon, which dominates the decoration, contrasts markedly with the fiery temper of the Yuan dragon (see no. 10). The trunk and limbs are here fleshed out and more massive, the scales more dense and crusty, the head, with flattened nose and pursed lips, larger and more erectly held and topped with a thick, hairy mane. Whereas the tense and sinewy Yuan serpent speeds forth with energetic abandon, this early Ming dragon strides with heavy, more measured steps. The clouds, with fungus or *ruyi*-shaped centers, are more formal and staid and are repeated in a row of eight around the neck. The base is ringed by upright banana leaves, and the frontal lion masks, positioned like four guardians on the shoulder, contribute to the stately air of this monumental vessel.[1]

It is generally agreed that the number of claws appearing on dragons in Ming porcelain decoration is significant, with five-clawed dragons thought to be reserved for use as an imperial emblem and four- and three-clawed dragons allotted to lesser beings. The imperial kilns produced vessels decorated with dragons of all three variations, and even among the reign-marked wares the same range is found. A Xuande-marked jar with a four-clawed dragon design excavated at Zhushan[2] as well as the present marked piece decorated with a three-clawed dragon were both most likely intended for court use, perhaps for imperial bestowal (like many of the Xuande emperor's paintings) on those who directly served their liege.

1. At least one other example is known, in the Metropolitan Museum of Art, New York (Suzanne G. Valenstein, *A Handbook of Chinese Ceramics*, New York: Metropolitan Museum of Art, 1975, cover and pl. 82).

2. *Zhongguo taoci*, no. 7 (1982), pl. 23, fig. 23.

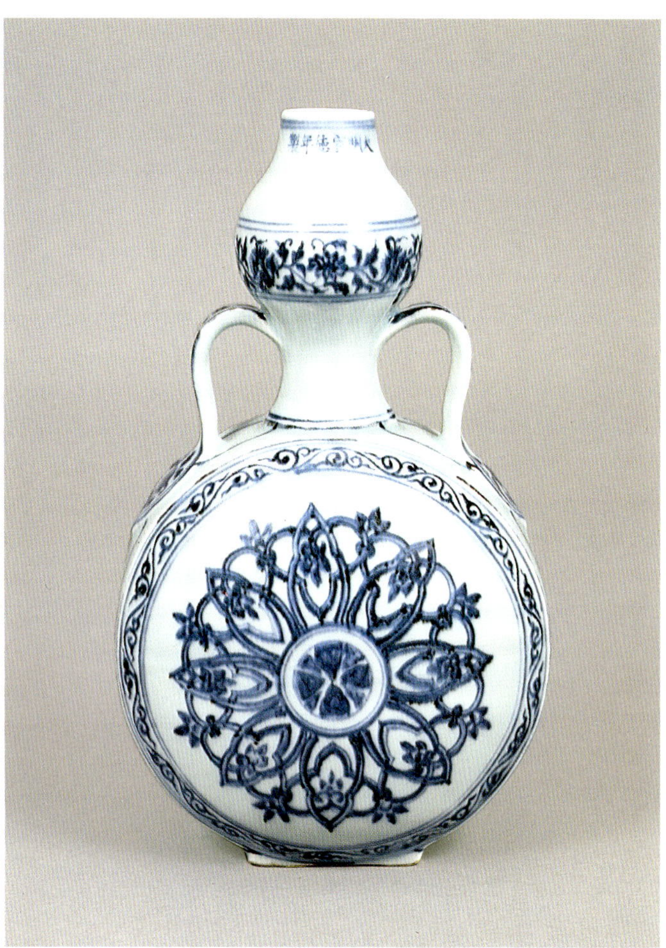

22

PILGRIM FLASK

Jingdezhen ware, underglaze-blue-decorated porcelain with rosette design

Ming dynasty, Xuande period (1426–35); Xuande six-character mark, *Da Ming Xuande nian zhi*

H. 25.8 cm (10 1/8 in.)

The flattened body of this flask is circular, its front and back faces convex. The constricted neck swells abruptly to the bulb-shaped upper section, which contracts to a narrow mouth beneath which the six-character mark is written horizontally. Two grooved strap handles arch from the neck to *ruyi*-shaped tabs of clay applied to the flat curving sides of the vessel. The low foot is rectangular in shape, and the recessed base is neatly glazed.

The rhythmic and lively floral scroll of alternating chrysanthemum and dianthus flowers on the upper bulb visually contrasts with the rigidly geometrical rosettes on the main body. On one side eight pointed panels radiate from a central *yin yang* medallion with palmette-shaped lotus placed between them. On the opposite side the pointed panels radiate from a central medallion, which contains petals pointed toward the center; the medallion in turn forms the focus for a ring of inward-pointing *ruyi* heads interspersed with trefoils. A chevron design on one side and a classic scroll on the other circle the edge, framing the wheellike rosettes. The cobalt blue, applied with ropy brushstrokes, has "heaped and piled" in some areas and streamed in the glaze in others. The thick glaze, bluish in tone, contains distinct bubbles and has an orange-peel texture.

The Idemitsu Museum has in its Persian collection a twelfth-century turquoise-glazed earthenware pilgrim flask so similar in form to the present piece that it clearly represents the Near Eastern shape on which the vessel type was based.[1] A fresh wave of Islamic inspiration was felt during the expansive, international years of the Yongle emperor's reign and led to the development of new porcelain vessel forms, which influenced such Xuande-period vessels as this flask.

1. *Treasures of the Orient* (Tokyo: Middle Eastern Culture Center, 1979), pl. 114.

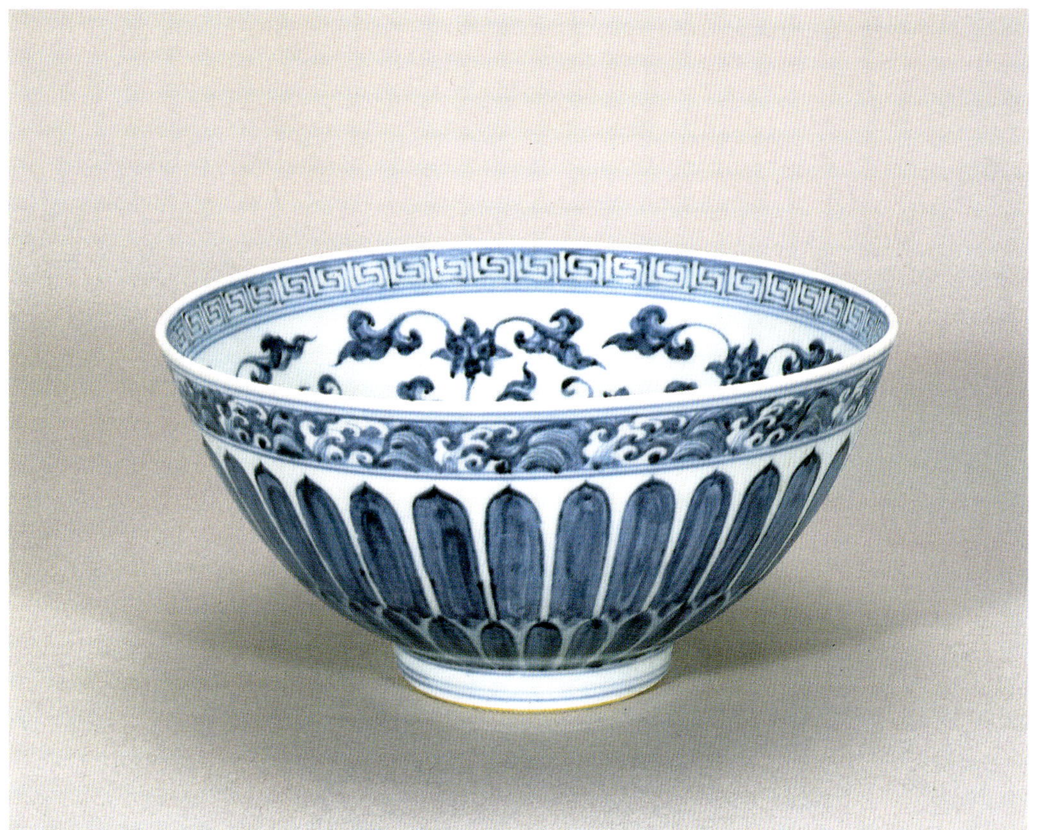

23

BOWL

Jingdezhen ware, underglaze-blue-decorated porcelain with floral design

Ming dynasty, Xuande period (1426–35), Xuande six-character mark, *Da Ming Xuande nian zhi*

D. 21 cm (8 1/4 in.)

This deep and sturdy bowl has a straight mouth, rounded sides curving to a straight foot, and a convex glazed base on which the six-character reign mark is written within a double ring. The exterior is decorated with two tiers of bold lotus petals and with a heavy wave band cresting in white against blue below the mouth rim. On the interior a meticulous key fret bands the top; in the cavetto a scrolling tendril with six, full-blossomed lotus flowers, lesser buds, and leaves is neatly arranged; and in the center a double circle frames a branch with two bursting pomegranate fruits, a single fluffy blossom, and carefully spaced leaves.

With the exception of the delicately painted undulating lotus stem and key fret, the floral design is created by thick and substantial brushstrokes, which sometimes overlap one another and elsewhere are interwoven. The blue appears "heaped and piled," especially in the lotus blossoms, but is otherwise comparatively light in tone. A slight haziness results from the numerous small bubbles within the glaze, and the glaze surface has a distinct orange-peel texture.

The use of underglaze-blue-decorated porcelain as imperial tableware during the Xuande period accounts for the great number and variety of cups, bowls, and dishes produced at the time, and the present piece is a handsome example of one standard type of large bowl.

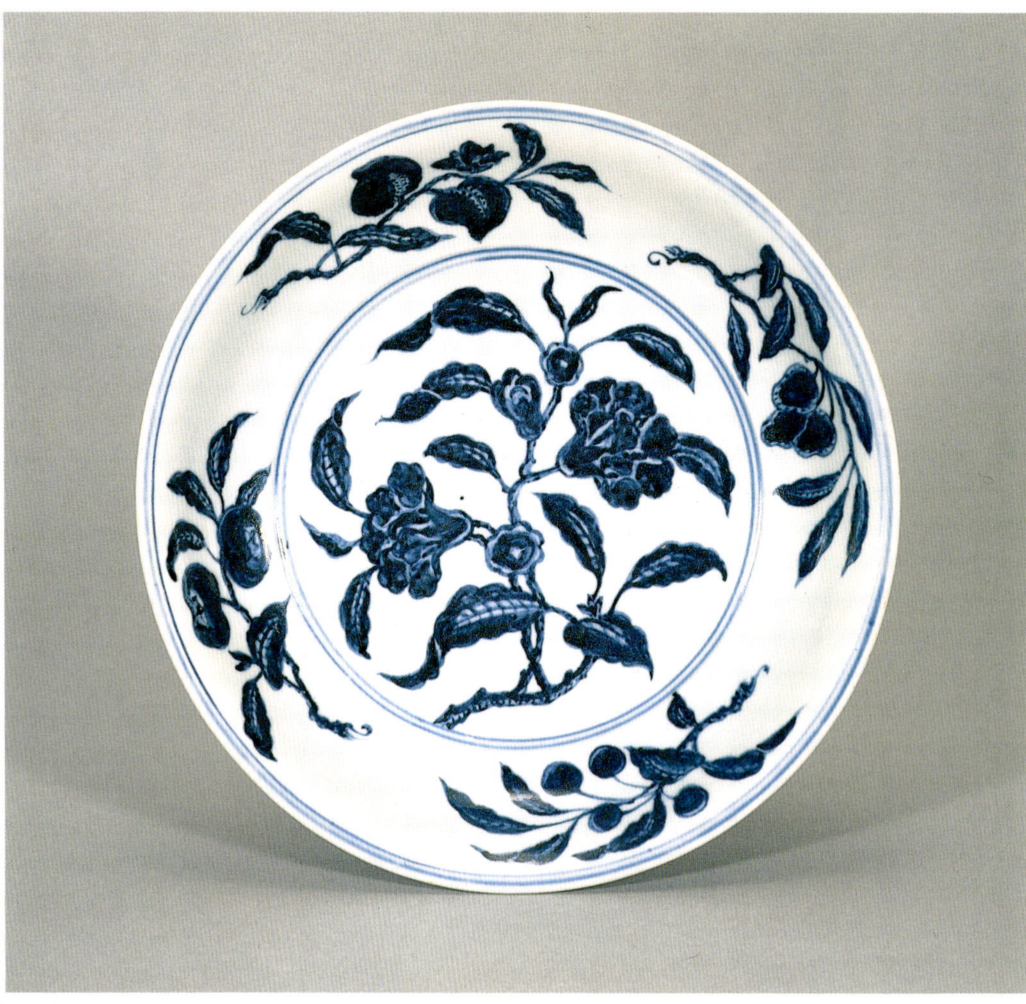

24

DISH

Jingdezhen ware, underglaze-blue-decorated porcelain with floral-and-fruit design

Ming dynasty, Xuande period (1426–35); Xuande six-character mark, *Da Ming Xuande nian zhi*

D. 29.8 cm (11 3/4 in.)

This shallow dish has rounded sides, an everted rim, and a wedge-shaped foot enclosing an unglazed recessed base, which is reddish orange in color and flecked with iron spots. On the flat interior a large blossoming pomegranate branch and in the cavetto four branches laden with peaches, lichee, cherries, and pomegranates are painted in underglaze blue. Four spiky lotus sprays with leaves symmetrically arranged around each blossom decorate the reverse, where the six-character reign mark is written in underglaze blue horizontally beneath the double line ringing the mouth rim. The blue is deep and rich in color and in many areas heavily applied, resulting in dense patches on the glaze surface. The cool, transparent glaze with typical orange-peel texture is much abraded on the interior due to extensive use.

The painterly technique of interweaving broad strokes of blue, which here plump the fruit and unfold the leaves and flowers, lends itself perfectly to creating images at once naturalistic and boldly decorative. Related to earlier and contemporaneous compositions based on strong central motifs surrounded by detached fruit or floral sprays, this design brings the motifs into closer focus. They appear larger and more forceful in relationship to the size of the piece. This change of scale, and the use of only four groups in the cavetto, results in an image that is quite original, a difficult feat given the immense variety and richness of the foregoing tradition.

Related examples from the Xuande period with a brown or yellowish underglaze painted decor appear to have been of limited appeal, whereas the innovative addition of an overglaze yellow enamel ground to the present underglaze-blue design was to gain a great following during the later fifteenth and sixteenth centuries.

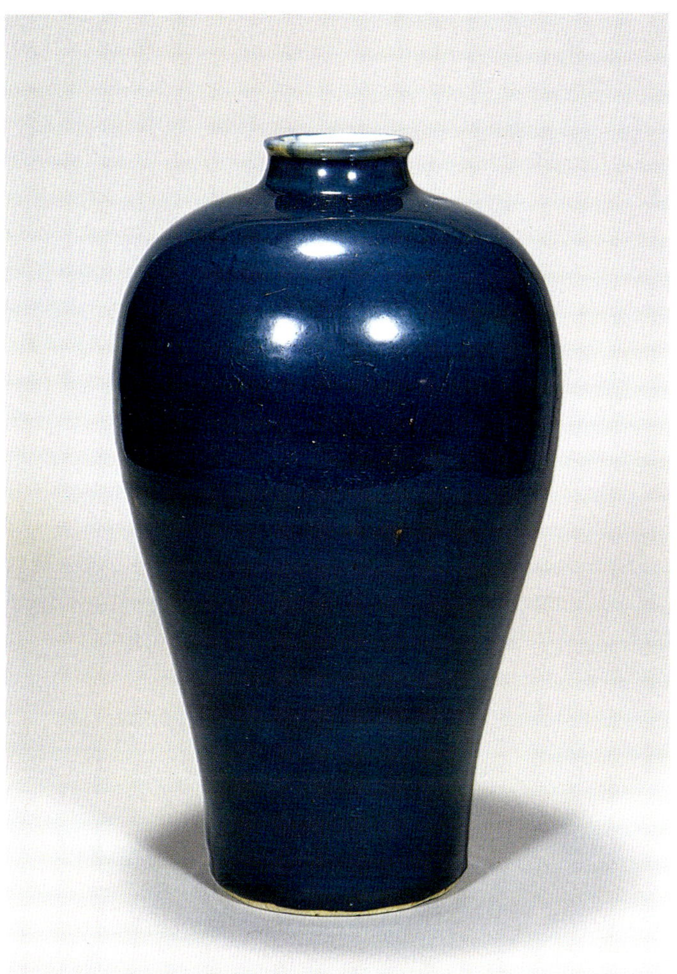

25

MEIPING

Jingdezhen ware, monochrome blue porcelain

Ming dynasty, first half 15th century

H. 32.5 cm (12 3/4 in.)

Swelling gently, this *meiping*'s body rises from a broad, sturdy base. The thick foot is somewhat rounded and slants toward the recessed unglazed base, where the dense white porcelain is flecked with dark iron stains. The wide neck opens to an everted and thickened lip rim. The vessel was glazed by dipping it into a glaze batch containing cobalt oxide, and slightly undulating areas around the body suggest that the thick glaze was applied in more than one coat. The color is otherwise a consistent, rich deep blue; only around the mouth rim is the glaze thinner and thus paler. There are minuscule holes in the surface of the glaze, but these are so widely spaced that visual disruption is minimal and the glaze appears smooth. Although the shape of the body is comparable to early fifteenth-century underglaze-blue-decorated *meiping*, the wide, short neck is distinctive and unusual and is like that of an underglaze-blue-decorated *meiping* in the Ardebil Shrine collection, attributed by John Pope to the fifteenth century.[1]

The treatment and appearance of the base of the present piece, its careful construction, sturdiness, and technical refinement suggest it was produced sometime during the first half of the fifteenth century.

1. John Alexander Pope, *Chinese Porcelains from the Ardebil Shrine* (Washington: Freer Gallery of Art, 1956), pl. 56, 29.420.

The rounded shoulders of this sturdy storage jar rise from a broad flat base. The cylindrical neck slants inward to a thick rounded lip. The interior, exterior, and base are covered with a deep brownish black glaze that is relatively thin, somewhat abraded and rough in areas, but with a strong luster. The piece was fired on large pads of clay, which left marks in the center and at four symmetrical points on the base. The two characters *neifu* (inner palace), in sharp relief on one side, appear creamy white under a thin layer of glaze. The jar, very finely potted with a stable earthbound appearance, is surprisingly light in weight for its size.

A number of Cizhou-type vessels, undecorated except for the characters *neifu* written on the shoulders in brown slip, have been discovered in Yuan-dynasty archaeological contexts.[1] These pieces are generally rough and uneven in potting and glazing, and the characters were written with a decided absence of neatness or style. The form of the present inscription, which has the strength and precision of a woodblock print, relates closely to those in underglaze blue on a pair of lidded, white porcelain *meiping* in the Museum of Oriental Ceramics, Osaka.[2] They are datable to the early fifteenth century and are generally believed to have been made for use within the imperial household. The court also ordered large numbers of wine jars from the Cizhou kilns during the early Ming period, and the present jar might be representative of the type.[3] The technical refinement, well-balanced form, and somber grace of the Idemitsu vessel accord with the high standards set by the early Ming court. A black-glazed *meiping* excavated from the Yuan stratum of the Guantai kilns near Cixian in Hebei province, with the characters *neifu* carved through the glaze on the shoulder, is a possible prototype for the present jar and perhaps a clue to its place of manufacture.[4]

1. Yutaka Mino, *Freedom of Clay and Brush through Seven Centuries in Northern China: Tz'u-chou Type Wares, 960–1600 A.D.* (Bloomington, Ind.: Indiana University Press, 1980), p. 170.

2. *Sekai tōji zenshū*, vol. 14, *Ming Dynasty* (Tokyo: Shōgakukan, 1976), pl. 180.

3. See Mino, op. cit., p. 11, for the *Minghuidian* passage concerning orders during the Xuande period for over fifty thousand wine containers each year from the Junzhou and Cizhou kilns. Feng Xianming of the Palace Museum, Beijing, believes such vessels were produced at the Cizhou kilns for the court during the early Ming period; none, according to him, remain today in the Palace Museum's collection. A similar though smaller (17.5 cm) black-glazed jar with a *neifu* inscription is housed in the Percival David Foundation. According to Margaret Medley, former curator of the collection, its provenance immediately preceding acquisition by the Foundation is unknown. The Foundation's turquoise-glazed storage jar with *neifu gongyong* in relief on the shoulder is known, however, to have been acquired from the imperial storehouse in Beijing. For the black jar see *Oriental Ceramics*, vol. 6, *Percival David Foundation of Chinese Art* (Tokyo: Kodansha, 1982), fig. 115, and for the turquoise-glazed jar see Margaret Medley, *Illustrated Catalogue of Ming and Ch'ing Monochromes in the Percival David Foundation of Chinese Art* (London: School of Oriental and African Studies, 1973), no. 518. In those publications both jars are attributed to the late fifteenth century.

4. *Wenwu*, no. 6 (1959), p. 60, fig. 11.

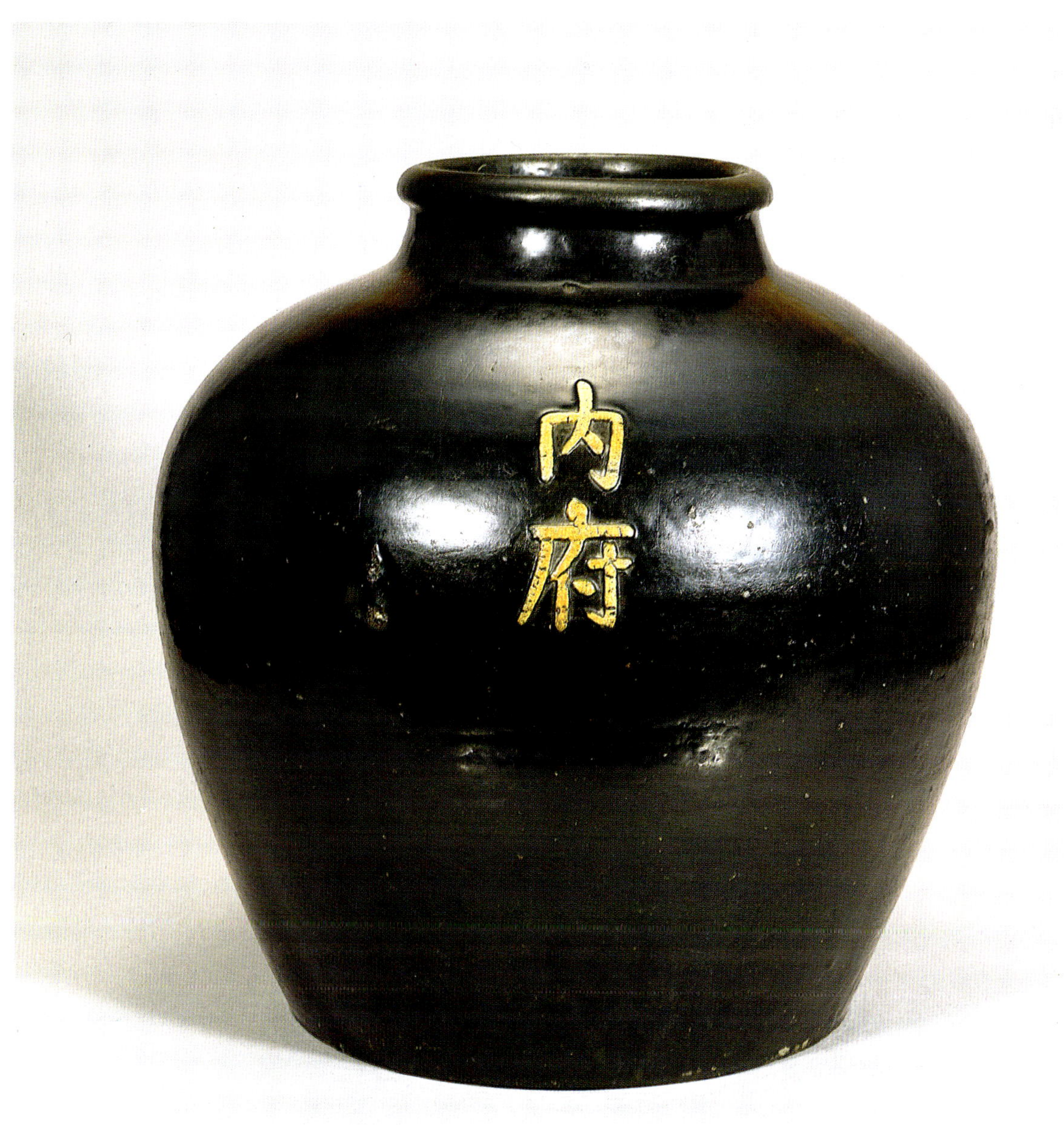

26

JAR

Cizhou-type ware, black-glazed stoneware with characters *neifu* in relief

Ming dynasty, early 15th century

H. 37.5 cm (14 3/4 in.)

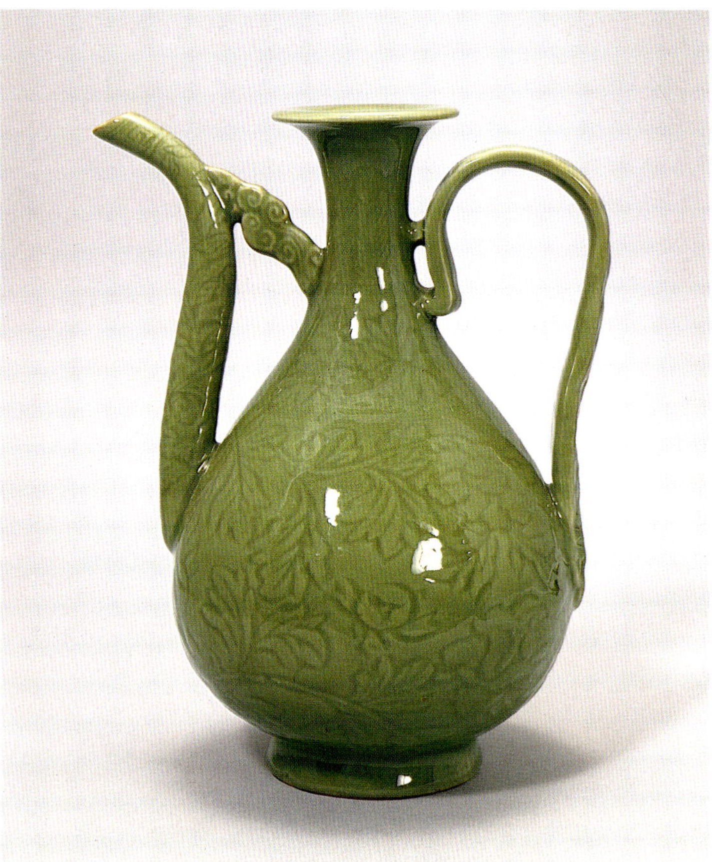

27

PEAR-SHAPED EWER

Longquan ware, celadon with carved floral decoration

Ming dynasty, early 15th century

H. 29.2 cm (11 1/2 in.)

The ewer has a low and broad ovoid belly, a slender neck, a strongly everted mouth, a strap handle, and a long curved spout bridged to the neck by a cloud-shaped strut. The sturdy beveled foot slants slightly outward and reveals a dense, pale gray body, which has burned reddish brown on the unglazed rim. The interior of the foot and the recessed base are neatly glazed. The piece is entirely covered with a carved design save for the mold-pressed strut and floral-decorated handle with a *ruyi*-shaped terminal. The bubbly, moss-green glaze is evenly applied and extremely bright, with some areas exhibiting a bluish iridescence.

The body is decorated with a leafy scroll featuring a large, lush peony and three buds on the verge of bursting into bloom centered on the front and back. Another floral scroll fills the wide shoulder band, and a collar of rising leaves appears around the neck. The floral theme is continued both on the spout and handle and is contrasted by a geometric key fret surrounding the tip of the spout and the foot.

Distinct from the more vigorous and expressionistic decoration of Yuan-period celadons, the motifs here were deeply carved with a studied precision, as if a more graphic effect were intended. The close correspondence of vessel shape and decorative scheme with underglaze-blue-decorated ewers produced at Jingdezhen in the early fifteenth century reveals the source for this new celadon style. Although the models were closely mimed—an underglaze-blue-painted ewer in the Topkapi Saray Museum could have served as the model for this vessel in almost every detail[1]—the decoration here is somewhat obscured by the celadon glaze. Although its immediate visual impact is less than that of the underglaze-painted designs, the ewer possesses a subtle and evocative appeal, one that was indeed appreciated in the Islamic world, where such celadons were acquired alongside the more visually stunning wares of Jingdezhen.

1. Regina Krahl, *Chinese Ceramics in the Topkapi Saray Museum, Istanbul*, vol. 2, *Yuan and Ming Dynasty Porcelains* (London: Sotheby's Publications, 1986), pl. 620, TKS 15/1412.

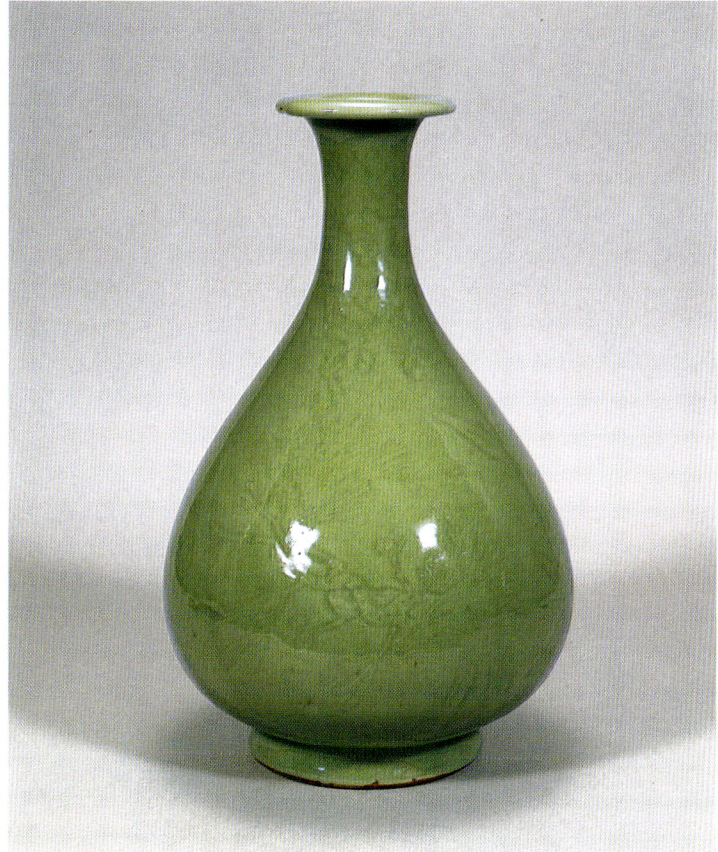

28

YUHUCHUN BOTTLE

Longquan ware, celadon with carved design of the "Three Friends of Winter"

Ming dynasty, early 15th century

H. 34 cm (13 3/8 in.)

This pear-shaped vessel has a narrow neck, an everted mouth, and a sturdy splayed foot. The gray body has burned brownish orange on the exposed foot rim; the recessed base is neatly glazed. Aside from the classic scroll on the foot and the *ruyi* band on the neck, the entire body is given over to unified scenes of carved bamboo leaves intermingled with blossoming prunus on one side and a bushy pine bough on the other. The pale yellowish green glaze is only semitransparent and has a bright sheen.

Pine, prunus, and bamboo, the symbols of the strength, purity, and uprightness of cultivated gentlemen, had been grouped by the thirteenth century as the "Three Friends of Winter" and have been portrayed as such by Chinese painters ever since. The representation of the subject by a Longquan potter might have been inspired by the decoration of underglaze-painted porcelains from Jingdezhen, where the theme was depicted on Yuan-dynasty wares and used not infrequently during the early fifteenth century. The "Three Friends," however, is rarely seen on Longquan celadons. The pictorial origin of the subject, which could be transposed directly and effectively in underglaze-painted decoration, might have militated against its successful translation to a carved design, which was then covered and partially concealed by a cloudy glaze. Here the secondary motifs are almost totally illegible. Despite the less-than-perfect marriage between pictorial theme on the one hand and technique and glaze on the other, the professional competence of Longquan potters is evident in the finely turned shape and careful finish of the present piece. The form of this vessel, with its relatively short neck and greatly distended lower body, is the source of its strength and commanding presence.

The relaxed, almost languid character of this *meiping*'s shape is distinctive. Its wide, slanted neck flows smoothly into the low, sloping shoulder; its lower body constricts and then flares to the vertical foot. The broad, unglazed foot rim reveals a dense white body flecked with iron stains. The bright moss-green glaze covering the carved surface contrasts with the pale bluish glaze of the recessed base.

The decorative composition is clearly related to underglaze-blue-decorated *meiping* produced at Jingdezhen during the early fifteenth century, and the similarity is some aid in dating these sparsely documented wares. Arranged in horizontal bands, the carved decoration includes a hollyhock scroll on the neck, a five-pointed cloud collar with formal lotus sprays in each lappet against a scrollwork ground on the shoulder, a flowering peach branch with wide-leafed bamboo naturalistically portrayed on each side of the main body zone, and a fungus scroll in a wide band around the base.[1] The reliance on painted models might also explain the development of the characteristic early Ming carving technique. In contrast to the standard Longquan method used in earlier periods, in which the clay was obliquely sliced away to create motifs standing in relief, here the carving tool was held perpendicularly to the surface to incise precise, even, and continuous outlines, producing a more clearly defined pictorial image.

Early Ming Longquan potters clearly derived shapes and decorative designs from the popular underglaze-painted wares of their Jingdezhen peers. Lest this relationship seem weighted in favor of the Jingdezhen potters, one should note that during the excavation of the remains of the Xuande imperial kilns at Zhushan in Jingdezhen, imitation Longquan celadon wares bearing underglaze-blue Xuande reign marks were discovered. The shapes and glazes were said to be indistinguishable from the Longquan wares, but they differed in their high degree of body whiteness and fineness.[2] Although the published "imitation Longquan" included only a limited number of examples, and none in the style observed here, extremely well-carved decorated examples, also indistinguishable from the products of the Longquan kilns, have been verbally reported to visitors at Jingdezhen. Given the character of the dense white body of this *meiping* and the white surface of the clay after firing, and considering too the nature of the bluish-colored glaze on the base, one is tempted to reconsider the stated provenance of this *meiping*.

1. An early fifteenth-century underglaze-blue-decorated porcelain *meiping* from a Ming-period tomb has precisely this decorative scheme, *Wenwu*, no. 6 (1972), pl. 6, fig. 1.

2. Xuande-marked imitation Longquan was discovered at the east wall of the Qing imperial depot and unmarked remains at the site of an early Ming-dynasty official building. *Zhongguo taoci*, no. 7 (1982), pp. 176, 179.

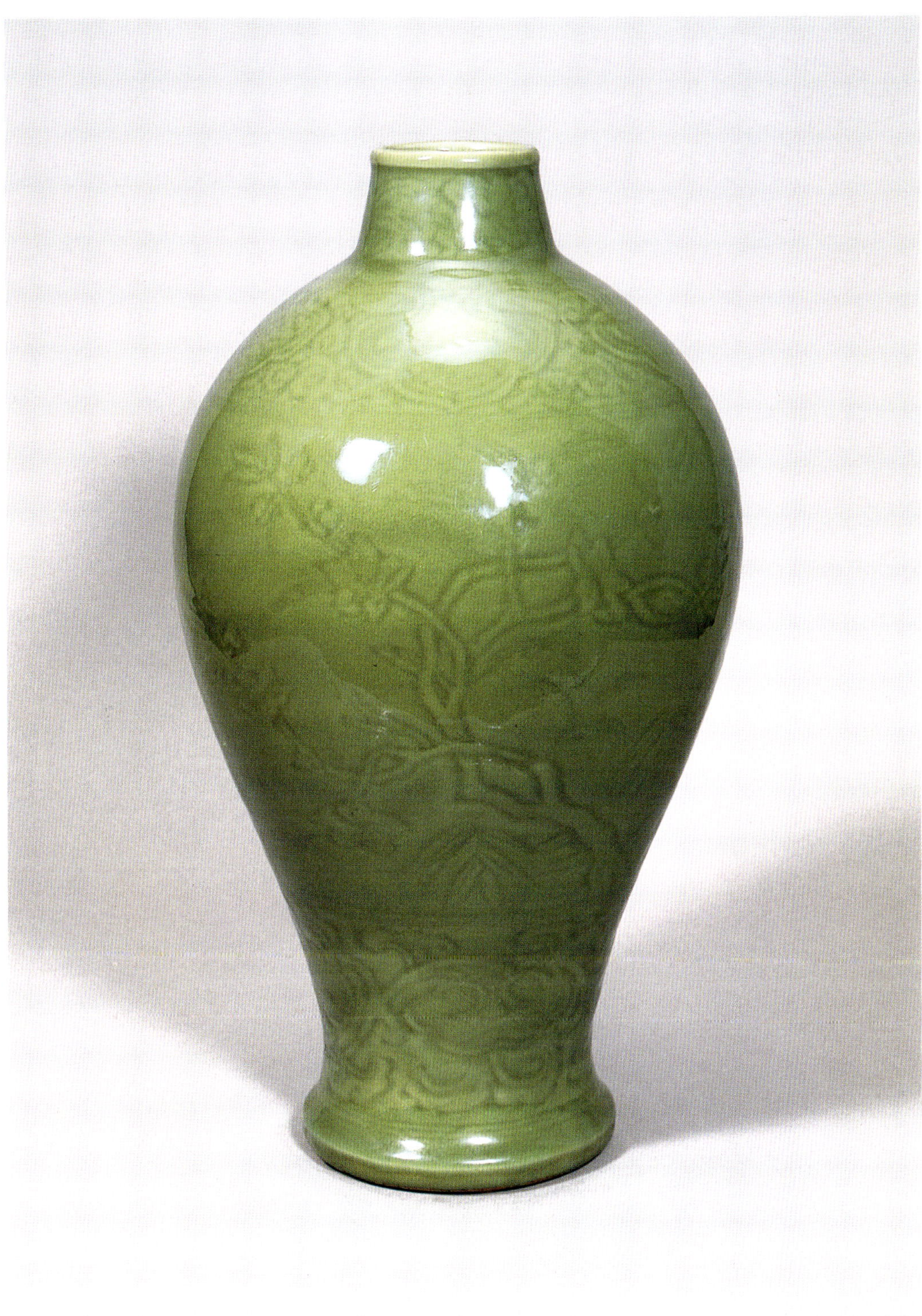

29

MEIPING

Longquan ware, celadon with carved floral design

Ming dynasty, early 15th century

H. 38.6 cm (15 1/4 in.)

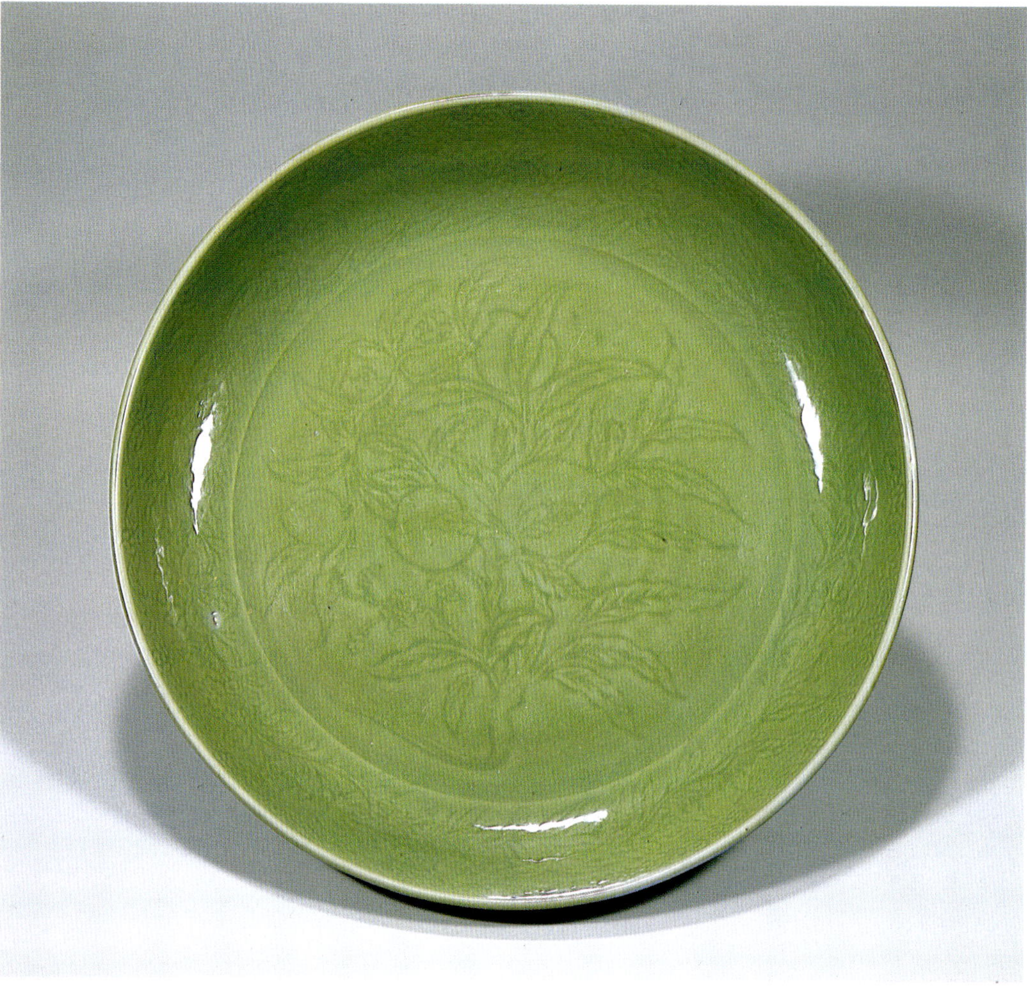

30

LARGE PLATTER

Longquan ware, celadon with carved fruit-and-floral decoration
Ming dynasty, early 15th century
D. 68.5 cm (27 in.)

This massive platter has rounded sides, a straight rim, and a low, narrow foot. The expansive interior field is embellished with a woody tree branch supporting succulent peaches, blossoms, and leaves. Well-controlled, descriptive linear incising produced organic and naturalistic forms, which twist, turn, and overlap to create a satisfying image, both ornamentally and pictorially. The narrow lotus scroll under the lip rim and bold leafy scroll sprouting lotus and other flowers are more difficult to read, a not uncommon phenomenon in early Ming carved celadons, in which the thick, bubbly glaze works against the realization of a clearly projected design. The rounded exterior wall bears eight independent floral, fruit, and fungus sprays.

The bright glaze, slightly olive in tone, covers the entire piece excluding a large ring on the base, which was left free of glaze to accommodate the stand that supported the piece in the kiln and prevented the base from sagging during firing. The pale grayish white body fired a deep orange on the exposed surface, and within this uncommonly neat ring are remnants of what might be a Persian or Arabic inscription. The sheer size of this platter indicates that it was destined to grace the dining carpet of some Near Eastern potentate, who had clear access once again to the marvelous ceramic wares of China after the restrictions on foreign intercourse imposed by the Hongwu emperor had been lifted during the early fifteenth century under the reign of the Yongle emperor.

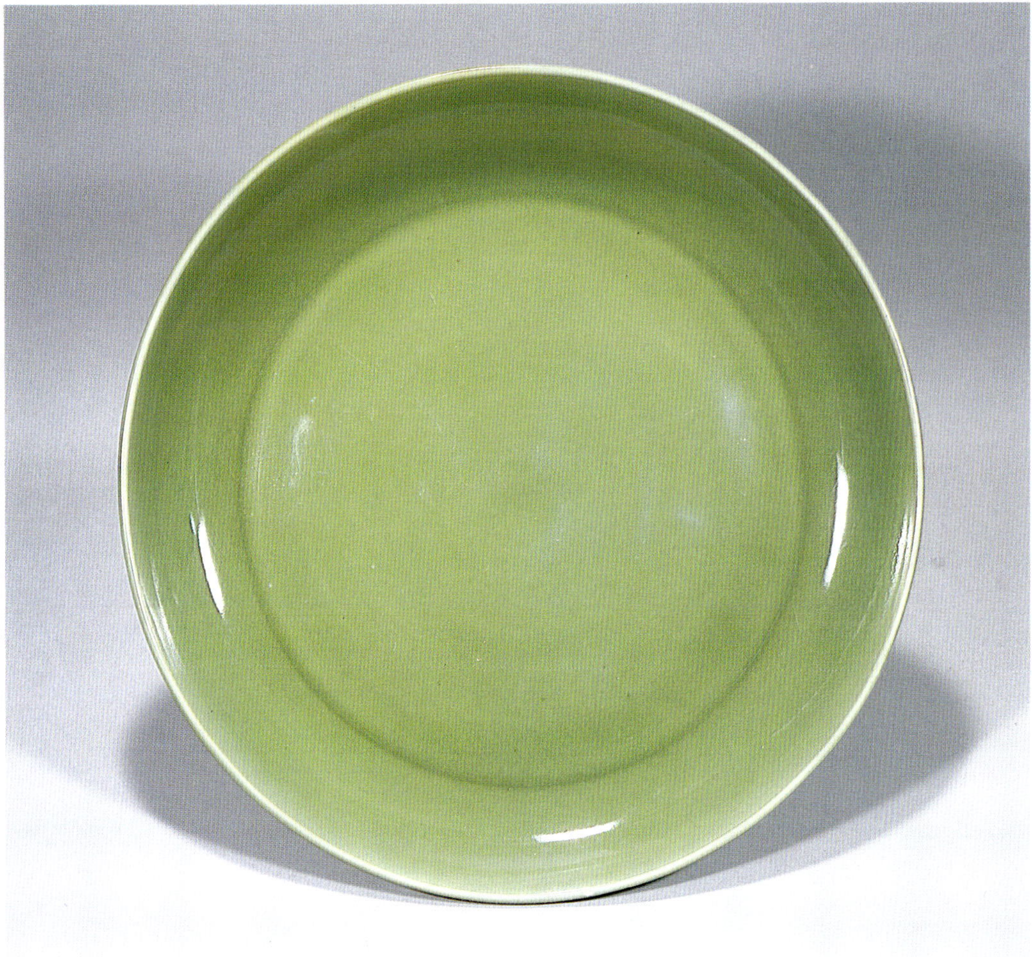

31

LARGE PLATTER

Longquan ware, celadon
Ming dynasty, early 15th century
D. 68.5 cm (27 in.)

Stunningly large, this platter has rounded sides, a straight mouth, and a glazed foot and base with the characteristic unglazed firing ring on the base burned to an orange color. Though the shape and dimensions are comparable to those of the massive underglaze-blue-decorated platters of early fifteenth-century Jingdezhen, this piece is completely without decoration. A sea of mirror-bright glaze, richly green and seductively deep, stands as its sole embellishment. Here glaze, shape, and size together speak eloquently of the masterful skills of the Longquan potters. This platter represents a last flourishing of the Longquan kilns before the marked decline in production and aesthetic standards that occurred by the later fifteenth century. Despite its overwhelming size it still distantly conjures in its elegant simplicity and reserve the splendors of the Longquan kilns during their halcyon days of the late Song period.

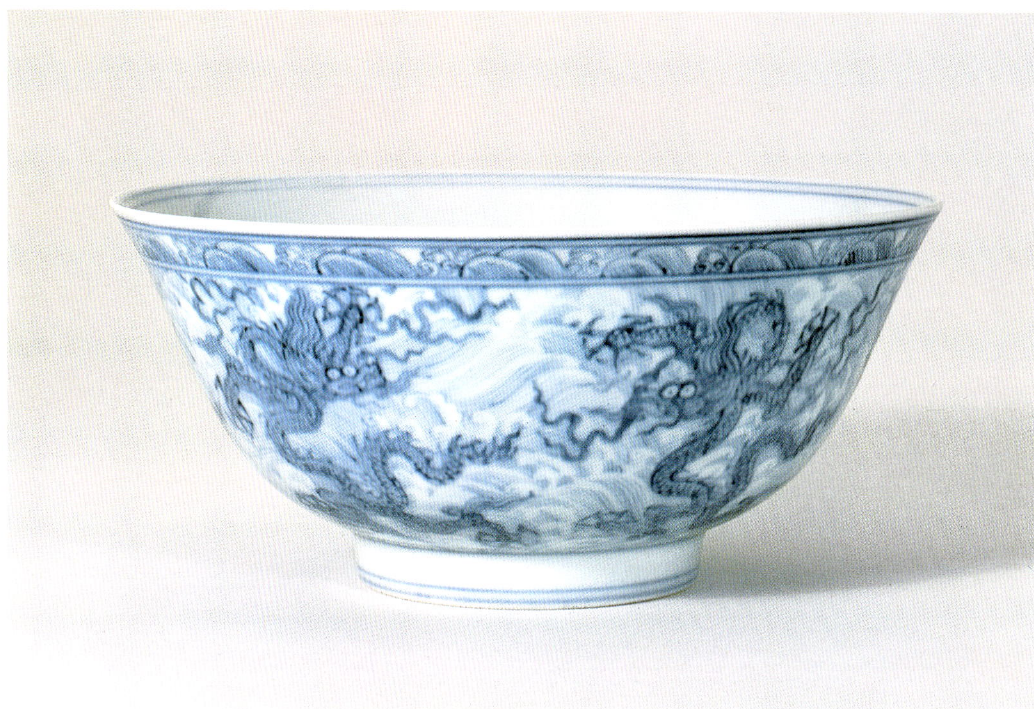

32

BOWL

Jingdezhen ware, underglaze-blue-decorated porcelain with dragon-and-wave design

Ming dynasty, Chenghua period (1465–87); Chenghua six-character mark, *Da Ming Chenghua nian zhi*

D. 18.3 cm (7 1/4 in.)

This thin, light, and gracefully formed bowl has gently sloping sides and rests on a straight ring foot. The reign mark is written within a double circle in underglaze blue on the recessed base. The white body, visible on the unglazed foot rim, is extremely fine and pure. The orange-colored hairline often seen at the juncture of body and glaze in Chenghua porcelain does not appear here. On the exterior wall five dragons patrol the depths of a churning sea; calm waves undulate and crest in a band bordering the mouth rim and a double ring encircles the lower foot. Inside the bowl another dragon with splayed body ascendant and head erect inhabits a circular field of frothy water bounded by a double ring. The blank cavetto is ringed twice below the lip. These cobalt-blue designs float beneath a clear glaze with a cool bluish tonality and a satiny sheen. Minute pores, like tiny pinpricks, are widely spaced and produce nothing of the textured feeling of earlier Ming glazes.

The basic scheme of dragons against a wave ground of fine, lightly drawn lines had been formulated in the decoration of a number of stem cups and bowls of the Xuande period. By the time the present bowl was made, the imported cobalt that had energized earlier motifs was no longer readily available. The best cobalt-bearing ore mined from native sources gave a less vibrant color and, as used by the potters at the imperial kilns, was further tamed by careful refining and pulverizing, by thinning it to a watery consistency, and by applying it in outline and wash. The blue here is therefore soft in color and the "heaped-and-piled" effect of earlier decoration absent; nevertheless the brushwork is, in contrast to much of the underglaze-blue-decorated porcelain produced during the Chenghua period, refreshingly vigorous and alive.

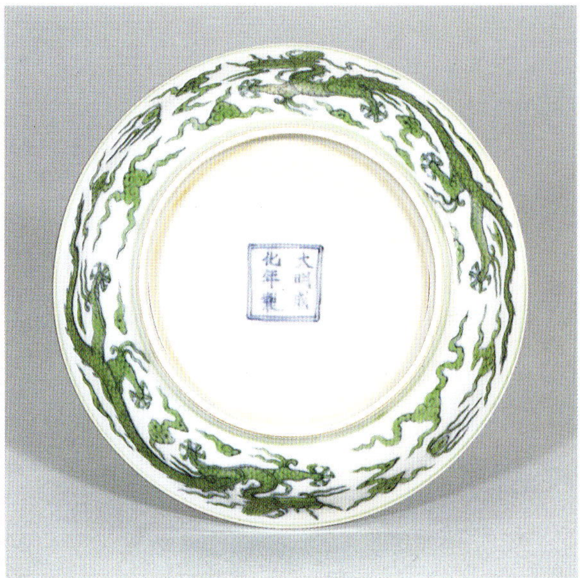

33

SHALLOW DISH

Jingdezhen ware, *doucai*-decorated porcelain with dragon-and-cloud design

Ming dynasty, Chenghua period (1465–87); Chenghua six-character mark, *Da Ming Chenghua nian zhi*

D. 19.9 cm (7 7/8 in.)

Delicately potted, thin and light, this shallow dish with low curving sides and everted rim was fashioned from extremely pure, dense white paste. The narrow ring foot encloses a glazed recessed base on which the six-character reign mark is written in pale cobalt blue within a double square. The satiny-bright glaze has a bluish cast on the undecorated interior and the exterior wall. The hairline edge between the glaze and the neatly wiped foot rim has a typical orange discoloration.

Glistening, translucent overglaze-green enamel was combined with meticulously drawn underglaze-blue outlines to produce the design: two dragons stretched luxuriously among clouds in leisurely pursuit of flaming pearls. The motifs were initially drawn with a fine brush in even, cobalt-blue outlines; after glazing and firing to the high maturing temperature of porcelain, copper-oxide enamel was applied to the glaze within the outlined areas and as narrow bowstring lines above and below the design and on the foot. The piece was then fired a second time at a lower temperature to fuse the enamel. The decorative combination of underglaze-blue outlines with overglaze-enamel color applied within outlines is known as *doucai* (contending colors). Normally involving more than the single enamel color used here, the procedure required precision and careful coordination. The enamel on this dish was applied so masterfully that it covers only the white ground within the outlined areas, with virtually no trespassing beyond the delicate blue boundaries.

That overglaze enamels were used in porcelain decoration by the later fourteenth century is known from Cao Zhao's mention of *wuse* (five-color) ware in his handbook for collectors, the *Ge gu yao lun*, published in 1388.[1] The combination of overglaze enamels with underglaze blue by the Xuande period is verified both by textual reference—for example, the sixteenth-century *Bo wu yao lun* mention of *wuse qinghua* (five color with blue decoration)[2]—and from extant examples. The inclusion of underglaze-blue outlines in the predominantly *wucai* design on a Xuande-marked bowl in the Sakya Monastery in Tibet is proof that the *doucai* technique was also in use by the early fifteenth century.[3] Chinese connoisseurs, however, have reserved their highest accolades for the supremely refined and harmonious *doucai* wares of the Chenghua era. Ceramic artists of that period produced these costly wares under incentive from the Chenghua imperial court, likely from the principal member of that lofty circle, the covetous Precious Consort Wan.[4]

1. See the text of the *Ge gu yao lun* (p. 40a) reproduced by Sir Percival David in *Chinese Connoisseurship: The Ko Ku Yao Lun* (London: Faber and Faber, 1971).

2. For reference to the *Bo wu yao lun* see Feng Xianming, et al., *Zhongguo taoci shi* (Beijing: Wenwu Press, 1982), p. 381). Additional references to Xuande "five-color" ware found in Ming-dynasty texts are discussed in *Chinese Porcelain: The S. C. Ko Tianminlou Collection*, pt. 2 (Hong Kong: Hong Kong Museum of Art, 1987), pp. 103–4, by Ko Shih Chao.

3. This bowl is discussed by Hu Zhaojing in *Wenwu*, no. 11 (1985), pp. 72–73. Ko Shih Chao (op. cit., p. 104) refers to two such bowls from the monastery collection, illustrated fig. 5, p. 110.

4. For a biography of the Chenghua emperor's favorite consort, Wan Guifei, see L. Carrington Goodrich, ed., *Dictionary of Ming Biography 1368–1644*, vol. 2 (New York and London: Columbia University Press, 1976), pp. 1335–37.

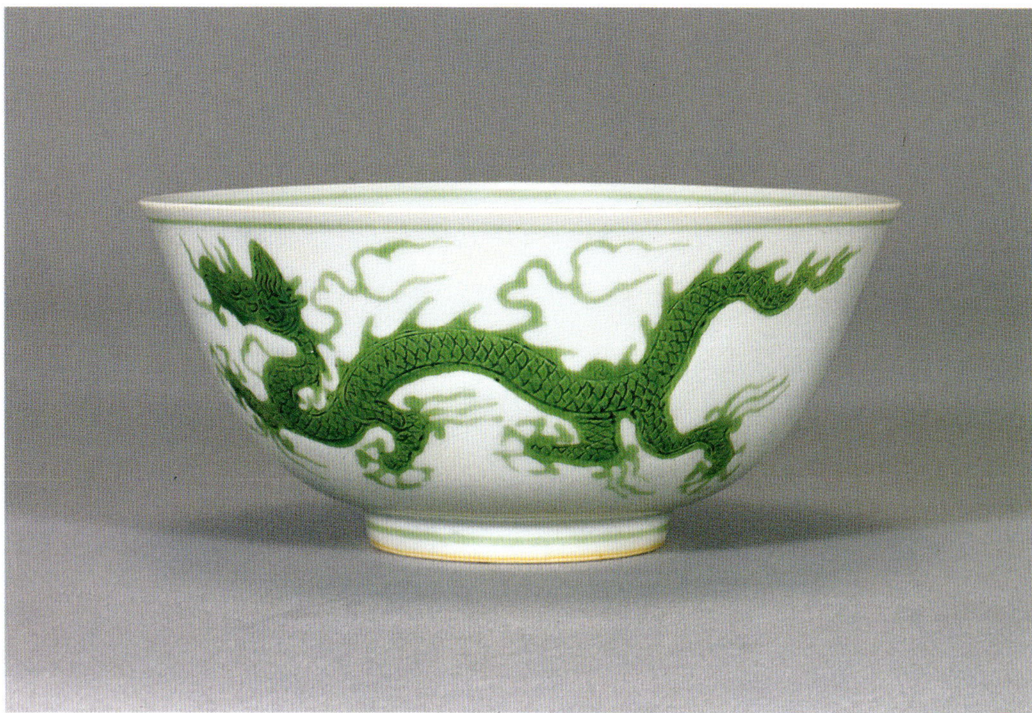

34

BOWL

Jingdezhen ware, green-enamel-decorated porcelain with dragon-and-wave design

Ming dynasty, Hongzhi period (1488–1505); Hongzhi six-character mark, *Da Ming Hongzhi nian zhi*

D. 18.4 cm (7 1/4 in.)

Finely potted, with gently rounded sides, this bowl has a straight rim and a delicate ring foot enclosing a recessed base, on which the six-character reign mark is written in underglaze blue within a double ring. The glaze is smooth and of a cool tonality, with a distinct orange line between the glaze and the unglazed foot rim. Two dragons stand out in green on the outer wall, and a third appears with similarly colored clouds and a pearl on the bottom of the interior. The sea of waves, intricately incised on the exterior wall, is barely visible beneath the luminous glaze.

The simple, restrained appearance of this bowl belies the complexities involved in its production. Each dragon, down to minute detail, and the background wave design were incised on the surface of the vessel with a fine point. A resist applied to the heads, trunks, and limbs of the dragons, and to the clouds and pearls on the interior, left these areas in biscuit after glazing and firing. Green enamel was subsequently applied to the glaze-free areas, brushed in fluid strokes over the glaze-covered streamers, spines, and claws of the dragons, and used to draw the bordering rings. The piece was then refired at a lower temperature. The single enamel shows up as three distinct shades of green: shimmering, light, and translucent where it was applied over the glaze, richer, more intense over the biscuit, and densest and darkest where the enamel filled in the deep incisions.

In standard underglaze-blue and overglaze-enamel dragon designs, clouds and waves provide a suitable environment for the beasts and function as decorative forms to occupy the compositional spaces between them. Here that environment is all but invisible, and the dragons seem motionless, suspended and frozen against the porcelain ground. Our interest is sparked not by the identity of these inert images but by the subtle technique and the rarefied design aesthetic. Though they originated during the preceding Chenghua reign, such green-dragon bowls were more widely produced during the Hongzhi period. There is little, however, aside from the reign mark, to distinguish this exquisite bowl from its predecessors, testimony to a continuity between the Chenghua and Hongzhi periods not only of style but of high technical and refined aesthetic standards.

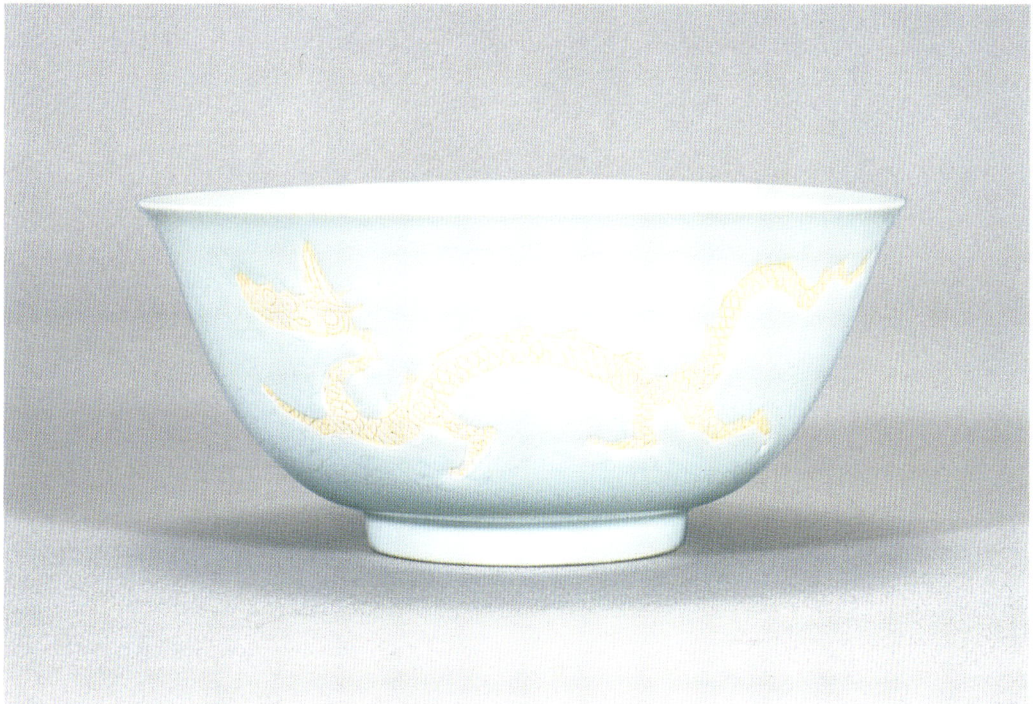

35

BOWL

Jingdezhen ware, white porcelain with dragon design in biscuit reserve

Ming dynasty, Hongzhi period (1488–1505); Hongzhi six-character mark, *Da Ming Hongzhi nian zhi*

D. 18.4 cm (7 1/4 in.)

This bowl has rounded sides, an everted mouth, and a ring foot surrounding a recessed base on which the six-character reign mark is written in underglaze blue within a double circle. The decorative composition, consisting of dragons, waves, and clouds, is exactly like that of the previous green-dragon bowl (no. 34). The absence of enamel, however, has left the dragons reserved in buff-colored biscuit against the grayish-tinged glaze. Although this condition might be interpreted as representing merely one stage in the production of a green-dragon bowl, the significant number of extant biscuit-reserve bowls, including some from the former Qing imperial collection, suggests they must have been considered finished products in their present state.

The contrast between the matt surface of the unglazed porcelain and the bright surrounding glaze is technically related to precedent wares—notably those from the Longquan kilns of the Yuan period—in which textural variety was used for ornamental purposes. In the manufacture of these earlier wares, the intent was to create stimulating and bold visual images, effects also achieved through the startling juxtaposition of the brick-red color of the biscuit and the green of the celadon glaze. By the later fifteenth century, however, subtlety, suggestiveness, and understatement were the aesthetic virtues in vogue, and this porcelain bowl, with its spiritlike dragons floating against the glaze, is eminently successful by that later standard.

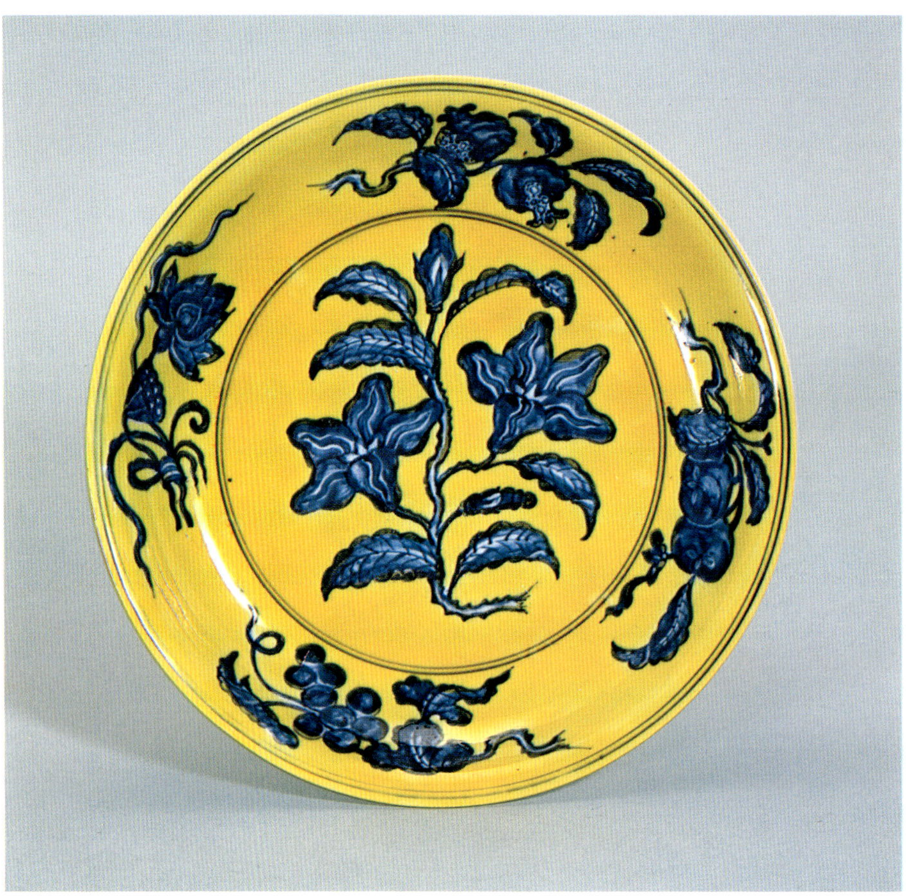

36

DISH

Jingdezhen ware, underglaze-blue and overglaze-yellow enamel-decorated porcelain with floral-and-fruit design

Ming dynasty, Hongzhi period (1488–1505); Hongzhi six-character mark, *Da Ming Hongzhi nian zhi*

D. 26.2 cm (10 3/8 in.)

Curved sides, an everted mouth, and a strong ring foot characterize this shallow dish. The underglaze-blue six-character reign mark is written within a double ring on the convex base, which is covered by a greenish-tinged glaze. The bold floral-and-fruit design on the interior and the floral scroll on the reverse were painted in cobalt blue. After the piece was coated with a neutral glaze and fired, the yellow enamel ground was brushed on and the piece fired a second time at a lower temperature. A large hibiscus branch with two blossoms, a bud, and leaves occupies the central zone of the interior; the four groups in the cavetto include fruiting pomegranate and persimmon branches, a grapevine, and a lotus bouquet. A scroll consisting of seven fluffy blossoms and leaves decorates the exterior. The blue appears watery but richly hued; in areas where the cobalt has been laid on thickly it is deep in tone. The yellow enamel, which slightly overlaps the blue in a few areas, is thinly and evenly applied.

Although this bold design and distinctive underglaze-blue composition set off by a yellow ground originated during the Xuande period, it was most frequently produced during the late fifteenth and early sixteenth centuries. (The Idemitsu Museum owns an example from each of the five reign eras during which the type was produced.) Previous to the Hongzhi period the base was left unglazed and the reign mark written in a horizontal white-reserve rectangular panel on the exterior below the mouth. Otherwise the group is by and large consistent, with some variation in the types of fruits and flowers. Technical and stylistic features vary according to period, as illustrated by a comparison between the present dish and the underglaze-blue design of the Xuande example of this composition (no. 24), which lacks the yellow ground. The central design of this dish is more compressed than that of the Xuande example, and the spray is suspended against the ground rather than growing from the side. Whereas the leaves and petals of the flowers turn rather naturalistically, as in the Xuande design, the simplification of the stem—two jagged outlines with no interior texturing—makes the branch here appear somewhat schematic. The brushwork is strong but that of the interior of the leaves is more systematic.

The high quality and attractive color of the yellow enamel is noteworthy but not surprising, since the yellow monochromes of the Hongzhi period are traditionally acclaimed as superior to those of any other Ming-dynasty reign.

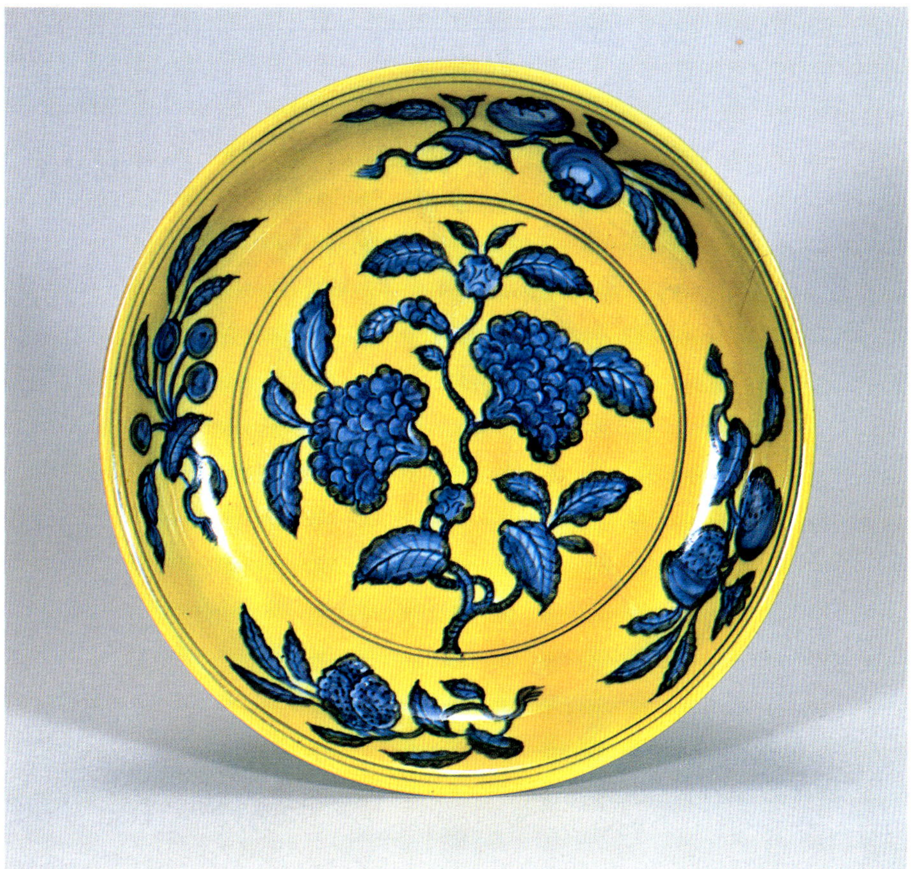

37

DISH

Jingdezhen ware, underglaze-blue and overglaze-yellow enamel-decorated porcelain with floral-and-fruit design

Ming dynasty, Zhengde period (1506–21); Zhengde six-character mark, *Da Ming Zhengde nian zhi*

D. 29.5 cm (11 5/8 in.)

This shallow dish has curving sides, an everted rim, and a ring foot surrounding the recessed base on which the six-character reign mark is written in underglaze blue. The unglazed foot rim has a strong orange discoloration and is somewhat roughly cut; what looks like a swastika was line-engraved on the base, probably by a Middle Eastern owner.

This early sixteenth-century floral-and-fruit design is a faithful reproduction of the scheme as it had appeared earlier, in the Xuande period (see no. 24); the interior bottom is decorated with a flowering pomegranate branch, the cavetto with fruiting peach, lichee, cherry, and persimmon branches, and the reverse with four lotus sprays. During the eight or more decades that intervened between production of the two pieces, outline-and-wash had become the standard underglaze-blue painting technique, here resulting in strong, clear, and relatively even outlines. The interior linear details of the central branch and leaves stand out clearly beneath the broad brushstrokes of blue wash. Because the painterly approach was eschewed, full realization of volumetric images was denied, although vestigial traces of the earlier method are found in the white highlights of the leaves, the petals of the central flowers, and the fruit. The leaves, however, twist in a two-dimensional plane, bending neither toward nor away from the viewer, and thus reinforce the flatness of the images. The background yellow intrudes on the underglaze design and in some areas completely washes over the entire motif.

In the final analysis the design is more generalized and schematic than in earlier pieces but more strongly formal. To note these stylistic features, as well as such minor shortcomings as the haphazardly applied enamel, leads to an historical understanding of this dish and to an appreciation of its position in the distinguished ceramic tradition.

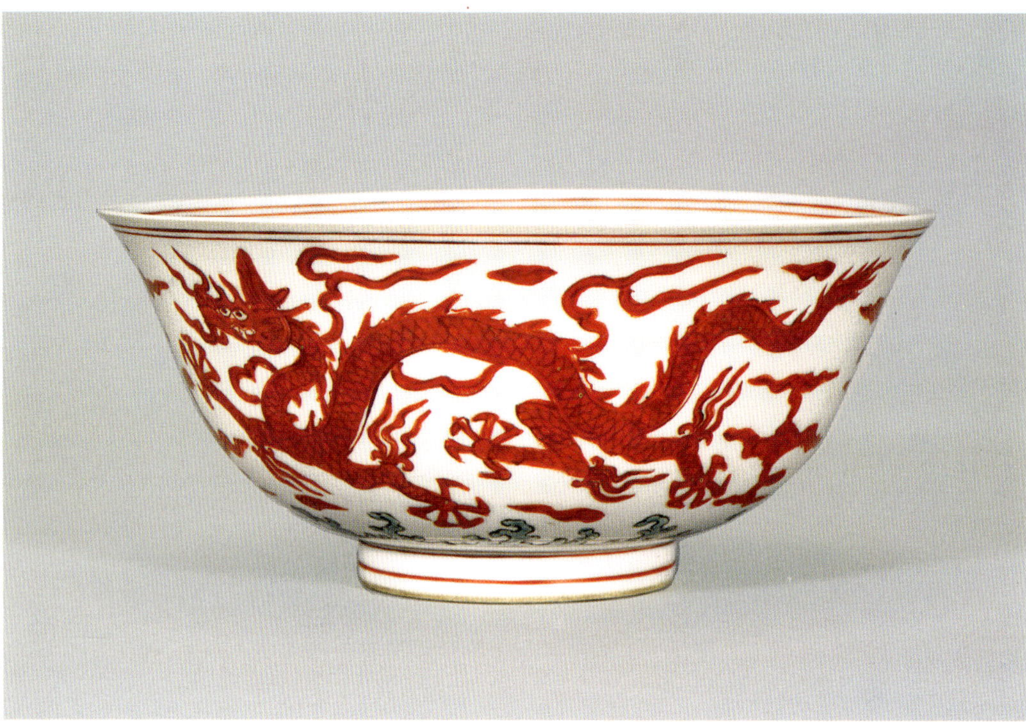

38

BOWL

Jingdezhen ware, overglaze-enamel-decorated porcelain with dragon-and-cloud design

Ming dynasty, Zhengde period (1506–21); Zhengde four-character mark, *Zhengde nian zhi*

D. 20.8 cm (8 1/4 in.)

This large bowl has curving sides, an everted mouth, and a ring foot enclosing the recessed base, on which the four-character reign mark is written in overglaze-red enamel within a double circle. The blemish-free glaze is smooth and sumptuously bright; only on the base, where the glaze is a honey color, is the application below the highest standard. On the exterior two dragons wheel above fingerlike waves; the space between the creatures is neatly charted by quatrefoil clouds. The dragons are outlined, colored, and detailed with overglaze-red enamel, which has a characteristically matt surface; the sepia-outlined waves are a translucent blue-green. At the bottom of the interior, within a field defined by double red-enamel circles and set off by the white of the undecorated cavetto, a third red dragon leaps among red clouds. The design is highly dynamic, and the dragons seem frenzied, even though the composition is statically balanced and some elements are repeated verbatim. Each dragon, for example, fits into a neat trapezoidal shape, and the streamers flowing from the dragons' backs and leg joints and the large clouds recur from section to section.

In its well-potted, finely balanced form, sumptuous glaze, and hearty, brisk design, this bowl combines the grace and perfection of late fifteenth-century potting techniques with the decorative robustness characteristic of porcelains produced during the post-Zhengde period. The four-character form of the reign mark, which occurs frequently on Zhengde porcelains of imperial taste and quality, might have been revived to associate these wares with their early Ming imperial ancestors.

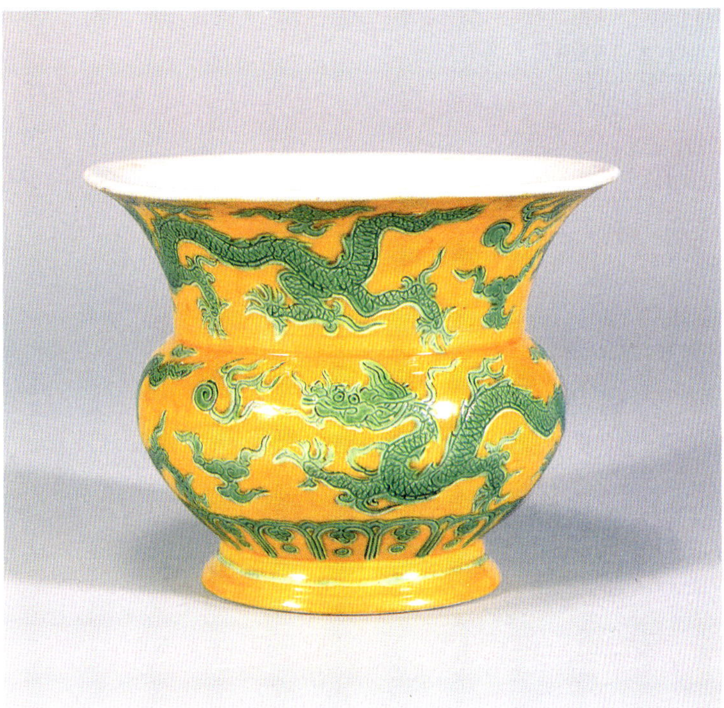

39

ZHADOU

Jingdezhen ware, yellow- and green-enameled porcelain with dragon-and-cloud design

Ming dynasty, Zhengde period (1506–21); Zhengde four-character mark, *Zhengde nian zhi*

H. 11.4 cm (4 1/2 in.)

The stout, bulbous body of this *zhadou* rests on a high, flaring foot with a reverse curve at the base and is surmounted by a funnel-shaped, broad neck with a strongly everted rim. This distinctive form was used to contain dining and tea-drinking refuse. The earliest known examples produced at Jingdezhen were decorated in underglaze blue and date to the first decades of the fifteenth century. During the Zhengde period a popular alternative to the underglaze-blue painting technique was to decorate *zhadou* with incised designs combined with green and yellow enamels.

The interior and the deeply recessed base, which bears the four-character mark in underglaze blue within a double circle, are covered in a greenish white, fairly thick glaze. The exterior surface—incised with a dragon-and-cloud design on both body and neck and a lotus-panel border above the foot—was left free of glaze. After the first high-temperature firing, enamels were applied to the biscuit to produce, after a second firing, a bright green design set against a rich yellow ground. The active, even agitated impression of the piece is due in no small part to the jostling colors and the incised lines emboldened by thickly accumulated enamel colors. Such an aesthetic—also evident in the overburdened surfaces of much contemporaneous underglaze-blue-decorated ware—perhaps represents an effort to inject vitality and sparkle into a tradition that had grown reserved and overly precious. The effort was not without effect; the potters of the succeeding Jiajing period followed suit in the creation of an unprecedented variety of kaleidoscopically colorful enamel-decorated porcelains.

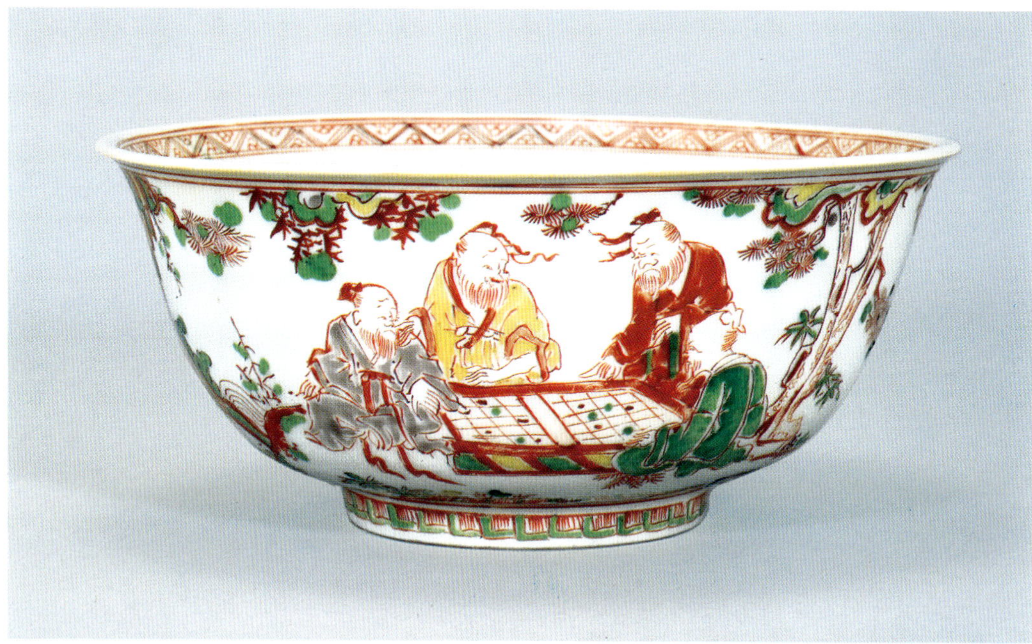

40

BOWL

Jingdezhen ware, overglaze-enamel-decorated porcelain with figural scene

Ming dynasty, first half 16th century

D. 22.2 cm (8 3/4 in.)

This deep bowl has gently rounded sides, a sharply everted mouth, and a straight ring foot. The deeply recessed base is coated with a glaze ranging from bluish white to a strong honey color. An informal garden scene with four gentlemen playing a sociable game of chess and another pair enjoying a stroll among the flowers, shrubbery, and rocks is painted on the exterior in overglaze enamels. Red is used throughout for varied and expressive outlines: fine and fluid lineament for the figures, thicker and bolder strokes for the rocks, clouds, fences, and contour lines of the ground. Yellow, green, aubergine, and red are deftly applied with broad brushstrokes, which are well controlled but sufficiently modulated to create light and lively images. One figure shows his delight at a brilliant move on the chessboard; the downcast grimaces and pouts of the others manifest their dismay. The scene is bordered above and below with a double red ring, and the foot is decorated with overlapping L-shaped elements that appear to be simplified leaves. The decoration on the interior bottom is less well preserved: two children, one with a yellow smock and the other in green, are seated against the white porcelain ground; the garden elements are arranged along the periphery of the circular field defined by a double red circle. A diaper band below the mouth frames the undecorated cavetto.

Stylistically this bowl appears to be a transitional piece between the reserve and control commonly found in later fifteenth-century overglaze-enamel-decorated porcelains and the boisterousness and flamboyance of those of the Jiajing period. Though the pot is somewhat sturdier and the smooth glaze less perfectly fired, the honey-tinted discoloration of the base is similar to that on a significant number of Zhengde-marked pieces, and it is not unreasonable to assume that this bowl was produced in the late Zhengde or early Jiajing period.

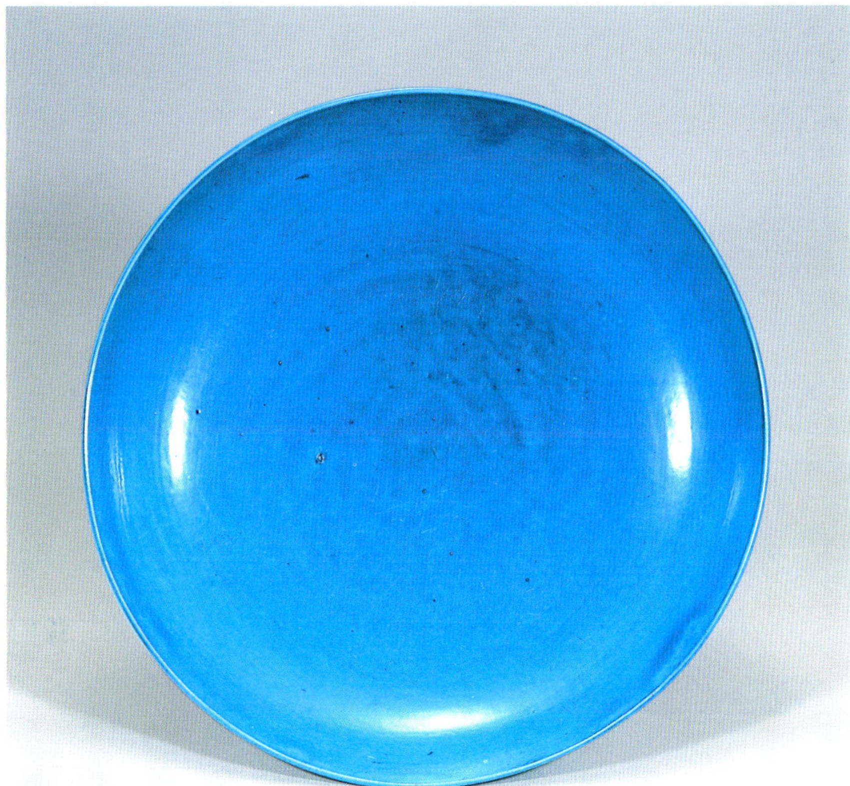

41

LARGE DISH

Jingdezhen ware, turquoise-glazed porcelaneous ware

Ming dynasty, first half 16th century

D. 50.6 cm (20 in.)

The widely curved sides of this dish open generously to an expansive interior. The inward slanting, undercut foot encloses an unglazed convex base, which has fired to a grayish brown color. Three inscriptions written in ink on the base are illegible. The turquoise color of the glaze applied to the interior and exterior walls of the biscuit-fired, somewhat coarse porcelaneous body was achieved by firing the copper-bearing alkaline coating at medium temperature in an oxidizing kiln. The glaze is not uniform but thins at the mouth and flows more thickly toward the foot, where it has accumulated in drops. Although there are pits and irregularities, and some crazing due to its high degree of instability, the glaze is a rich, brilliant color and has a good sheen.

As a glaze color, turquoise, or *kongcui* (peacock blue), was far more popular and widely produced in the Islamic world, where the inscriptions on the present piece might have been written. In China turquoise appeared only rarely during the Ming dynasty as a monochrome glaze color, although its use can be traced at least to the thirteenth century—possibly by way of Islamic influence—in the wares of the Cizhou kilns in the north. It continued to be used there, though infrequently, through the sixteenth century. In referring to an "extremely beautiful" color of Chenghua-period glazes, the author of the *Nan yao bi ji* used the term *feicui*, which is most likely the same peacock-blue color seen here.[1] Extant Chenghua-period porcelains with a turquoise glaze were produced by applying the colored glaze to a prefired, neutrally glazed vessel, and presumably the same procedure was followed in making the vessels of which fragments were found during excavation of early fifteenth-century sites at Zhushan in Jingdezhen.[2] The color was also used extensively in *fahua* vessels, which apparently originated in the north, perhaps as early as the fourteenth century. The majority of extant examples appear to be sixteenth century in date (see nos. 57 and 58). A similar date for the Idemitsu piece is likely, though its provenance remains in question.[3]

1. Feng Xianming, et al., *Zhongguo taoci shi* (Beijing: Wenwu Press, 1982), p. 389; for the *Nan yao bi ji* reference see also the *Meishu congshu* (Taiwan ed.), vol. 16, p. 321.

2. *Zhongguo taoci*, no. 7 (1982), pp. 176–77.

3. A turquoise-glazed dish measuring 43.1 cm in the Percival David Foundation of Chinese Art, London, appears from the catalogue description to be similar to the Idemitsu piece and is dated there to around 1500. See Margaret Medley, *Illustrated Catalogue of Ming and Ch'ing Monochrome in the Percival David Foundation of Chinese Art* (London: School of Oriental and African Studies, 1973), A511.

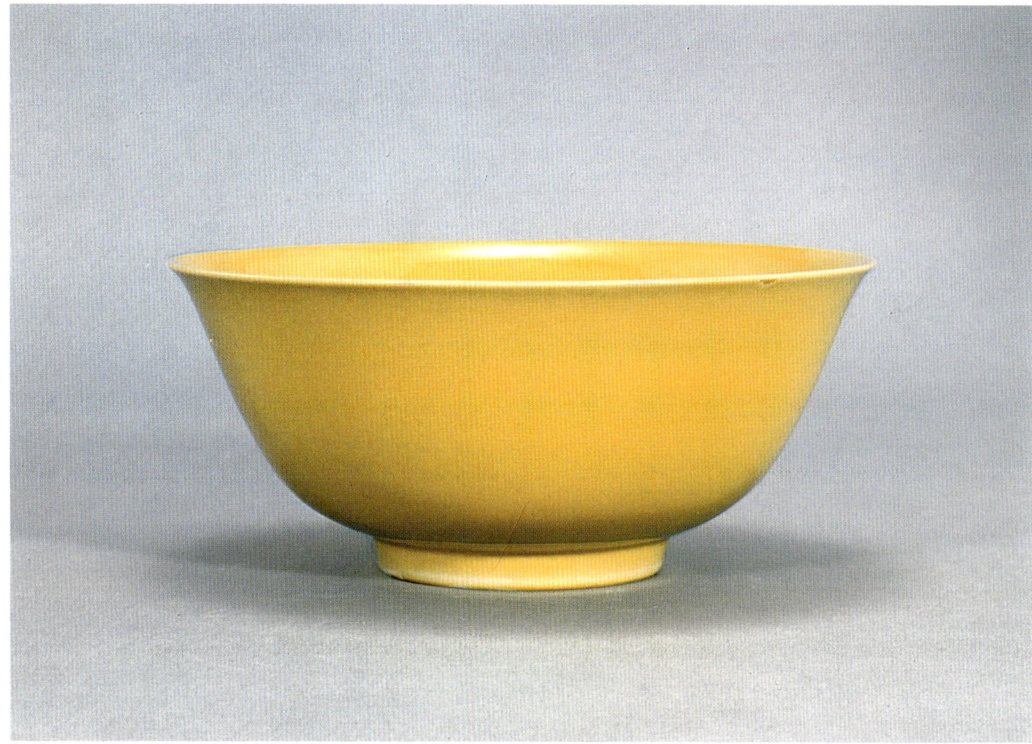

42

BOWL

Jingdezhen ware, yellow-glazed porcelain

Ming dynasty, Jiajing period (1522–66); Jiajing six-character mark, *Da Ming Jiajing nian zhi*

D. 19.9 cm (7 7/8 in.)

The sides of this finely potted bowl curve to an everted mouth; its ring foot tapers. A colorless glaze covers the interior of the foot and the convex base, on which the six-character reign mark is written in brilliant blue within a neatly drawn double circle. The sole embellishment is the yellow enamel glaze, which covers both the exterior and interior of the piece.

According to research carried out at the Shanghai Institute of Technology, iron-rich hematite ore was used to produce the yellow color. Yellow monochrome porcelains were made in one of two ways: the enamel was applied to the surface of a prefired, unglazed porcelain vessel or, as here, to a prefired, neutrally glazed porcelain. In either case, the piece was fired a second time at 850 to 900 degrees centigrade in an oxidizing atmosphere.[1] Whereas the color of the biscuit-glazed ceramics is a deep egg-yolk yellow, here the overglaze color has a pale lemony tone. The yellow coating was thinly and evenly applied and is palest around the mouth rim and foot. The surface has a pearly luster, and due to the high translucency of the yellow layer, the marks of the shaving tool used to pare the vessel are visible.

Yellow monochromes were used as imperial sacrificial vessels in ceremonies performed at the Altar of the Earth. The long association of this color with the earth derives from the special character and appearance of the northern Chinese terrain, and its link with imperial authority can be traced back to the legendary third millennium B.C. sovereign Huangdi, the "Yellow Emperor." The color appears to have been developed as a monochrome in the early fifteenth century, and though Hongzhi monochrome yellow porcelains are often accorded the highest rank by connoisseurs, the present piece is evidence of extremely high-quality production during the Jiajing period.

1. See Feng Xianming, et al., *Zhongguo taoci shi* (Beijing: Wenwu Press, 1982), p. 389.

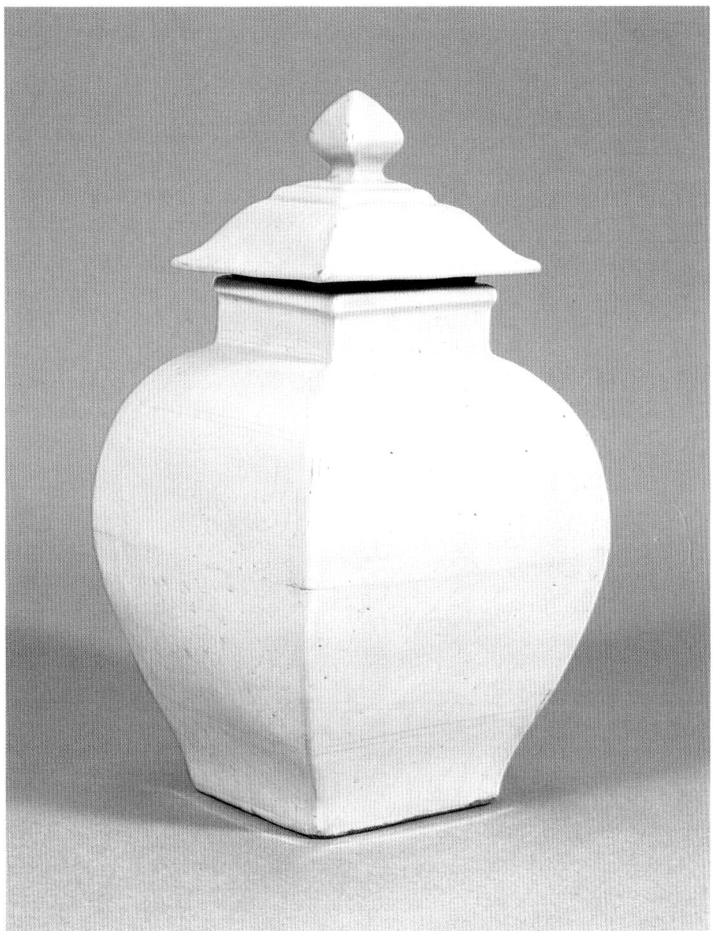

43

SQUARE COVERED JAR

Jingdezhen ware, monochrome white porcelain with incised dragon design

Ming dynasty, Jiajing period (1522–66); Jiajing six-character mark, *Da Ming Jiajing nian zhi*

H. 27.1 cm (10 5/8 in.)

This four-sided jar is square in section; its swelling body narrows at the base and curves inward to join the high neck. The unglazed foot encloses a deeply recessed base, on which the six-character mark is written in bright blue within a double square beneath a greenish-tinged glaze. The square lid with sloping sides is set into the thickened mouth, extends well beyond the rim, and is topped by a pointed knob. The slight distortions in shape and the imperfect fit of the lid might have resulted from attempting to combine sharply angled edges with the curving contours of the swelling and contracting form. The design was incised on the surface and covered by a grayish glaze.

A pair of dragons with ascendant and descendant bodies gravitates around a central pearl on each of the four sides. Pendant *ruyi*-shaped motifs form a frieze on the shoulder. Lotus panels containing heart-shaped elements and simple circles and rectangles fence the lower body. A key fret supports the rectangular geometry of the neck. The cover has a bold floral scroll symmetrically arranged and centered on each of its four sides. The decorative design of the vessel is thus a conventional successor of the horizontally tiered composition popular since the fourteenth century.

This piece, like the porcelains of the fifteenth century with *anhua* (hidden decoration), requires more than a passing glance to be appreciated. Unlike those earlier wares, however, the incised lines here are irregular, sometimes jerking and erratic. This hesitancy and unsteadiness in the lineament is common in this relatively rare group of Jiajing-period white monochromes, which includes examples in both the Palace Museum in Beijing and the National Palace Museum in Taipei. A certain lack of precision had come to detract from the perfection of even the porcelains intended for court use during the Jiajing period, but the spirited assault on traditional vessel forms waged by the potters of the sixteenth century also resulted in positive departures, such as the shape of the present jar.

This heavy, stout jar has a wide short neck with a rounded mouth rim and rests on a narrow beveled foot. The six-character reign mark is written in bright cobalt blue beneath the greenish white, pitted glaze on the convex base. A coat of yellow enamel was applied to the prefired porcelain body, which had been covered with a neutral glaze. The design was sketched out in sepia enamel, the background then brushed in with iron-red enamel, and finally further details added in sepia before a second firing at a lower temperature. The result is both a festive and lively interplay of rich, sunny colors and a subtle contrast of vibrant yellow images against a matt red ground. The enamel around the mouth rim has been worn away by contact with the original cover.

The two dragons, their popping eyes transfixed on the pearl booty before them, tramp the fungus-laden red skies with a cloud canopy above and tri-pronged rocks and lapping waves below. The main features of the typical Jiajing dragon are all here: lumpy brows and straining eyes, here haloed by sharply fringed lashes, thick tresses sweeping from beneath the necks into high coiffures, and strongly curving bodies propelled by widely stretched limbs.

The rock formation, a central peak flanked symmetrically by two lesser ones, is akin in shape to the ideograph meaning "mountain." By the early Song period (960–1127), Chinese landscape painters used this arrangement to convey on silk or paper an impression of the majesty and permanence of the natural world. Not until the sixteenth century, however, did the tripartite mountain, already cast in the hieratic form seen here, appear as a common motif in ceramic design.

The shape of each cloud, related to the *ruyi* form, also long predates the sixteenth century as a decorative design used by craftsmen in almost every media. The insistent transfiguration of the shape into the form of the *lingzhi* (fungus of immortality) is characteristic of the Jiajing-period decorators' compulsion to create images suggestive of longevity and reflects the emperor's personal preoccupation with attaining everlasting life. Thus the skies are overgrown with fungus springing from the sea; even the pearls are encased in aureoles related in shape to the sacred fungus.

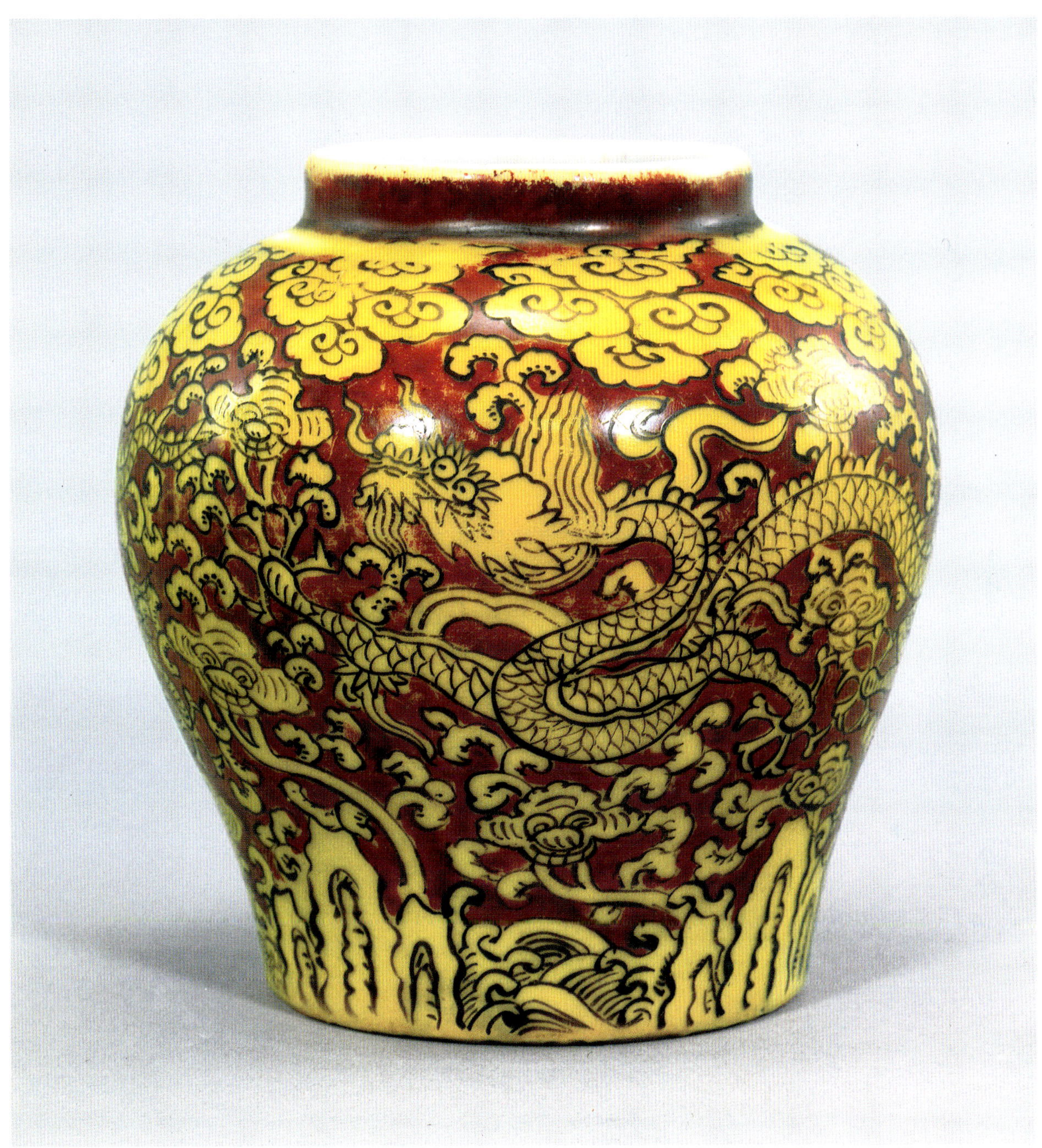

44

JAR

Jingdezhen ware, overglaze-yellow and red-enameled porcelain with dragon design

Ming dynasty, Jiajing period (1522–66); Jiajing six-character mark, *Da Ming Jiajing nian zhi*

H. 13.7 cm (5 3/8 in.)

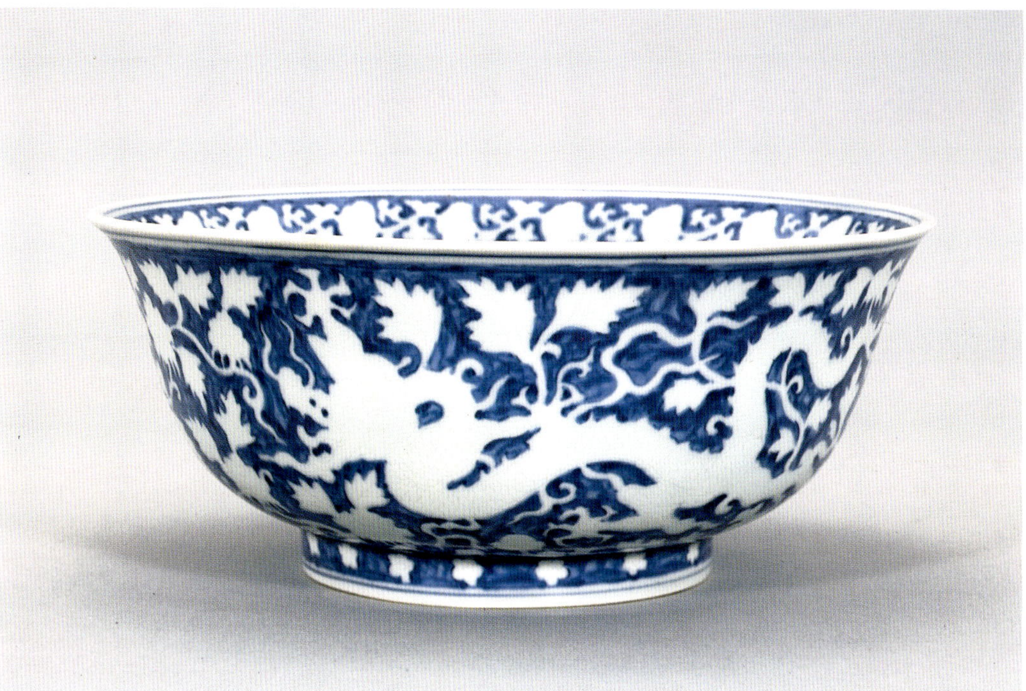

45

LARGE BOWL

Jingdezhen ware, porcelain decorated with white-reserve-on-blue dragon design

Ming dynasty, Jiajing period (1522–66); Jiajing six-character mark, *Da Ming Jiajing nian zhi*

D. 28.1 cm (11 1/8 in.)

Finely potted yet quite sturdy, this large bowl with deep, rounded sides and everted mouth is forceful in appearance. The high ring foot encloses the neatly glazed base, on which the six-character reign mark is written in underglaze blue within a double circle. The dragons and floral scrolls on the exterior and bottom interior, the five-petaled florets on the foot, and the band of fungus along the inner mouth rim were outlined and detailed by steady, precise incisions with a pointed tool. Fluid cobalt pigment was brushed on as a background, leaving the motifs in white against a brightly colored blue ground after glazing and firing. The cavetto, which is undecorated save for the fungus scroll around the mouth rim, was likewise brushed with blue. Two characteristics of Jiajing-era production at the imperial kilns are apparent here: one is the use of high-grade imported cobalt, the so-called *huihui qing* (Mohammedan blue); the other is exhaustive pulverization of the ore to yield a smooth and textureless pigment. Whatever irregularities in color are present here—the appearance of dappling, or light versus dark patches—resulted from applying the pigment with a large brush.

The dragons, with puffed-up heads, beady eyes, forelimbs thrown upward, and claws splayed, appear to fling themselves through fields of peony and lotus, although in fact the meandering foliage springs from the dragons themselves. The symbolic potency of the beast, the denizen of wind and cloud-filled skies as well as the ocean depths, is somewhat diminished by this gay, florid background, but throughout the later Ming such environments are not uncommon for the imperial emblem.

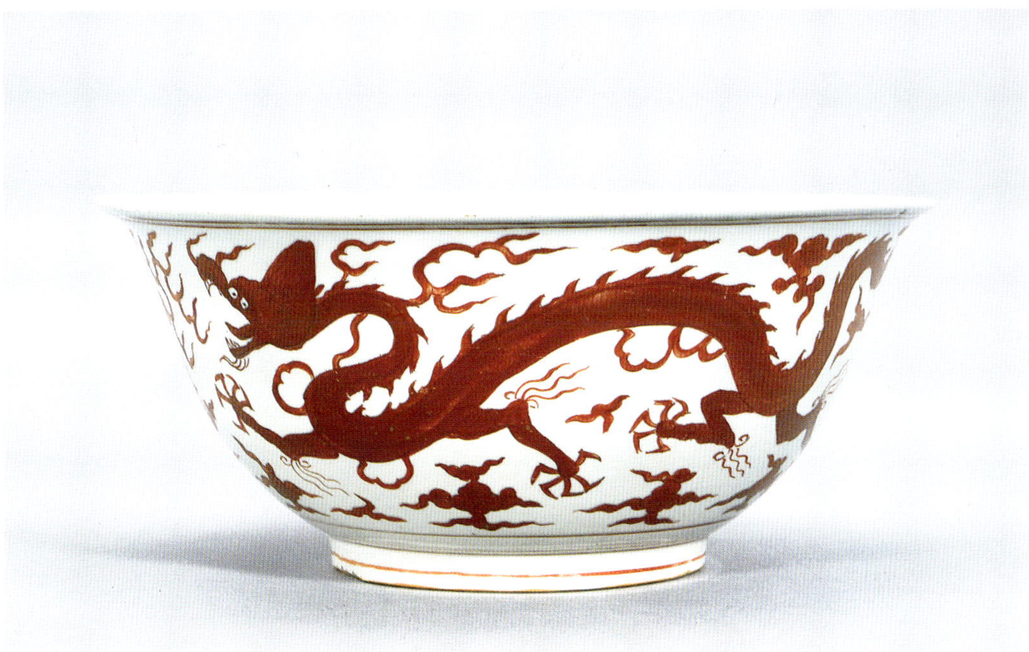

46

LARGE BOWL

Jingdezhen ware, overglaze-red-enameled porcelain with dragon-and-cloud design

Ming dynasty, Jiajing period (1522–66); Jiajing six-character mark, *Da Ming Jiajing nian zhi*

D. 37 cm (14 5/8 in.)

This large bowl, with deep sides curving to the everted mouth, is similar in shape, decorative technique, and design to the earlier Zhengde-period bowl (no. 38). Here, however, the sheer size of the vessel, with the motifs elongated and expanded to fill the swollen surface, conveys a feeling of luxuriousness and expansiveness in tune with other products of the Jiajing-period kilns at Jingdezhen. Some minor technical imperfections in comparison to the Zhengde-period bowl—kiln grit adhering to the unglazed foot ring, the loose appearance of the clay body beneath some areas of the glaze—are at worst forebodings of characteristics that became more frequent during the course of the later Ming, but detract not at all from this impressive vessel.

Against the carefully arranged ground of formalized clouds, a pair of dragons pursues the pearls symbolizing their beneficence, although these giants appear more the lustful recipients than the gracious harbingers of bounty. Their swelling brows, bulging eyes, over-ripe faces, and pompadour topnotches are features they share with other dragons of their generation. The rich, tomato-red enamel is heavily applied, but the expanses of matt color are relieved and the dragons enlivened by superficial incising of scales and other anatomical details. The use of red to the exclusion of all other colors and the completely plain interior represent simplifications of Zhengde-period design, and indeed the monochromatic red scheme harkens back to the overglaze-red-enamel dragon dishes produced during the reign of the first Ming emperor. This bowl thus takes its place in a long lineage, extending from the late fourteenth century and continuing on long after the Jiajing period, as a splendid example of the prevailing aesthetic of its time.

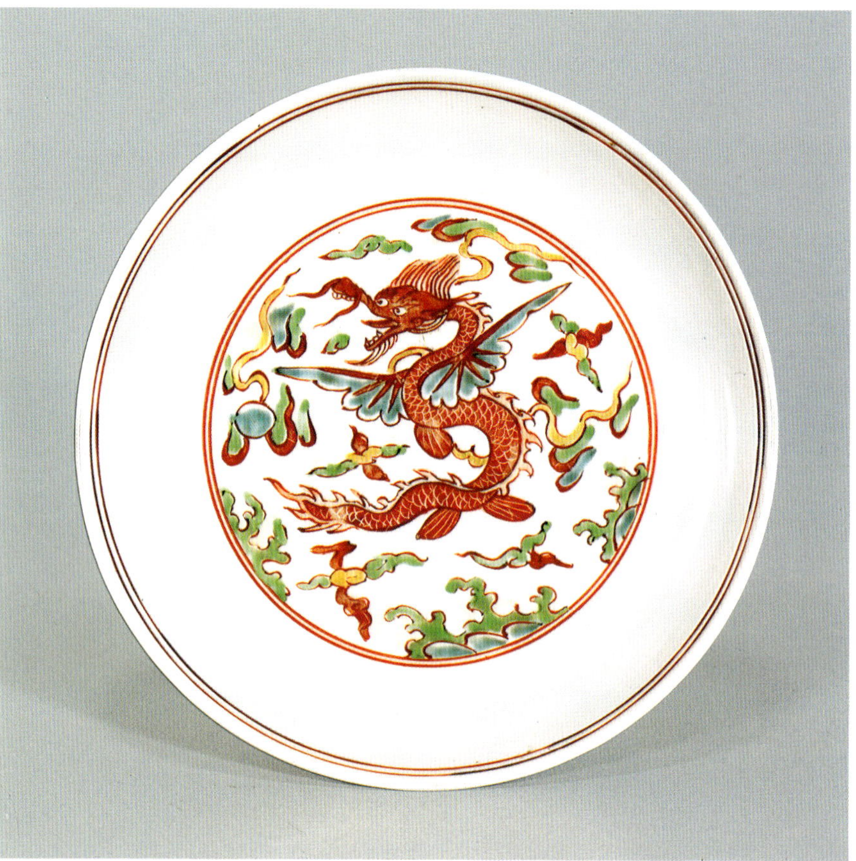

47

DISH

Jingdezhen ware, overglaze-enamel-decorated porcelain with flying-dragon design

Ming dynasty, dated 1541?; four-character inscription, *Xinchou shang·yong*

D. 20.5 cm (8 1/8 in.)

This dish with curved sides rests on a foot that slants inward and is steeply cut on the interior. The four-character inscription, *Xinchou shang yong*, "[in the] Xinchou [cyclical year] presented for use," is written in overglaze-red enamel on the convex base. Painted in enamels over the smooth glaze are colorful dragons with scaly, fishlike bodies, fins in the place of legs and claws, and large batlike wings. The scales of the red dragon bodies are incised down to the white ground; the jagged yellow spines and turquoise wings are outlined in red. Two of the dragons are outstretched over splashing waters in pursuit of pearls on the exterior; in the center of the dish, enclosed within a double red circle, a single winged dragon has risen out of the waves and soars amidst clouds before a dazzling pearl. Aside from the red, which is matt, the delicately applied green, yellow, and turquoise enamels are quite lustrous.

The extraordinary flying fish-dragon (*feiyu*) might be related to the wondrous fish-dragon who bore a certain brilliant scholar of the Tang dynasty (618–907) from the depths of the Yellow River, in which he had drowned himself in despair, to a glorious rebirth in the firmament as Kui Xing, the chief star in the Great Dipper (see no. 84).[1] A number of bowls and dishes to which this piece relates both technically and stylistically are variously marked with overglaze-red enameled inscriptions reading *Shang yong* (Presented for use), *Zhao Fu zhi yong* (For use in Zhao principality), or *Zhao Fu zhi zao* (Made for Zhao principality). The Idemitsu piece is distinguished by the inclusion of the characters *xinchou* in its inscription; these correspond to a date in a sixty-year cycle, in this case the years 1421, 1481, 1541, 1601, and so on. The overglaze-enamel decoration manifests a continuation of the refined style of the later fifteenth to early sixteenth centuries, but the physical and technical characteristics of the dish make the year 1541 the most likely date for its manufacture.

1. A small *gui*-shaped incense burner with similar flying dragons painted in overglaze enamels, and with a cyclical date corresponding to 1564, was in fact dedicated to the temple of the God of the Northern Skies. The piece is illustrated and the inscription translated by Sheila Riddell in *Dated Chinese Antiquities: 600–1650* (London: Faber and Faber, 1979), p. 122, fig. 111.

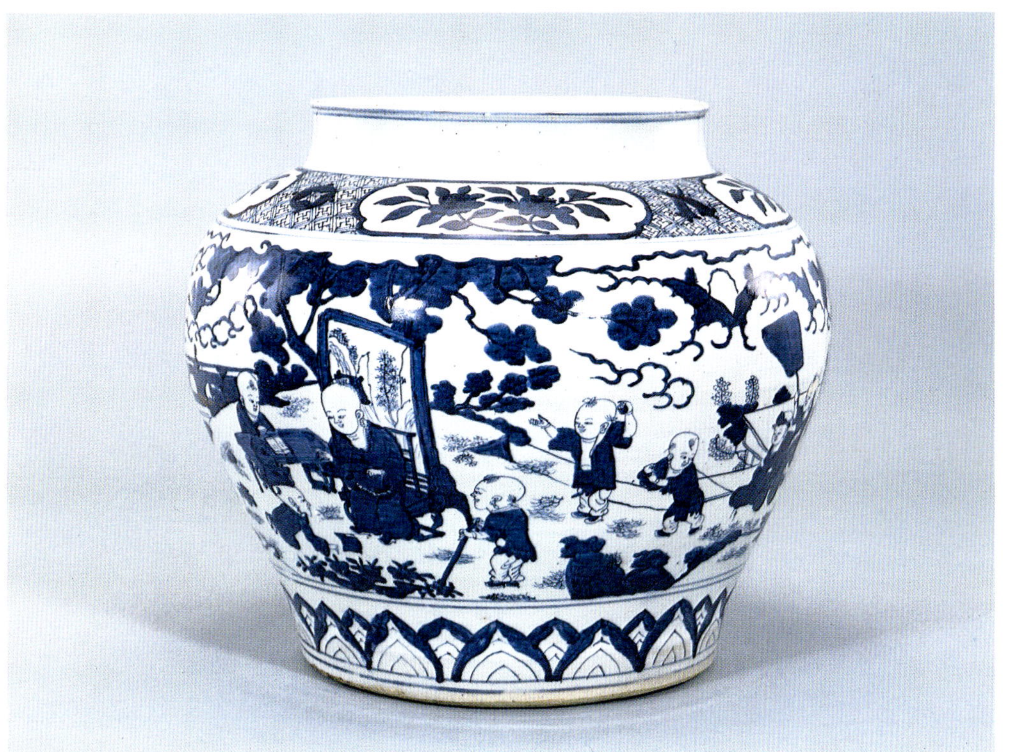

48

LARGE JAR

Jingdezhen ware, underglaze-blue-decorated porcelain with scene of children at play

Ming dynasty, Jiajing period (1522–66); Jiajing six-character mark, *Da Ming Jiajing nian zhi*

H. 33.5 cm (13 1/4 in.)

A perfect playground for sixteen frolicsome children is provided by this high-shouldered, broad-based, sturdily potted jar. Only the wide neck, which curves inward to the thickened lip, is free of ornament, but this would have gone unnoticed when the jar was fitted with its original, fully decorated lid. The unglazed foot, irregularly cut and encrusted with a bit of kiln grit, reveals a somewhat impure body, and the haphazardly glazed recessed base, on which the six-character reign mark is written in underglaze blue, is marred by numerous gas holes and iron spitouts. The hasty finishing of this piece might have been prompted by the great demand for these widely popular vessels, which had great decorative and symbolic appeal.

On the shoulder, ripened fruit and floral sprays are set in four quatrefoil panels against a diaper ground on which auspicious objects are superimposed. The plump, pointed leaves in two overlapping tiers forming a fence above the foot have a playful, casual air suitable to the scene that unfolds above them. There, within a terraced garden with ornamental rocks, trees, shrubs, and flowers, little boys gambol about, some playfully assuming the guises and enacting the roles of the adults they will one day become. The decoration throughout is painted in the deep violet-blue, *huihui qing* (Mohammedan blue), of the Jiajing period. An artful contrast to the heavy washes of color, which all but completely mask outlines and obscure details, is provided by the simpler linear renditions of the garden screen, the sloping ground, the grass, and the faces of the happily engaged children.

This lighthearted subject of children at play was propitious and conveyed wishes for success and male progeny. The symbolism is enforced by the bats metamorphosing from the ribbony clouds, which in turn appear to spring from the pine. The bat was a symbol for both longevity and happiness and a rebus for good fortune; the characters for "bat" and "good fortune" are both pronounced *fu*. The pine is also a symbol of longevity, and the swastika, *wan*, which is the basic unit repeated in the diaper ground of the shoulder, was also emblematic of good fortune and virtue.

The theme of children at play occurs in paintings of the Southern Song period (1127–1279) and in Song ceramic decoration. The theme was depicted in underglaze-blue-decorated porcelain at Jingdezhen from the early fifteenth century. During the Jiajing period elements from those earlier designs were coalesced into a standard pattern, which was repeated by and large verbatim, as can be seen from the numerous examples of such jars still surviving today.[1]

1. In 1980 an additional example, complete with cover, was added to the extant children-at-play jars, excavated in the Zhaoyang district in Beijing (*Wenwu*, no. 9, 1982, pl. 8, fig. 2).

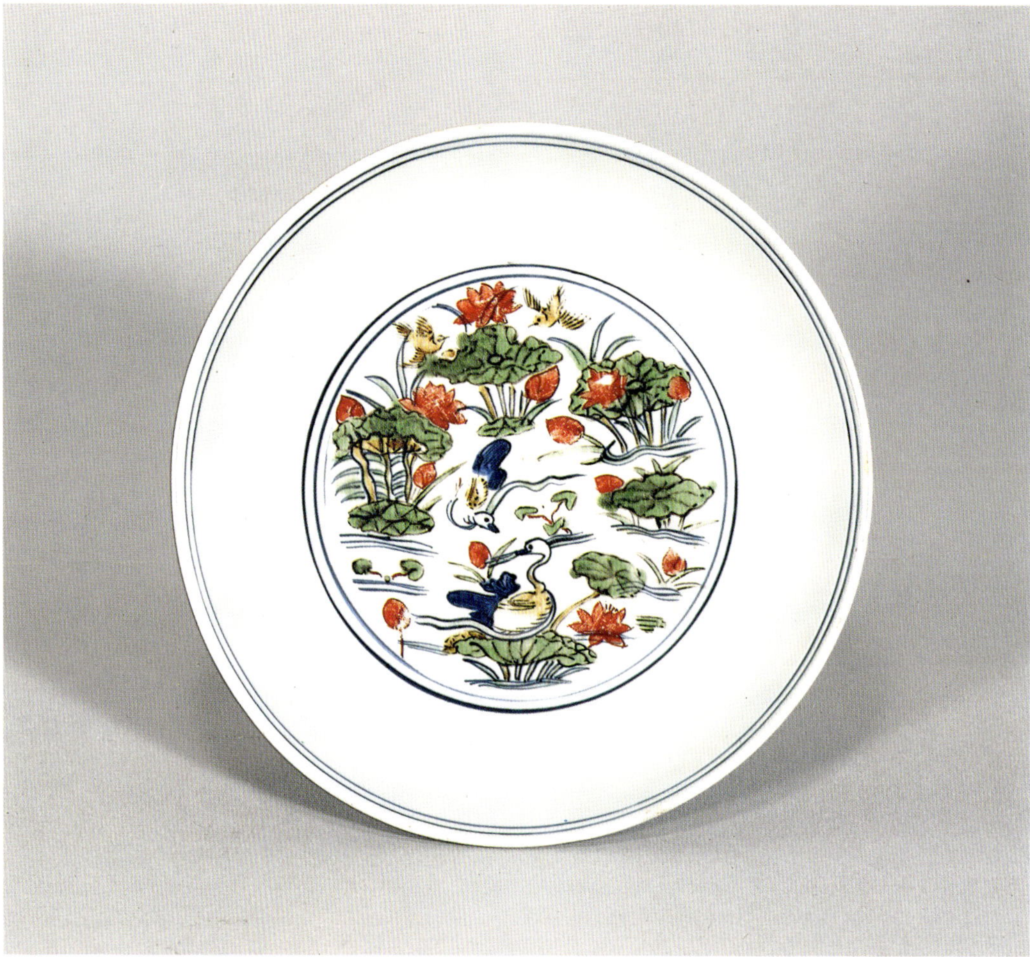

49

DISH

Jingdezhen ware, *wucai*-decorated porcelain with lotus-pond-and-waterfowl design

Ming dynasty, Jiajing period (1522–66); Jiajing six-character mark, *Da Ming Jiajing nian zhi*

D. 22.8 cm (9 in.)

This finely potted, shallow dish has wide, curving sides, an inward-slanting, low foot cut straight on the interior, and a recessed base, on which the six-character reign mark is written in cobalt blue beneath the smooth, bright glaze. On the interior of the dish a colorful scene of waterfowl flying above, swimming upon, and at watch beside a lotus-filled pond is enclosed by a double underglaze-blue ring, which is mirrored by another double ring at the top of the undecorated cavetto. A similar scene unfolds horizontally along the exterior of the dish and is also enclosed by blue rings with a single blue line on the foot. A significant portion of the design was outlined with underglaze blue before the addition of the enamel color in a modification or simplification of the *doučai* technique of the Chenghua era (see no. 33); the delicate blue rings framing the scene and demarcating the foot also relate to those earlier wares. Here, however, the brilliant swabs of blue coloring the lotus leaves and the wings, tails, and bills of the ducks are characteristic of standard Jiajing-period *wucai* (five-color) decorated porcelain, as is the use of overglaze sepia for outlines. Though the bright greens, yellows, and reds produce a light and charming scene, the combination of those enamels with the underglaze-blue outlines is far less meticulous than in the precedent wares. Such designs might be lacking in precision, but these zestfully colored porcelains were extremely popular and are viewed today as a hallmark of Jiajing-period achievement. In contrast to the more robustly decorated pieces typical of the time, the present dish stands somewhat apart in its delicate potting, impression of lightness, and reserve and could well have been made during the early years of the Jiajing period.

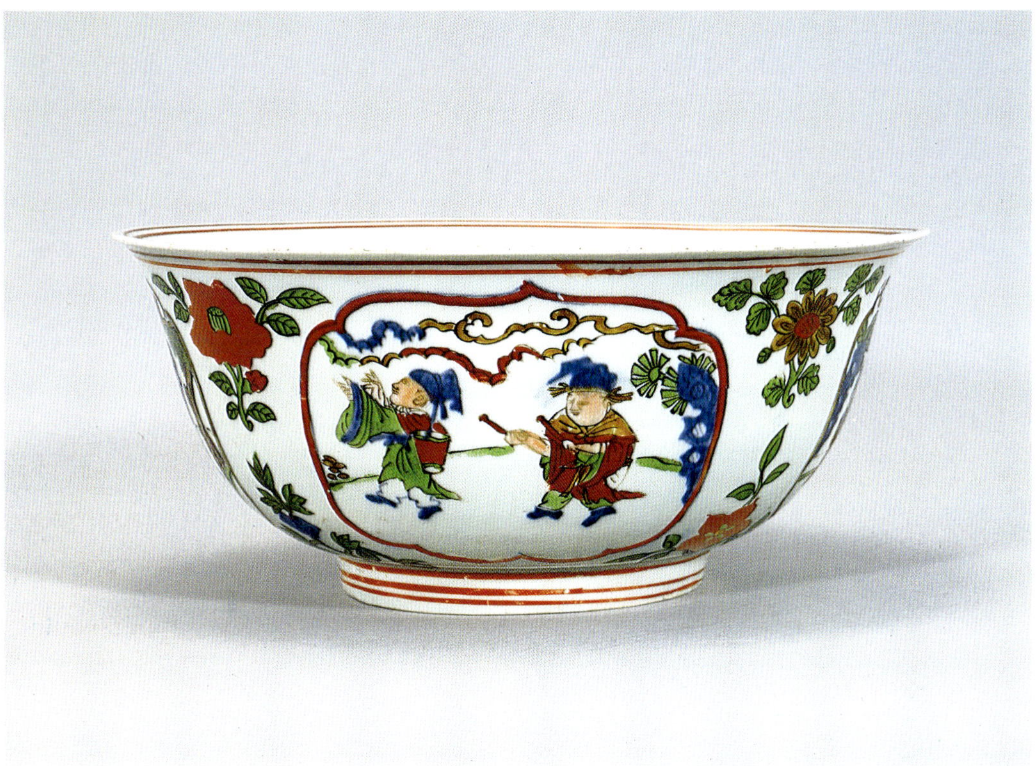

50

LARGE BOWL

Jingdezhen ware, *wucai*-decorated porcelain with figural scenes

Ming dynasty, Jiajing period (1522–66); Jiajing six-character mark, *Da Ming Jiajing nian zhi*

D. 30 cm (11 7/8 in.)

Large and deep, this bowl has curving sides, a gently everted mouth, and a wide ring foot. The underglaze-blue six-character reign mark is written on the recessed base. The glaze is bubbly, smooth, and bright. The underglaze-blue and overglaze-enamel decoration on the exterior consists of four lobed and pointed panels containing figural scenes; plump floral sprays surrounded symmetrically by leaves are placed at the upper and lower interstices between the panels. Another figural scene appears on the bottom of the interior, and the cavetto is undecorated.

The buffoonish figures are stunted in stature and wear floppy hats and whimsical expressions. One character has his fingers to his lips as if about to give out a loud whistle; his companion waits in joyful expectation. Two figures toy with fans, a puppet dangles from strings in another scene, and in the last, one chap with sticks in hand bounces nimbly after his mate, who carries a drum on his back. In the bottom interior of the bowl, in contrast to the amusing scenes of the exterior, a more sober scene is depicted: a scholar sits in relaxation, approached by a servant carrying a fan.

The more expansive palette of the sixteenth-century decorator is evident here in the appearance of a deep brownish red, a dark mustard yellow, and brown, in addition to the standard enamel colors. Hats, sleeves, and other details are broadly brushed with the resonant blue characteristic of the Jiajing period. Fine underglaze-blue outlines, however, are used for such details as the faces and hands of the figures and the well-drawn small puppet. The four exterior panels are framed by double underglaze-blue lines, now partially obscured by the red and yellow enamels that were painted over them.

Panels, medallions, and cartouches in a variety of shapes had long functioned as compositional devices in ceramic decoration, frequently acting as windows through which scenes drawn from life or the imagination could be viewed. During the Jiajing period these vignettes often focused on human or superhuman figures. Some of the figures here are clearly children; others appear to be dwarves or foreigners, but are likely children masquerading as such. The Chinese were fascinated by the bizarre and exotic physiognomies of foreign ambassadors, traders, and monks and took delight in depicting them, sometimes even as caricatures, in both the fine and applied arts.

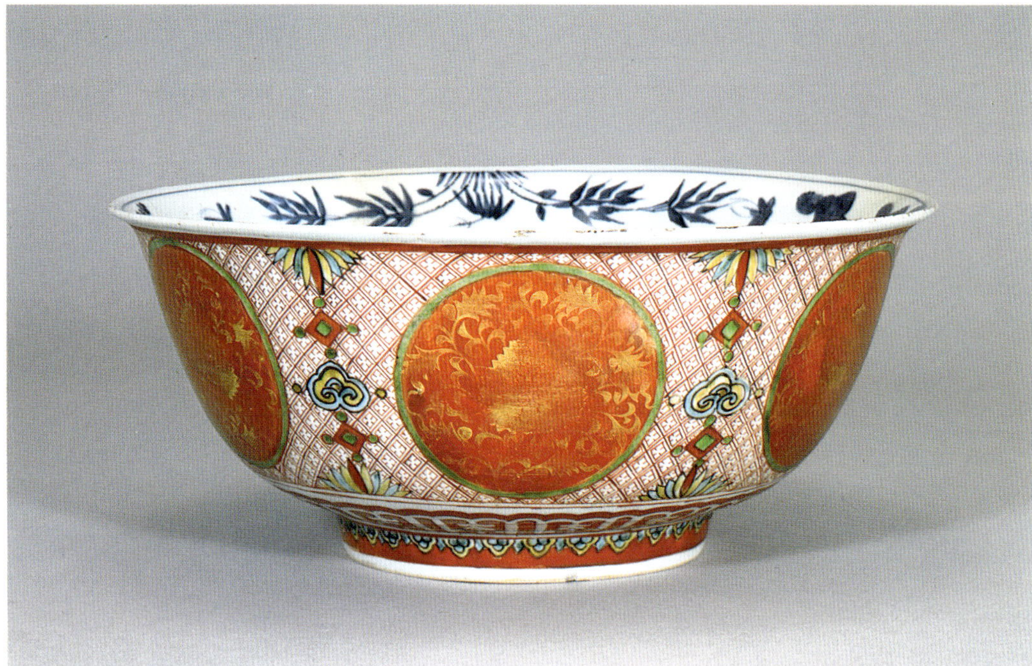

51

LARGE BOWL

Jingdezhen ware, *kinrande* porcelain with peony design

Ming dynasty, Jiajing period (1522–66); Jiajing six-character mark, *Da Ming Jiajing nian zhi*

D. 29.8 cm (11 3/4 in.)

This large bowl has rounded sides, an everted mouth, and a foot that slants slightly inward. The six-character reign mark is written within a double ring in underglaze blue on the deeply recessed base. After the pine, plum, bamboo, and the character *shou* were painted in cobalt on the interior, the bowl was glazed and fired. Large, circular medallions were then painted in solid red against a red diaper ground, which is studded with auspicious emblems and bordered below by lotus panels and *ruyi* heads produced with red, yellow, green, and turquoise overglaze enamels. After a second, lower-temperature firing, powdered gold combined with an adhesive was brushed on the red ground of the medallions to form the peony designs, with details scratched through the gold to the red.[1]

The decoration on the interior was executed in the outline-and-wash technique, using motifs common in underglaze-blue-decorated porcelains of the Jiajing period. On the bottom of the interior, the trunk and branches of a pine tree are contorted in the shape of the character *shou* (longevity), and indeed, the pine itself was an emblem conveying the same meaning. Pine, prunus, and bamboo—together known as the "Three Friends of Winter"—were elongated to fit sequentially into a narrow band below the mouth rim.

The orderly arrangement of medallions containing gilt floral designs, the meticulously drawn diaper ground, the half-flowers and additional decorative devices, and the borders of lotus panels and *ruyi* heads are typical of *kinrande* wares in general. The name *kinrande*[2] (gold-brocade style), the Japanese term by which this group of wares is widely known, aptly describes the ornateness and gold embellishment characteristic of the style. Although a small quantity of *kinrande* porcelains remained in China, a fair number were exported to the Near East and points farther west during the sixteenth century. By far the largest number went to Japan, and the basic style might have been devised specifically to accord with contemporaneous Japanese taste.

On the basis of a very small number of marked pieces, including the present bowl, *kinrande* is believed to have flourished during the Jiajing period. The style influenced not only the decoration of provincial wares of later Ming China, notably the Swatow group, but also the *ko-Imari* porcelains of seventeenth-century Japan and even the wares created by Japanese studio potters active in the late Edo period.

1. The standard method for decorating porcelains with gold was to cut gold leaf to a desired shape and apply it by means of an adhesive to the glaze or enamel ground. Painting in gold was a technique often used to redecorate wares on which the delicate and easily abraded gold leaf had worn away.

2. Fujio Koyama in *A Selection of Outstanding Kinrande Porcelains in Japanese Collections* (Tokyo and Kyoto: Unsodo Publishing, n.d.), introduction, n.p., explains that the term *kinrande* originated in sixteenth-century Japan as a descriptive appellation for the brocade textiles used as decorative borders for scrolls and for making bags in which tea ceremony utensils were stored; only from the seventeenth century does the term *kinrande* appear in tea ceremony diaries and in inventories of tea utensils specifically in reference to ceramic vessels.

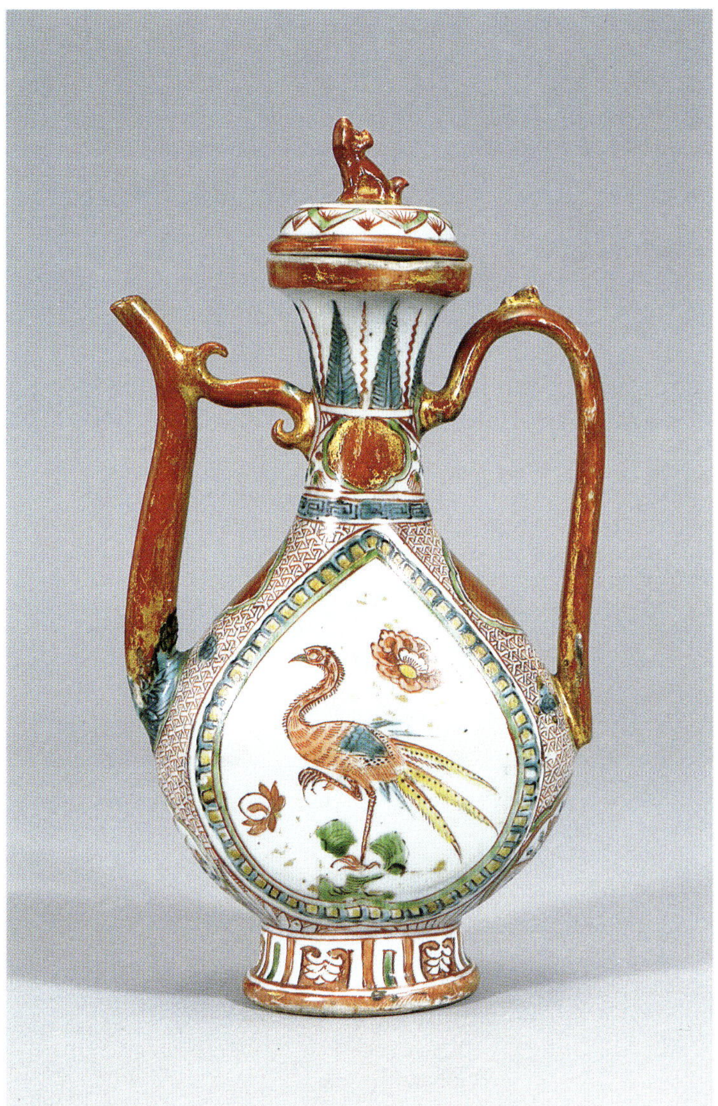

52

EWER

Jingdezhen ware, *kinrande* porcelain with bird-and-flower design

Ming dynasty, second half 16th century

H. 26 cm (10 1/4 in.)

The flattened pear-shaped body of this ewer contracts to a round, flaring neck with a straight mouth and is mounted on a high splayed foot. The long, curved spout is attached to the body with an S-shaped strut. Small rings designed to accommodate a metal chain have broken from the top of the high, arched handle and from the animal-shaped knob atop the snugly fitting lid. The roughly trimmed foot is thick, and the unglazed rim reveals an impure, grayish white body. The deeply recessed base and the interior of the vessel and the lid are covered with a glaze dotted with iron specks. The vessel is light in weight and was somewhat distorted in firing.

Typical of *kinrande* porcelain, red enamel with gold appliqué prevails in the color scheme, although a good portion of the gold has worn away, and the composition is dominated by medallions set against a diaper ground. Large tear-shaped panels on the front and back correspond in shape to the profile of the ewer and contain peacocks and flowers painted in red, turquoise, green, and yellow enamels. The flowers, which now float somewhat awkwardly against the white ground, would have been anchored by the original gold, of which only tiny flecks remain. Traces of gold on the birds also indicate the original, far more elaborate appearance of the vessel in pristine condition.

Technical shortcomings of the vessel might suggest a date later than the Jiajing period, when the majority of *kinrande* vessels were produced. But even if Jingdezhen had begun to suffer the consequences of depleted natural resources and diminished imperial interest, the popular domestic and export markets continued to inspire creativity. Here, the teardrop shape of the panels with peony and birds depicted in colorful enamels set against a gold and white ground, or what might have been an entirely gold ground, is an inventive and rare variant among surviving *kinrande* porcelains.

This large, ovoid jar has a wide neck and rounded mouth, high looping handles (one of which is a later replacement), and low-slung shoulders. The slightly recessed, unglazed base is rough and of buff color. After a preliminary, high-temperature firing of the neutrally glazed vessel, the exterior was covered entirely with iron-red enamel; after a second firing, at a lower temperature, the decoration was produced in gold. The main body zone is dominated by two large arch-shaped panels against a feathery-leafed peony ground. On one side a stately peacock and its mate pose among lush peonies; on the other is a pair of ducks, one swimming and the other about to alight on a lotus pond. A formal floral scroll decorates the shoulder, a band of pointed leaves encircles the neck, and lotus lappets surround the base.

The complex design might have been produced with a technique other than the usual cut gold-leaf method: it seems that the design was drawn on the surface using a brush dipped in clear, colorless adhesive, and extremely thin sheets of gold were then applied to the surface. Gold not held in place by the adhesive was blown or brushed away, leaving only the design in gold.[1] Throughout, the gilded areas were incised with fine lines, which define in exquisite detail the botanical and anatomical features of flowers, leaves, and birds.

The Idemitsu jar has attracted attention because of its stunning design, excellently preserved gold, and exceptional shape. The bird-and-flower scenes and secondary zone motifs are more complex but not unrelated to the decoration on two *kinrande* ewers in China, one covered in red and the other in brownish red enamel before the gold designs were applied.[2] Although unusual, the shape of this jar is not unique. It relates, for example, to that of a monochrome yellow, two-handled ovoid jar of the Hongzhi period in the Palace Museum in Beijing and to that of a Jiajing-marked, monochrome blue vessel with incised design in the Baur collection in Switzerland.[3] Dating for the present *kinrande* jar is suggested by a paragraph in the *Taoshuo* which describes Longqing-era wares of Jingdezhen; "wine jars with gold-applied peacocks and peonies"[4] were a specialty of the time.

1. This possibility was suggested by Teresa Kobayashi, Tokyo.

2. The red-enameled ewer is on view in the Shanghai Museum of Art and the other, discovered in a drainage ditch of a temple in Shaanxi province, illustrated in *Wenwu*, no. 12 (1979), pl. 1.

3. The Hongzhi piece is on view in the porcelain section of the Palace Museum in Beijing and the Baur vessel illustrated by John Ayers in *The Baur Collection: Chinese Ceramics*, vol. 2, *Ming Porcelains, and Other Wares* (Geneva: Collections Baur, 1968), A168.

4. Zhu Yen, *Taoshuo* (preface, 1774), chap. 6, in *Meishu congshu* (Taiwan ed.), vol. 7, pt. 2, p. 205.

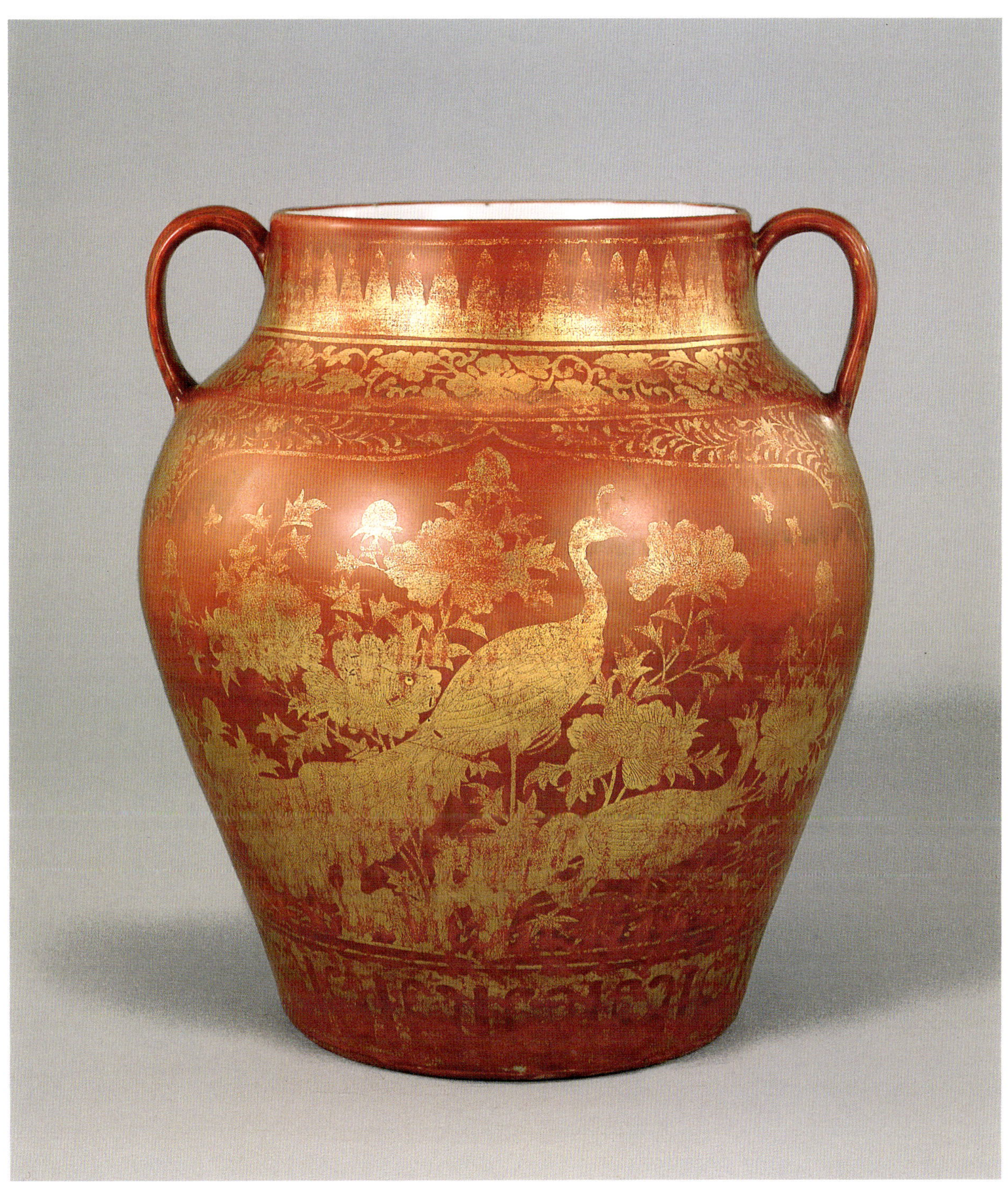

53

LARGE JAR WITH HANDLES

Jingdezhen ware, *kinrande* porcelain with bird-and-flower design

Ming dynasty, Longqing period? (1567–72), second half 16th century

H. 31.3 cm (12 3/8 in.)

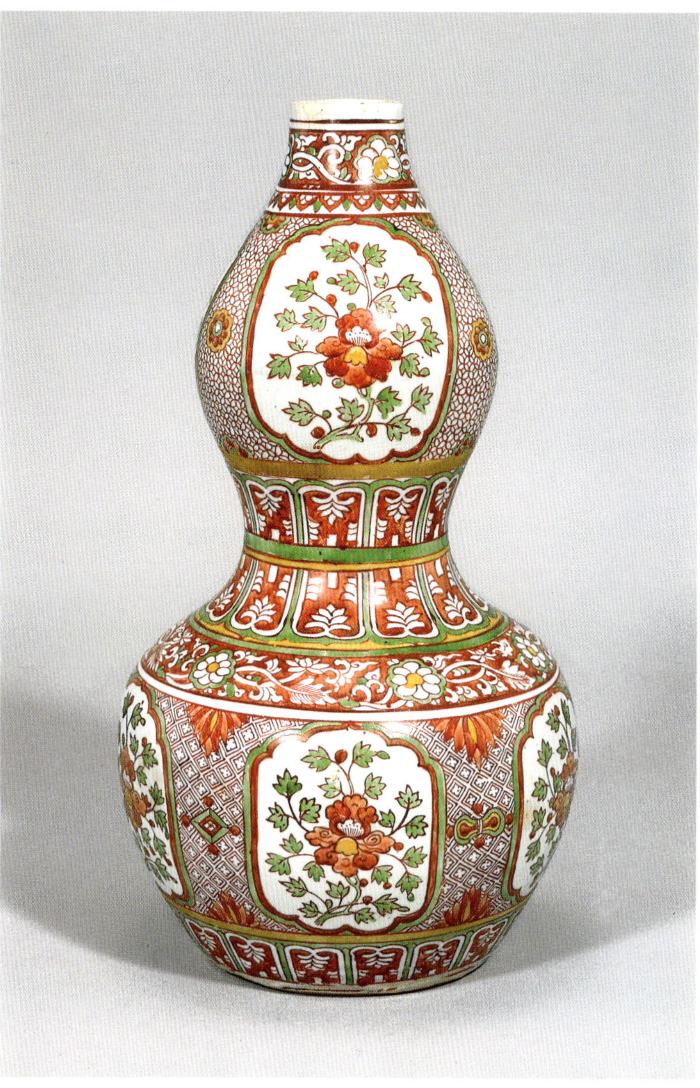

54

GOURD-SHAPED BOTTLE

Jingdezhen ware, overglaze-enamel-decorated porcelain with floral design

Ming dynasty, second half 16th century

H. 33.7 cm (13 1/4 in.)

An elongated upper bulb, a contracted waist, and a broad lower section distinguish this gourd-shaped bottle. The recessed base has a thin, irregular coating of transparent glaze, and the body has burned a pale orange color. Seven cracks running across the foot were filled in and touched up with green enamel. The vessel surface is completely covered with floral patterns: lotus-lappet bands and floral scrolls in reserve against solid red grounds, elongated cartouches occupying a red diaper ground on the upper and lower bulbs, each framing a similar fluffy flower surrounded by numerous small leaves, and half-chrysanthemum and auspicious emblems superimposed on the diaper ground.

This enamel palette, dominated by red and with a characteristic absence of underglaze blue, was commonly employed during the sixteenth century at privately operated Jingdezhen kilns that catered to popular markets. Some examples of such wares are very close in decorative scheme to *kinrande* porcelains, as is the present piece, and though apparently influenced by the basic schemes current in *kinrande* decoration, gold was not used in their designs.

An interesting feature of this bottle is its gourd shape. A special container for the liquor of immortality, the gourd is carried by Shou Lao, the supreme god of immortality, as well as by lesser immortal beings and by Daoist adepts. During the Yuan dynasty, when popular Daoism had attracted a large following, ceramic vessels shaped in imitation of the natural gourd were produced both at the Longquan and Jingdezhen kilns. Here the lower bulb of the gourd is lower-slung and stouter than those of earlier vessels. Numerous variants of the gourd shape were produced in ceramics during the Jiajing period,[1] and though the shape had long been popular, its symbolic associations were especially relevant in light of the reigning monarch's obsessive quest for immortality.

1. Nine variations are diagramed by Geng Baochang in *Ming Qing ciqi jianding*, Ming vol. (Hong Kong: Zhonghua shuju, 1984), p. 107, fig. 114.

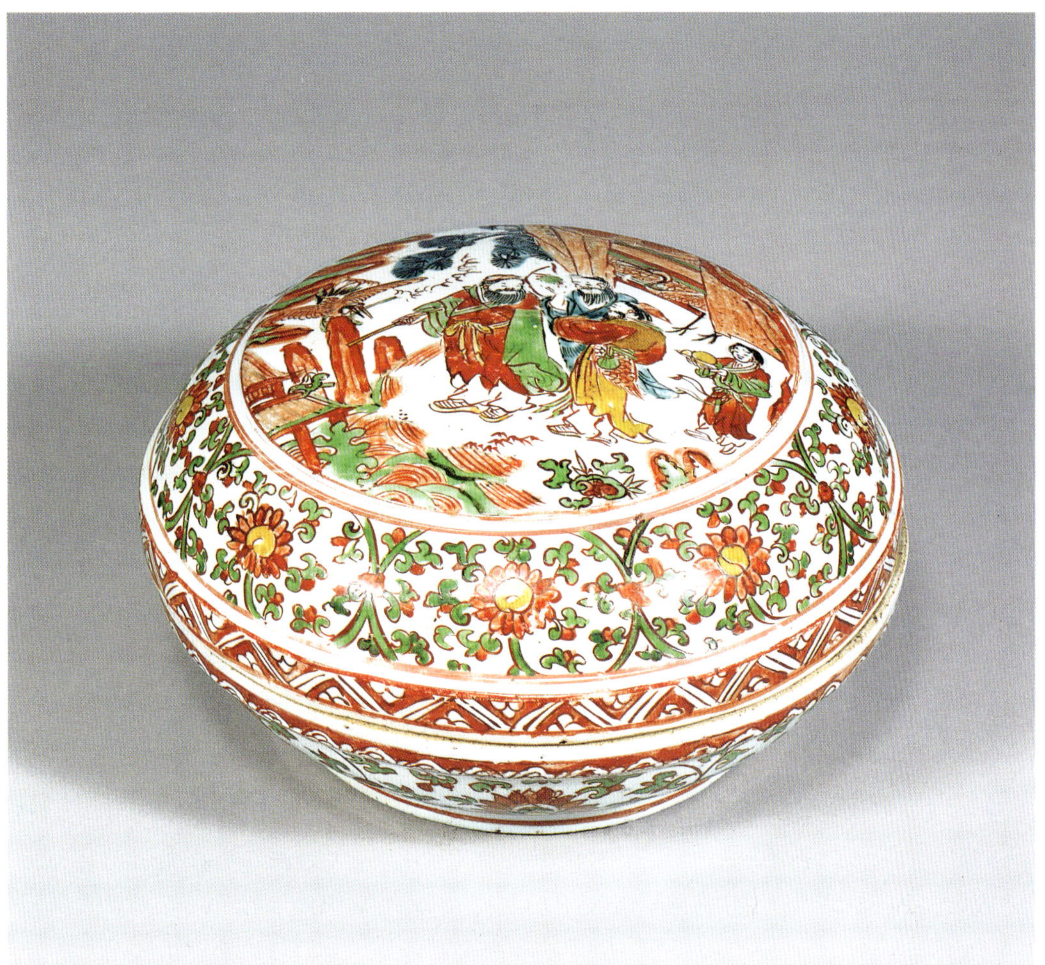

55

ROUND COVERED BOX

Jingdezhen ware, overglaze-enamel-decorated porcelain with scene of "The Three Laughers at Tiger Stream"

Ming dynasty, Jiajing period? (1522–66), 16th century

D. 21.3 cm (8 3/8 in.)

This box and cover were heavily potted from a coarse paste. The foot of the receptacle is somewhat dark and gritty, and its glazed base is convex. Pits and iron spitouts mar the surface of the greenish-tinged glaze, especially on the interior of the cover and bowl. The casually and hastily executed enamel decoration effectively masks the irregular glaze on the exterior. Lively versions of conventional floral scrolls, lotus on the bowl and chrysanthemum on the cover, were dashed on in red, yellow, and green. The figures in the slightly raised central field of the lid most likely represent "The Three Laughers at Tiger Stream," a theme popular in painting since the tenth century, soon after the legend was first recounted, but one extremely unusual in ceramic decoration.

Assuming the identification of the theme is correct, the portly figure pointing to the bridge is the late fourth-century Buddhist monk Huiyuan; he is accompanied by the eminent Daoist thinker Lu Xiujing, in a feathered waist wrap, and the illustrious poet and Confucian literatus Tao Yuanming, holding his favorite flower, the chrysanthemum. Huiyuan had vowed never to cross Tiger Stream, the boundary between the secluded Donglin temple he established on Mount Lu and the dusty world beyond. One day he was visited by Lu and Tao, and so engrossed were they in conversation that, while seeing his guests off, Huiyuan crossed the bridge over Tiger Stream, its rushing torrent depicted here in red and green enamel. Hearing the roar of tigers, Huiyuan realized his transgression, and he and his companions burst into laughter.

In contrast to the subject as depicted in paintings, the scene here is filled out with decorative elements that create a complete design for the circular field of the box lid. A crane is perched on the bridge post, another emerges from the rocks to the left; a servant stands off to one side. Also present are clouds, trees, and a moon—characteristic elements of porcelain decoration produced during the mid and later Ming period for popular markets at home and abroad. Though the "Three Laughers" theme would have been most fully appreciated by a literate audience, this charmingly decorated and useful container would have readily appealed to a much broader clientele.

Wide-shouldered and high-necked, this jar has a thick, rounded mouth rim and a rounded lid capped by a pointed knob. The body contracts above the thickened foot ring, which slides into the recessed convex base. The coarse texture of the body is revealed on the unglazed, vaguely trimmed foot rim and base, which are a light reddish buff color. The overglaze-enamel decoration consists of a figural scene in the main body zone bordered by predominantly floral and geometric bands. Lions with bushy manes and tails romp through a large-blossomed floral scroll around the base; five lobed cartouches containing fungus, chrysanthemum, peony, lotus, and carnation are placed against a diaper ground studded with half-flowers and fungus on the shoulder; a long-leafed floral scroll in white reserve against red decorates the neck; and four diaper-filled triangles linked by jeweled tassels drape the lid.

A vast cast of characters, superbly individualized in physical features, mood, and expression, is assembled in the decoration of the main scene: a red-faced judge at his bench with a bevy of attendants, animated figures in contest before him, hot-tempered henchmen in heavy armor, flashing swords and bows and arrows, spirited dappled horses, a city under siege. Details are so exquisitely painted as to invite and reward the closest scrutiny. Every article of clothing and armor, headwear, and footwear is cut, woven, stitched, embroidered, or welded to perfection. The enamels themselves present a marvelous kaleidoscope of color: reds, oranges, apricots, and flesh tones; fresh green, chartreuse, and turquoise; golden yellow, pale and dark brown, and stunning black.

A small number of similar vessels, undoubtedly the products of a single workshop, differ from one another only in the events presented in the central zones.[1] The characters depicted and the episodic nature of the scenes are reminiscent of the heroes and rogues, the intrigue and action, that fill the pages of such fictionalized histories as *The Romance of the Three Kingdoms* and *Water Margin*, which enjoyed a great vogue in mid and late Ming China. Their popularity makes it likely that each of these dramatic scenes is based on a specific event described in those texts. Although secondary motifs and technical features of the group suggest a date in the second half of the sixteenth century, the sophistication of the figural scenes would be exceptional for that early date.

1. These are in the Hakutsuru Museum, Hyogo, published in *Chinese Art of the Ming and Ch'ing Periods* (Tokyo: Tokyo National Museum, 1963), no. 345; in the Guimet Museum, Paris, illustrated by Daisy Lion-Goldschmidt in *Ming Porcelain* (London: Thames and Hudson, 1978), pl. 146; and two examples are in the Toguri Museum, Tokyo (*The Commemorative Exhibition of the Opening*, Tokyo, 1987, nos. 27 and 28, pp. 42–43).

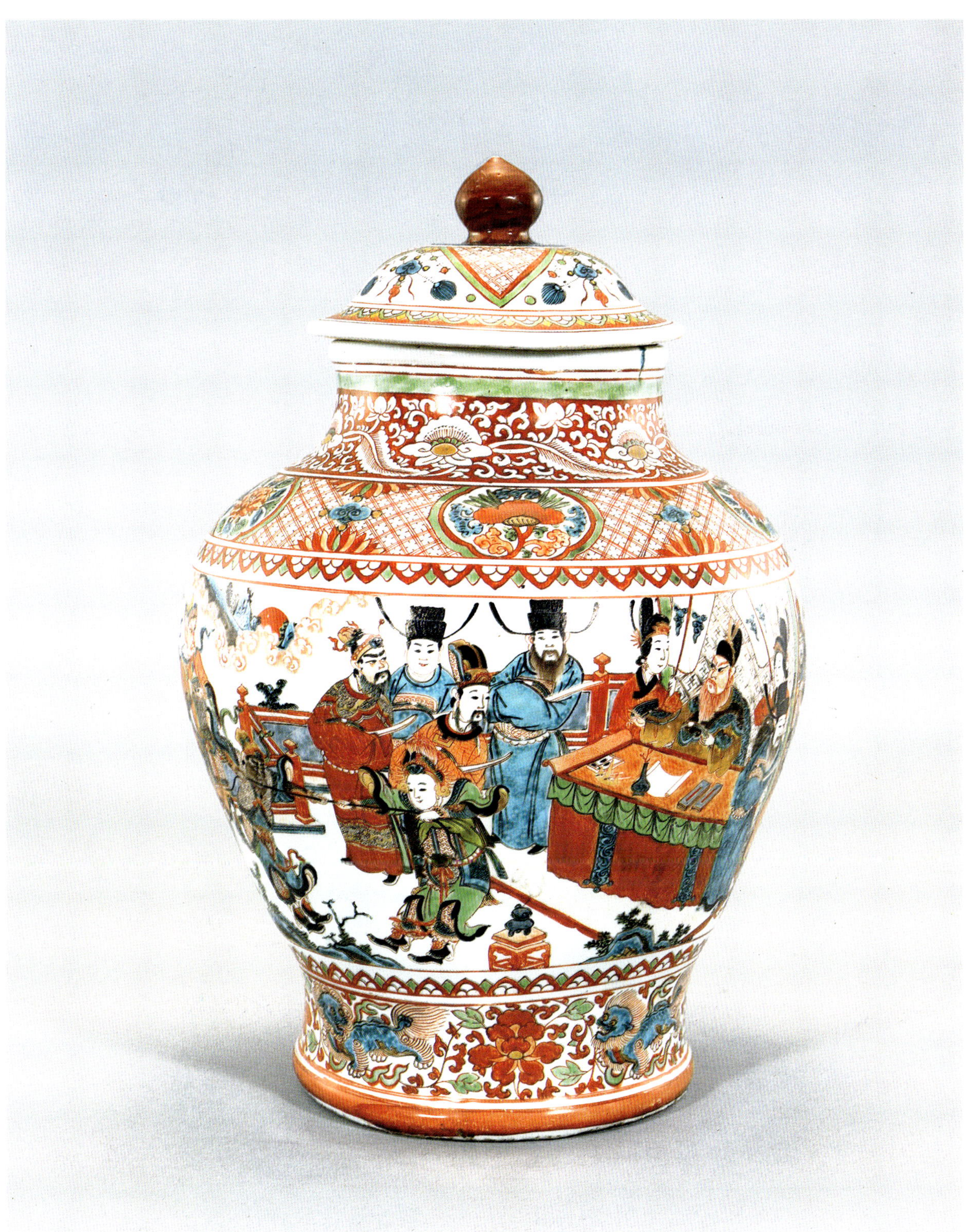

56

COVERED JAR

Jingdezhen ware, overglaze-enamel-decorated porcelain with figural scene

Ming dynasty, second half 16th century

H. 38.2 cm (15 in.)

This jar has high, rounded shoulders, a neck slanting inward to a thickened mouth rim, and an everted foot. The wide rim of the foot and the slightly recessed base are unglazed; in those areas the heavy stoneware body has fired to a buff color. A central pictorial scene is bordered below by lotus lappets and on the shoulder by a cloud collar supporting jeweled tassels, with four elongated fungus-shaped clouds on the neck. Gentlemen, afoot or mounted on horses, and attended by their servants, are spaced between rocks, trees, flowers, and bamboo; the lofty mountain location of the handsome pavilion is suggested by the ribbony clouds that envelop it. The design was laid out with slip trailed on the surface to form the raised borders and the discrete cells forming the motifs. After a first, high-temperature firing, colored enamels (or low-firing glazes) were applied within the cells, the background filled with a solid cobalt-colored glaze, and the interior glazed bright green. After a second firing at a lower temperature, the design appeared in light yellow, bluish green, and aubergine, neatly and clearly embedded in the inky blue of the background. The decoration is precise in its execution and exacting in its detail, which accounts for the peculiarly inert, frozen, and airless quality of the design.

This distinctive style is known by the term *fahua*. *Fahua* can be translated as "ruled design," in reference to the raised boundaries of the decoration, but the word was most likely derived from the term used for cloisonné-technique enamelwares, *falang* (*fa* designates the western region from which cloisonné was introduced to China). Probably dating to the early twentieth century, the earliest literary source mentioning *fahua* notes that these wares "budded in the Yuan and flourished in the Ming."[1] This text identifies a northern provenance for *fahua* ceramics and names as producers Fuzhou and Huozhou in Shanxi province and Xi'an in Henan province. These wares were ranked and those from Fuzhou accorded superiority: "The blue is the deep color of sapphires, the purple the deep color of rose quartz, and the yellow like translucent gold amber." Although kiln-site evidence has not yet been reported, a long history of lead-glazed ceramic production in these regions makes such a provenance likely.[2] The popularity of this strongly decorated northern ware is indicated in part by the imitations that potters at Jingdezhen were inspired to produce as early as the sixteenth century.[3]

1. *Yinliu Zhai shuoci*, in *Meishu congshu* (Taiwan ed.), vol. 3, no. 6, p. 203.

2. *Zhongguo taoci quanji*, vol. 28, *Shanxi taoci* (Kyoto: Shanghai People's Art Publishing House and Bi-no-Bi, 1984).

3. Feng Xianming, et al., *Zhongguo taoci shi* (Beijing: Wenwu Press, 1982), p. 397.

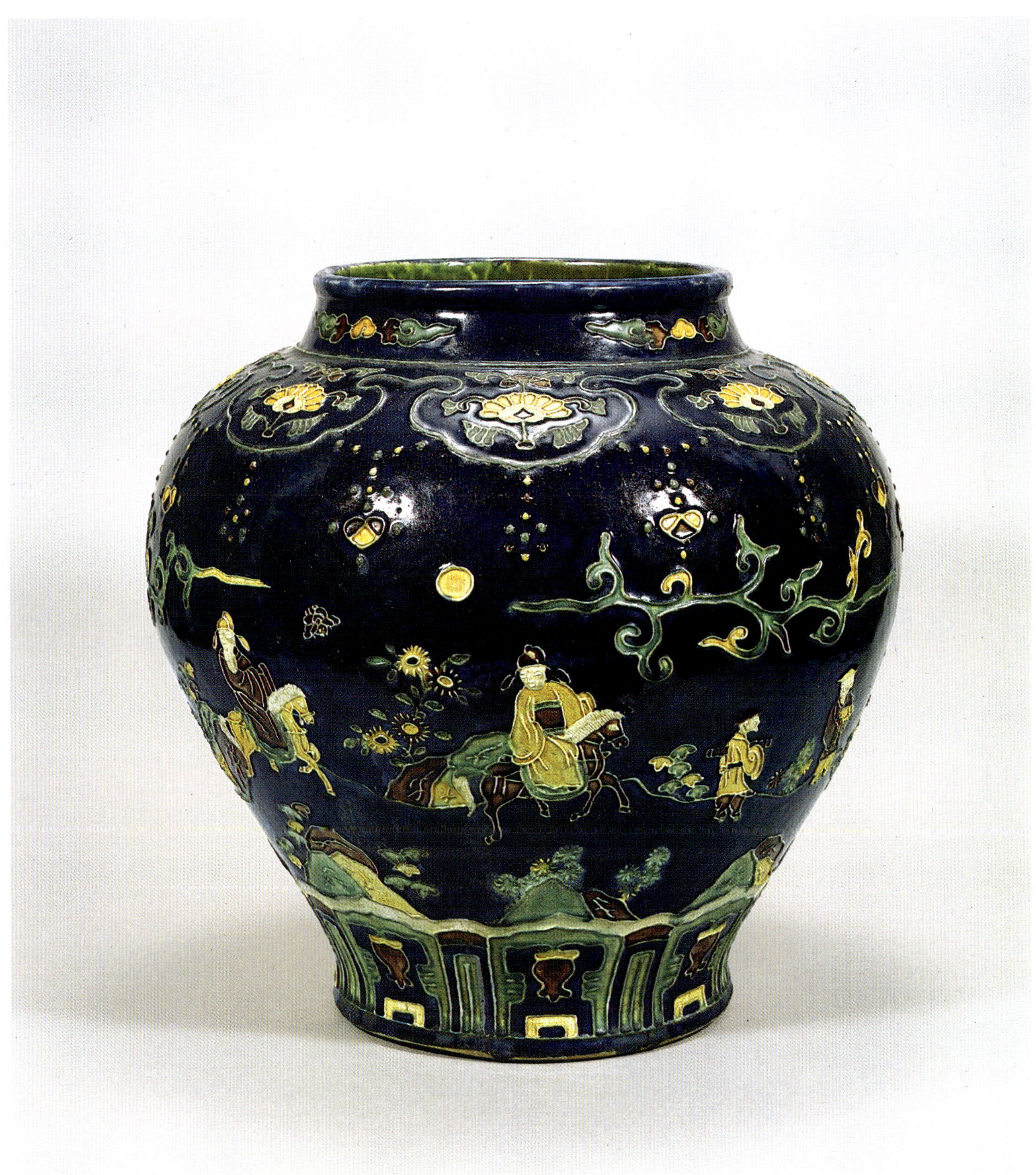

57

LARGE JAR

Fahua ware with figural scene

Ming dynasty, 16th century, Shanxi province?

H. 36.2 cm (14 1/4 in.)

These tall vases have swelling shoulders, trumpet-shaped necks and flaring mouths, everted feet, and handles naturalistically modeled in the form of elephant heads. The unglazed foot of each vase is wide and flat and has fired to a pale brownish color. The light bluish-colored glaze thickly applied to the recessed bases has crackled, degraded, and extensively peeled away, exposing soft, porous, pinkish buff bodies. The tall, large-blossomed lotus plants vertically aligned on the front and back of each vase were outlined with threads of clay applied to the body. At least the lotus blossoms were covered with white slip before the addition of colorless and peacock-blue glazes to the design. A purplish glaze extends over the background; a yellowish buff glaze coats the interiors of the vessels and the handles. The vases appear to have been fired at a quite low temperature. The glaze coating is bright, minutely crazed, and has separated and peeled from some of the protruding edges.

The application of trailed slip to produce raised borders for motifs that were then filled in with low-firing glazes is the decorative technique known as *fahua*. However, the relationship between the technique and that used for cloisonné enamelwares is less direct here than for the previous piece (no. 57). The outlines of the lotus blossoms are more suggestive than definitive; this impressionistic effect is due to the application of turquoise glaze over the borders and its diffusion around the outlines of the flowers. A comparison with the compositions of Ming cloisonné ware suggests that the unified pictorial fields found here should be dated to the later Ming period, perhaps to the late sixteenth century. If the author of the *Yinliu Zhai shuoci* was correct in his claim that *fahua* wares produced at Pingyang in Huozhou, Shanxi province—which he ranked below the others—had clay bodies that were "halfway to pottery" (i.e., low-fired wares or earthenwares), then these vases might well have been produced in that region.[1]

1. *Yinliu Zhai shuoci*, in *Meishu congshu* (Taiwan ed.), vol. 3, no. 6, p. 203.

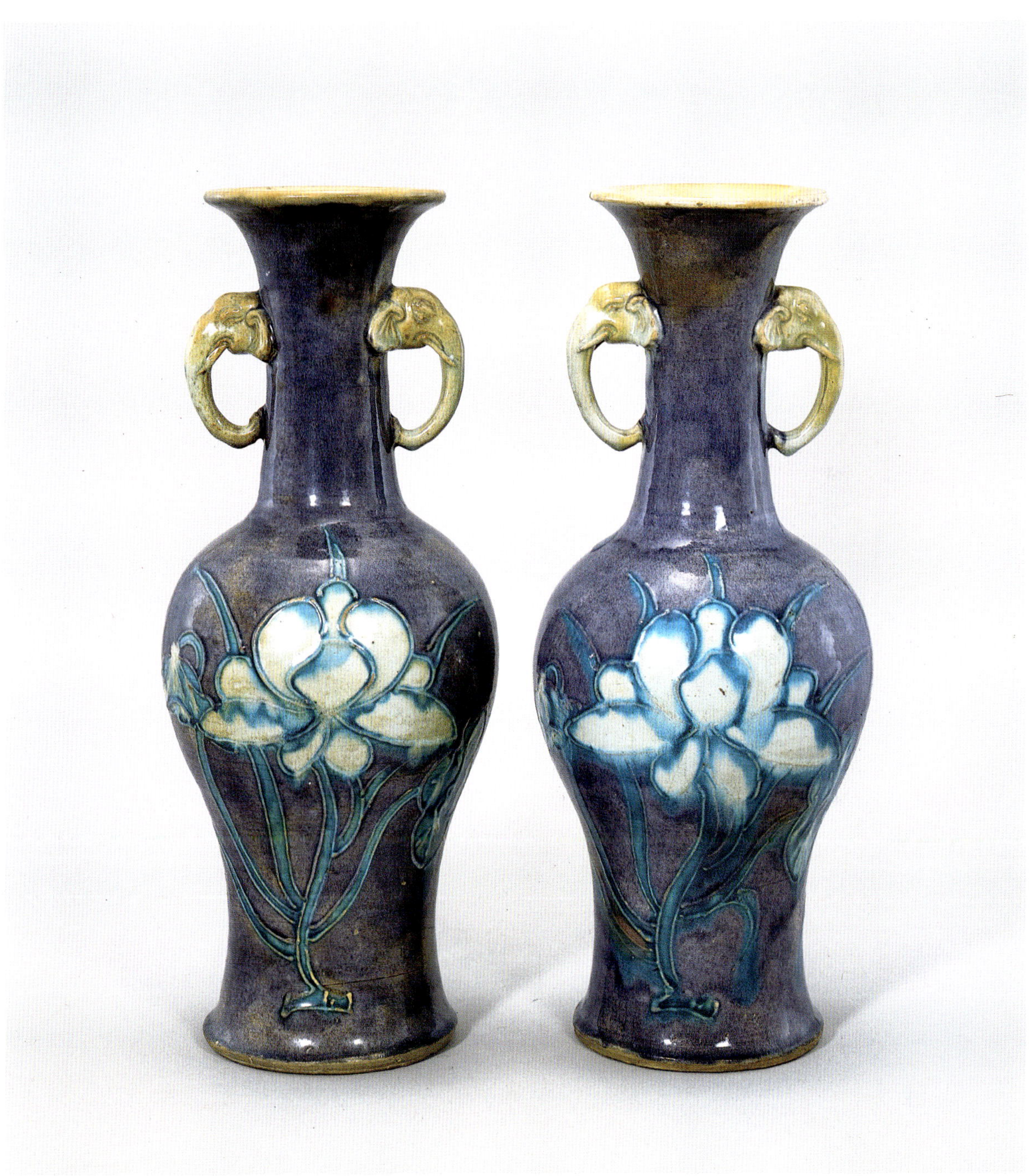

58

PAIR OF VASES

Fahua ware with lotus design

Ming dynasty, 16th century, Shanxi province?

H. 44.1 cm (17 3/8 in.) and 43.8 cm (17 1/4 in.)

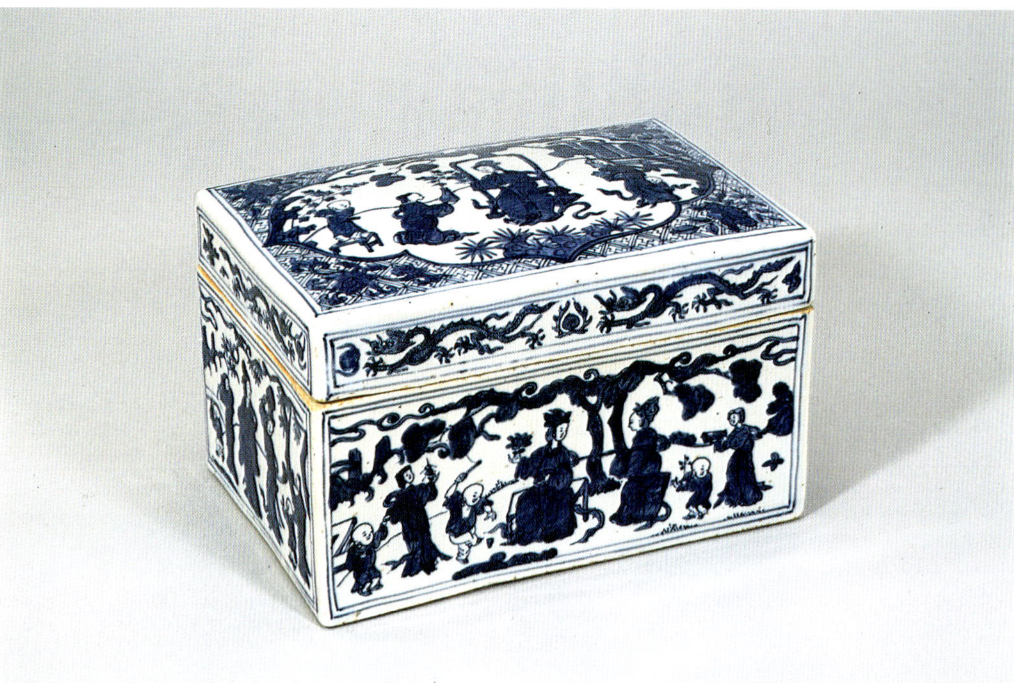

59

RECTANGULAR COVERED BOX

Jingdezhen ware, underglaze-blue-decorated porcelain with figural scenes

Ming dynasty, Longqing period (1567–72); Longqing six-character mark, *Da Ming Longqing nian zao*

L. 23.4 cm (9 1/4 in.), W. 16.2 cm (6 3/8 in.), H. 16.1 cm (6 3/8 in.)

This deep rectangular box and its cover are sturdily constructed from thick slabs of clay. The strong foot and flat, recessed base are unglazed save for a circular depression cut in the center of the base, where the six-character underglaze-blue reign mark is written within a double circle. The thick glaze, which is tinged grayish blue, has separated from some of the sharp edges. The body has burned a buff color on the exposed areas.

The designs on the cover and the four sides are variations on the single theme of finely dressed and fancifully coiffured gentlewomen engaging in pleasurable conversation and admiring the flowers gathered within their elegant garden. The sides of the box are filled with scenes bordered by conventional double lines; the cover scene is enclosed within a quatrefoil frame set against a swastika-patterned ground with a lotus, a camelia, a chrysanthemum, and a fourth flower, perhaps a morning glory, in each corner. The grand dame of the scene is seated in front of a wind screen, delighting in the vase of flowers presented to her by a kneeling figure. A boy perched on a stool reaches to pick more flowers from a blossoming tree, and off to the side an attendant looks on, another small child peeping out from behind her abundant skirts. Large trees spread their branches over the happy gatherings, their branches looping and curling, merging into clouds, and taking on the appearance of bat wings. Dragons slink along the sides of the lid, as if in procession.

The entire design was painted with a dark cobalt blue in outline and heavy wash; the painting style is thus a continuation of that practiced during the preceding Jiajing period. A noteworthy feature, and perhaps an innovative one, is the subject of the decoration. Also distinctive is the substitution in the reign mark of the character *zao* for *zhi*. Although the two characters are synonymous, the latter was invariably used in the marks of all other Ming reign periods; only during the Longqing period was *zao* the preferred character, an anomaly that has yet to be explained.

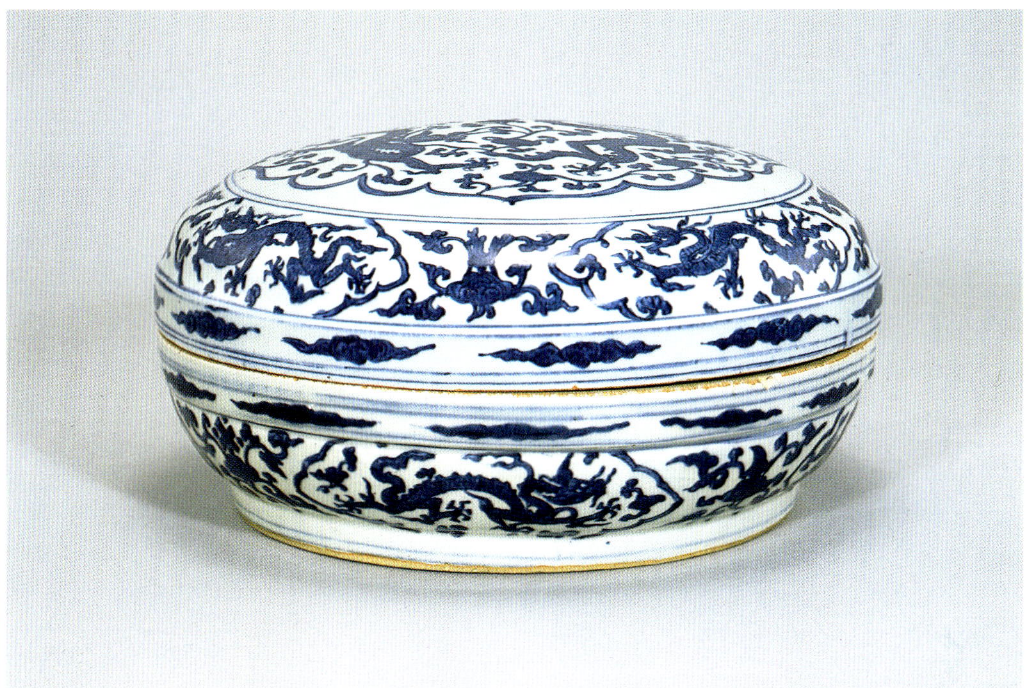

60

ROUND COVERED BOX

Jingdezhen ware, underglaze-blue-decorated porcelain with dragon design

Ming dynasty, Longqing period (1567–72); Longqing six-character mark, *Da Ming Longqing nian zao*

D. 33 cm (13 in.)

The bottom and lid of this covered box were formed in molds. The circular top of the lid is slightly raised, as are the bands where top and bottom neatly fit together. The unglazed mouth rims and foot rim reveal a smooth body, speckled with dark dots and burned slightly orange where glaze and body meet. The recessed base bears the six-character reign mark written in cobalt blue within a double circle beneath a greenish white glaze.

A formalized scene of paired ascendent and descendent dragons set against a dense fungus ground occupies the fanciful, multilobed quatrefoil panel of the raised central field of the cover. Within the four elongated panels, and repeated on the exterior of the bowl, single dragons undulate against grounds of scrolling or detached fungus sprays. Auspicious emblems mounted on fungus pedestals are hieratically stationed between panels. Elongated, stylized clouds border the juncture of box and lid. The application of the intensely deep, smooth blue with a heavily laden brush resulted in thick, generalized, and coagulated images. At the same time, the decoration, especially that of the lid, tends toward the denseness and hyperactivity of design that came into full play during the succeeding Wanli period (1573–1619). Here, however, the rococo medallion is displayed against sufficient white ground to produce a compositional elegance uncommon in late Ming porcelain decoration.

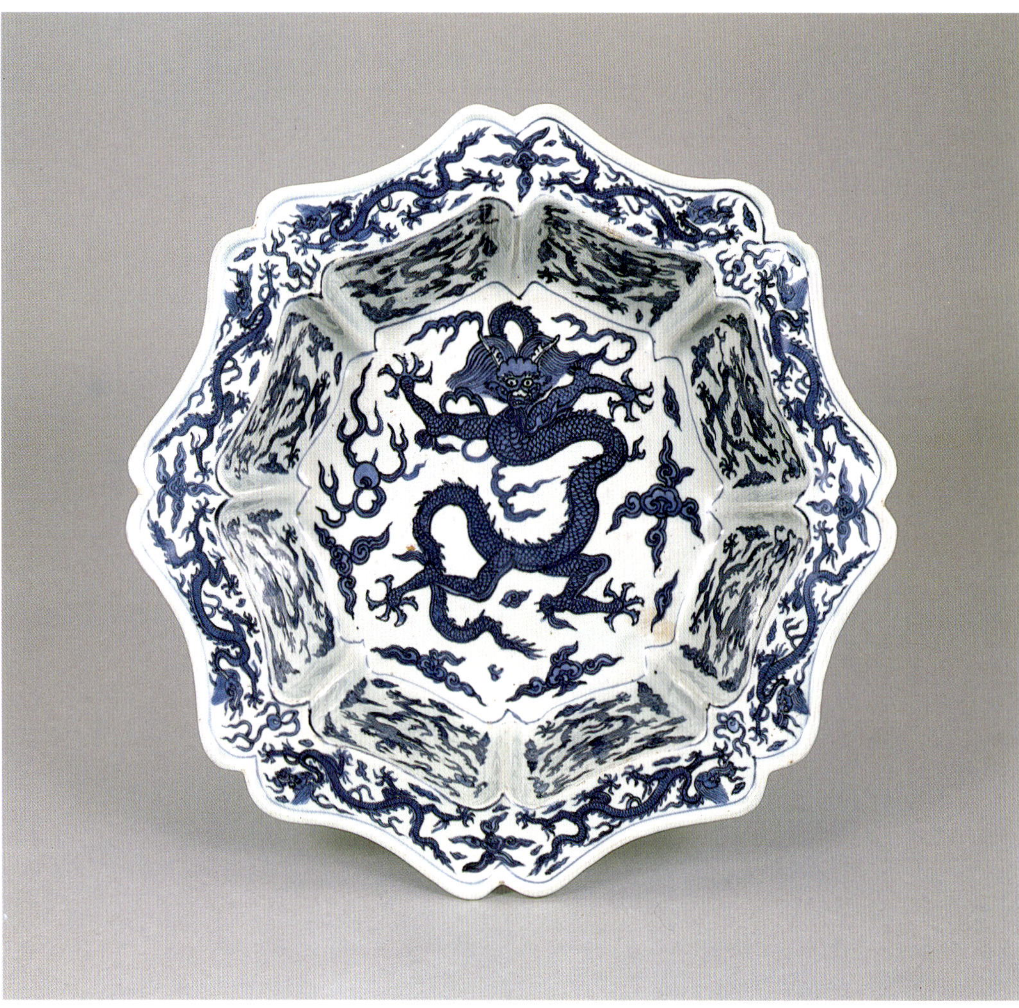

61

OCTAGONAL BASIN

Jingdezhen ware, underglaze-blue-decorated porcelain with dragon design

Ming dynasty, Wanli period (1573–1619); Wanli six-character mark, *Da Ming Wanli nian zhi*

D. 37.4 cm (14 3/4 in.), H. 11.1 cm (4 3/8 in.)

The bracket-shaped rim of this deep, octagonal basin is clearly articulated. The foliation extends down the steep walls of the cavetto and through the foot, which encloses a flat, recessed base. The foot and base are unglazed except for a circular depression in the center of the base, where the reign mark is written in underglaze blue within a double circle. The walls are thick, the piece heavy, and the paste somewhat coarse. The vivid blue design is covered with a thick, bright, transparent glaze.

Seventeen dragons decorate the mouth, cavetto, and interior bottom of the basin. Confronting dragons, seemingly in dispute over the pearls between them, are stretched in four pairs on the rim; an ascendant dragon writhes in each section of the cavetto with head turned toward his pearl. The central beast is splayed vertically, his great head emerging from a strongly arched neck. The eyes of this domineering dragon stare directly out from the strictly frontal face; his horns are silhouetted against his mane, which flows to each side from a part at the center of the head. The pearl, ignored, simply floats in space, as do the scudding clouds. Within the eight exterior wall sections lotus blossoms and pod pedestals support the eight emblems of Buddhism: shell, wheel, knot, paired fish, vase, flaming jewel, umbrella, and canopy. A lotus scroll undulates on the reverse of the flattened mouth rim.

Each motif was outlined in deep blue and colored in with a paler, contrasting shade applied flatly, smoothly, and evenly. The lotus-pod pedestals and emblems on the reverse were painted in various shades of blue, and the lotus scroll on the back of the flattened rim was outlined and painted with extraordinary care. Traditional sources note the Wanli-period potter's ability to fashion a multitude of shapes. This basin exemplifies that enriched repertoire and the style of underglaze-blue painting perfected, but rarely so splendidly practiced, during that period.

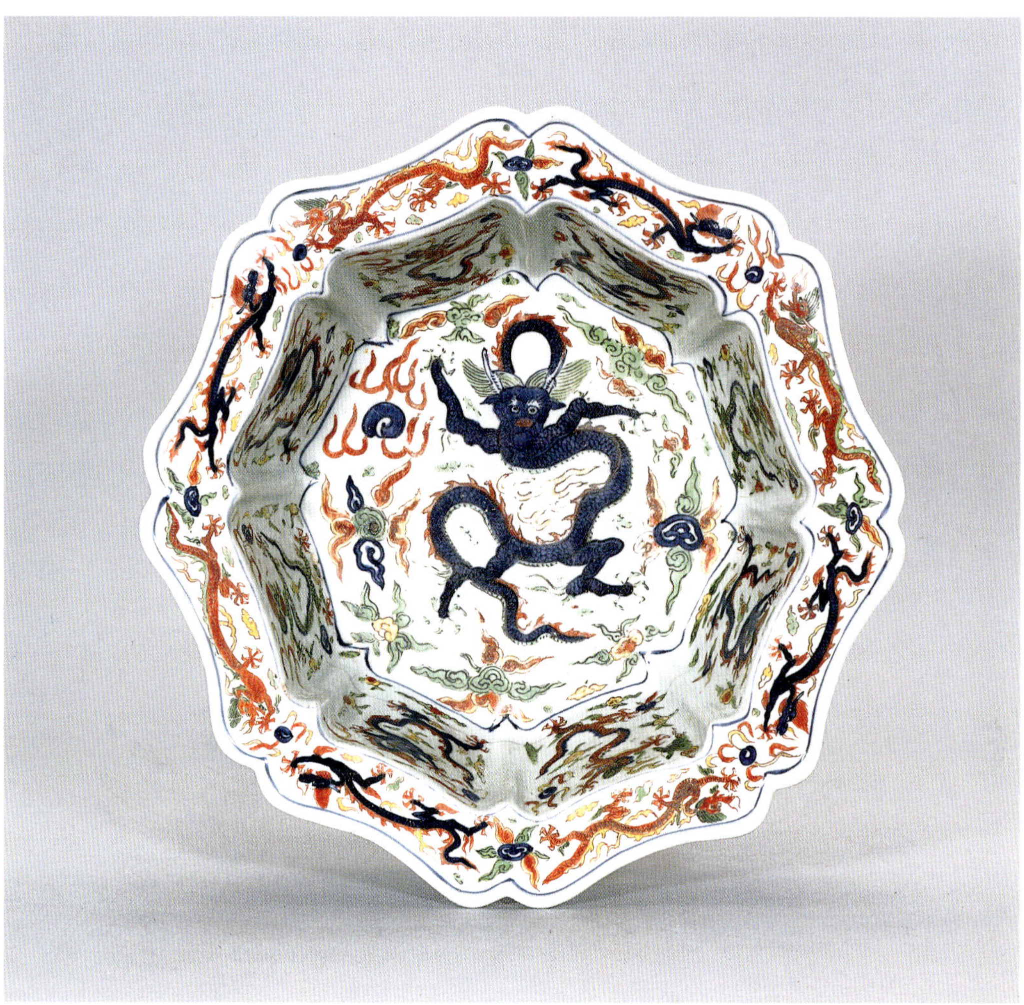

62

OCTAGONAL BASIN

Jingdezhen ware, *wucai*-decorated porcelain with dragon design

Ming dynasty, Wanli period (1573–1619); Wanli six-character mark, *Da Ming Wanli nian zhi*

D. 37.5 cm (14 3/4 in.), H. 10.9 cm (4 1/4 in.)

This deep, octagonal basin has a bracket-shaped rim, cavetto, and foot. Both the foot and recessed base are unglazed save for a circular depression, which contains the six-character reign mark written in underglaze blue within a double circle. The thickness of the walls, the weight, and the body paste are similar to those of the previous piece (no. 61). The decoration uses the same motifs, similarly arranged: seventeen dragons in the interior, lotus and Buddhist emblem groups on the exterior, and a floral scroll on the bottom of the mouth rim. The major difference is the use here of overglaze enamels of the *wucai* palette, applied in the colorful style characteristic of the Wanli period. Yellow, red, and green, with sepia outlines, join with underglaze blue in a hectic design, where sobriety yields to festiveness and studied technical precision to lively bravura.

This boisterous design directs attention away from the body and glaze, both of which fall far short of perfection. Such technical deficiencies, often apparent in porcelains of the Wanli period, were most likely unavoidable, given the diminished supplies of high-grade raw materials and a work force overburdened by extraordinary demands for ceramics at home and abroad. The court's requirements for extravagant quantities of wares and for difficult-to-fashion luxury objects and novelties were far greater and more pressing than its concern for quality, a situation that contributed to a general decline of technical and aesthetic standards. Although the dragon throne itself was more often than not left vacant by the notoriously neglectful emperor, weakening the dynasty's mandate and opening the way for its collapse, at least in the porcelains produced during the Wanli emperor's reign the symbols of imperial authority were kept manifest and alive.

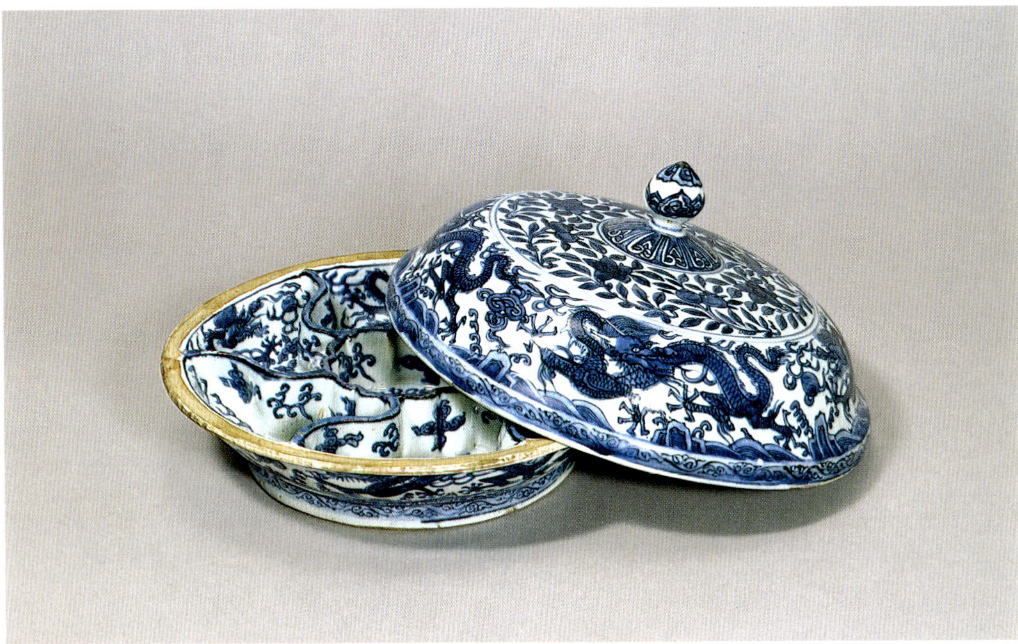

63

ROUND COVERED DISH

Jingdezhen ware, underglaze-blue-decorated porcelain with dragon-and-floral design

Ming dynasty, Wanli period (1573–1619); Wanli six-character mark, *Da Ming Wanli nian zhi*

D. 23.6 cm (9 1/4 in.)

The interior of this dish is divided into six side sections by curving walls, which radiate from a central lobed compartment. The unglazed foot ring and mouth rim are discolored, and some kiln grit adheres to the foot. The sides of the high, dome-shaped cover, which sits generously over the dish, curve out to a straight rim. The greenish-tinged glaze covering the interior of the cover and also the recessed base, on which the six-character reign mark is written in underglaze blue within a double ring, contains large surface holes and impurities. The thick glaze has separated from some areas along the upper edges of the compartment walls.

The underglaze-blue decoration was outlined and washed in deep blue with lighter contrasting tones. Within the outer field of the cover and around the exterior of the dish, a skyborne procession of pearl-chasing dragons is shown above the tripartite rocks and wave arcs so common in late Ming ceramic decoration. Also characteristic are the elongated snouts, jaws, and tongues of the dragons, who are here particularly animated and thoroughly enjoying their mischievous pursuit. Plums, five-petaled flowers, and lichee fruit, on stems sprouting numerous small fat leaves, occupy the inner ring-shaped area of the lid. The painting of the fruit and flowers is staid and controlled; that of the dragons and rocks is more energetic.

In the classic scrolls banding the foot and the edge of the lid, the blue looks smudged and the design is blurred. But none of this detracts significantly from the lively and ornamental quality of this and similar dishes, which were structured to contain sweetmeats and handsomely decorated to enliven a table setting.

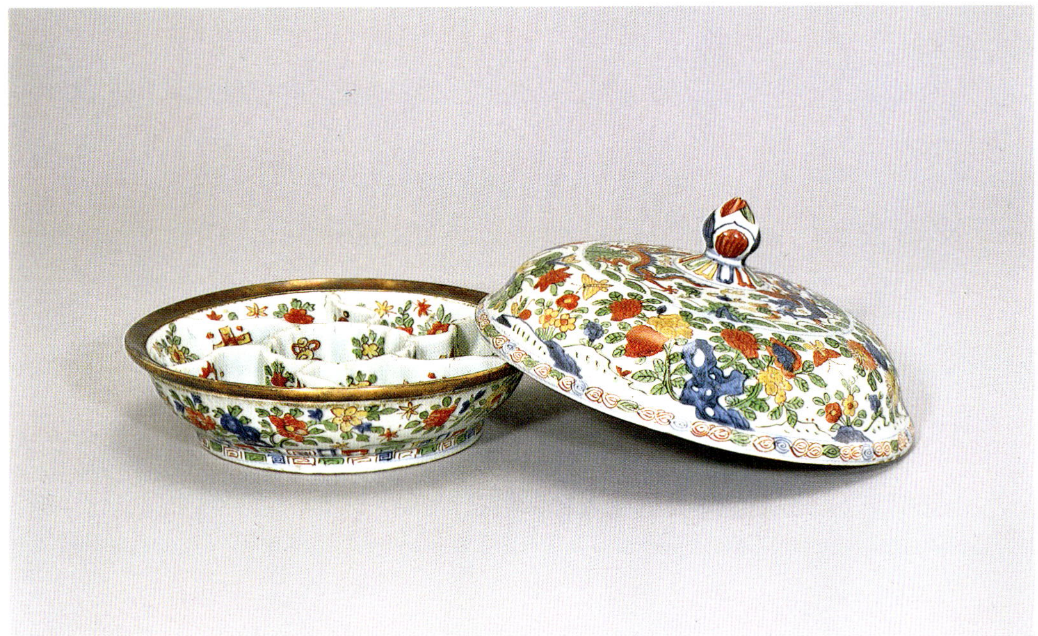

64

ROUND COVERED DISH

Jingdezhen ware, *wucai*-decorated porcelain with dragon-and-floral design

Ming dynasty, Wanli period (1573–1619); Wanli six-character mark, *Da Ming Wanli nian zhi*

D. 22.8 cm (9 in.)

This *wucai*-decorated covered dish with interior compartments is constructed, like the previous example (no. 63), from a coarse and impure paste. The roughly trimmed foot slides into the base, and the glaze has a strong greenish tinge; the six-character reign mark is written on the base in underglaze blue within a double ring. The piece is heavy, due in part to the wide protective metal band fastened to the mouth. The decoration is arranged as in the previous piece but is predominantly floral, with one pair of dragons confined to the inner ring on the lid. Clusters of five-petaled flowers, a clump of lotus, and peony and chrysanthemum bushes, with moths flitting between them, spring from the sepia-lined ground on the outer ring, and plump flowers rise from rocks on the exterior of the bowl. Simplified flower-and-rock groups are contained within the compartments, with other flowers and auspicious emblems scattered among them and on the upright walls. The decoration was produced with underglaze blue of a grayish tonality and overglaze enamels, which appear quite soft in tone, due in part to long usage of the piece. The spiral pattern on the rim, the key fret on the foot, and the simplified lotus panels around the foot were painted with alternating colors, characteristic of Wanli-period design. The perfunctory, even naive execution of these latter motifs and the parting of the glaze from sharp edges are not unlike features prevalent in porcelains produced for the Japanese market during the early seventeenth century. But whereas such characteristics were appreciated by the Japanese in accordance with their admiration of the rough, the natural, and the accidental, in China such features reflected a diminished state of the art.

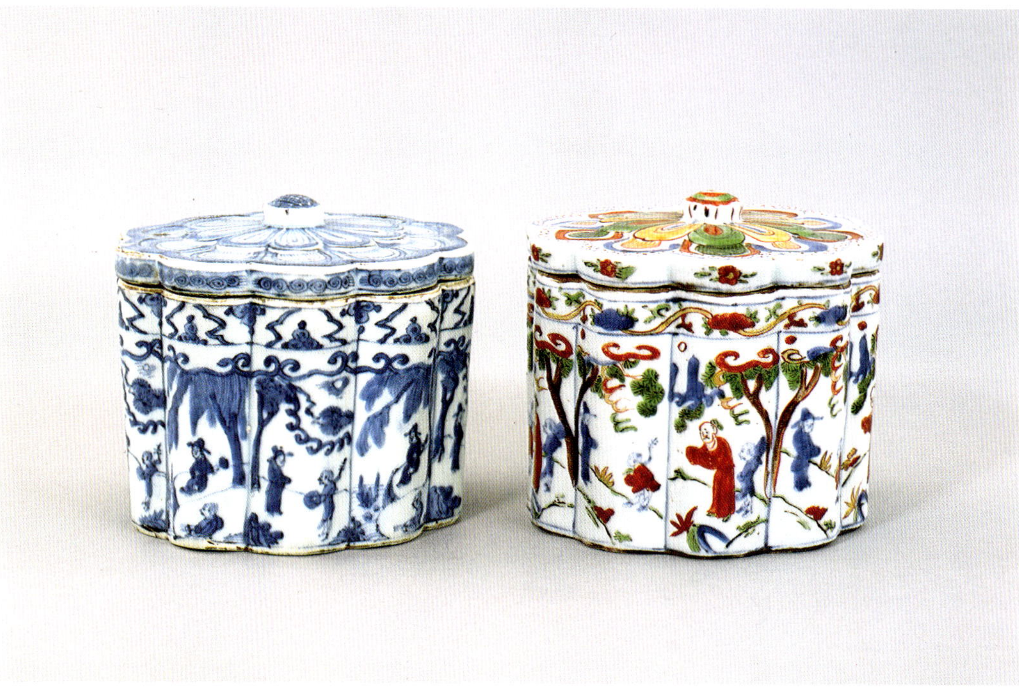

65

COVERED TEN-LOBED BOXES

Jingdezhen ware, underglaze-blue-decorated porcelain and *wucai*-decorated porcelain with figural scenes

Ming dynasty, Wanli period (1573–1619); Wanli six-character marks, *Da Ming Wanli nian zhi*

D. 14.3 cm (5 5/8 in.) and 13.7 cm (5 3/8 in.)

The thick, vertical walls of these boxes are lobed in ten sections; the covers are similarly lobed and tiered and capped by short cylindrical knobs. The vertical sides of the lids fit flush with the walls of the lower sections, thus producing well-integrated, compact, and harmonious shapes. Sturdy, unglazed foot rims enclose recessed bases, on which the underglaze-blue six-character reign marks are written within double circles. A grayish green glaze, which is particularly pitted on the base of the *wucai* piece, covers the interiors of the boxes and their lids.

On the exterior walls of each box a similar though not identical scene is repeated five times. Scholarly figures, attendants, and simple landscape elements are framed by adjacent trees and stylized clouds. The underglaze-blue-decorated piece has a more varied theme and two distinct types of trees—pines and willows. Viewed from above, each box looks like an open flower, the lobed and raised tiers corresponding to rigid petals. The effect of the *wucai*-decorated lid, painted in a delightful alternation of red, yellow, green, and blue, is especially striking and attractive.

Although not particularly taxing for the decorator, and not repaying very close scrutiny of detail, these interestingly shaped boxes do have an immediate and captivating decorative appeal.

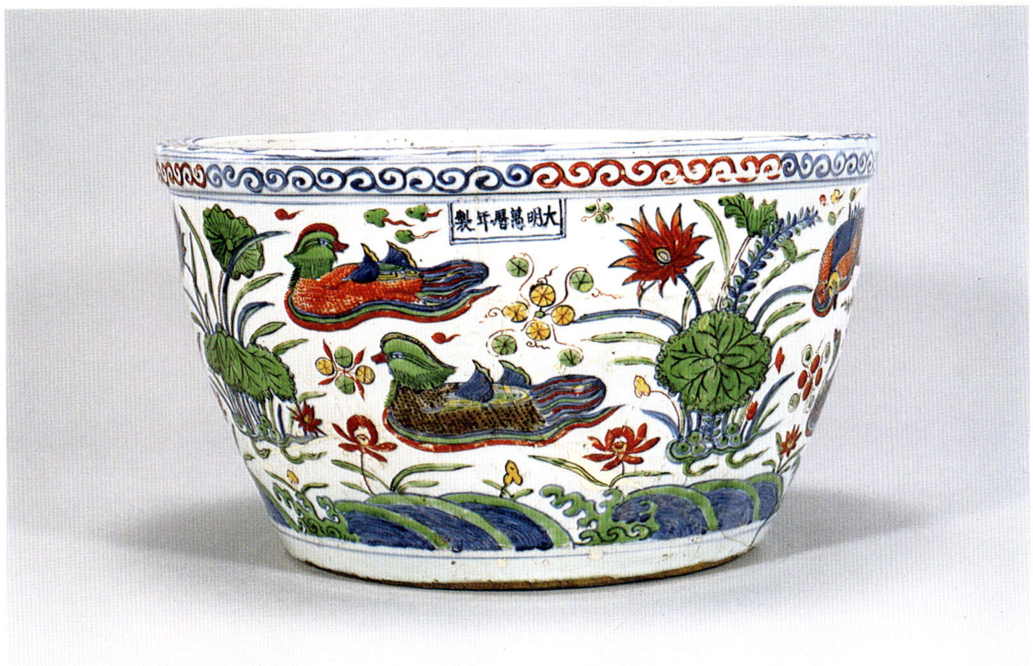

66

LARGE FISHBOWL

Jingdezhen ware, *wucai*-decorated porcelain

Ming dynasty, Wanli period (1573–1619); Wanli six-character mark, *Da Ming Wanli nian zhi*

D. 44.2 cm (17 3/8 in.), H. 25.1 cm (9 7/8 in.)

This massive, cylindrical fishbowl has steep, slightly curved sides, a broad, sturdy base, and a thickened mouth with a flat, horizontal rim. The bowl, at some point broken, had been mended with metal clamps; these were subsequently removed, the holes filled in, and the break mended with an adhesive. The glaze is dull, especially that covering the interior. The six-character reign mark is written in underglaze blue beneath the mouth within a double-lined horizontal panel. The slightly recessed base is unglazed and has burned a buff color.

The large-scale design of ducks swimming in a lotus pond is perfectly proportioned to suit the size of the piece, just as the subject is well tailored to the bowl's practical and decorative functions. The bold design consists of four pairs of ducks of substantial form, generously spaced between large lotus leaves, blossoms, and waterweeds. What might in another context seem simplistic and trite—the overlapping, rounded waves and fingerlike crests, the thick scroll around the mouth—appears here as assertive and intriguing boundaries for the scene. Deep, bright underglaze blue was used lavishly and effectively to outline a substantial portion of the design and to color solid areas. The overglaze enamels provide bright contrasts in red, green, yellow, and brown with additional outlines and details in black and red. As is typical of late Ming wares, subsidiary bands, in this case around the mouth, were decorated in alternating colors—here red and blue.

One can easily envision this piece gracing a courtly garden or verandah, and such an environment, as well as long use, might have contributed to the present condition of the glaze.

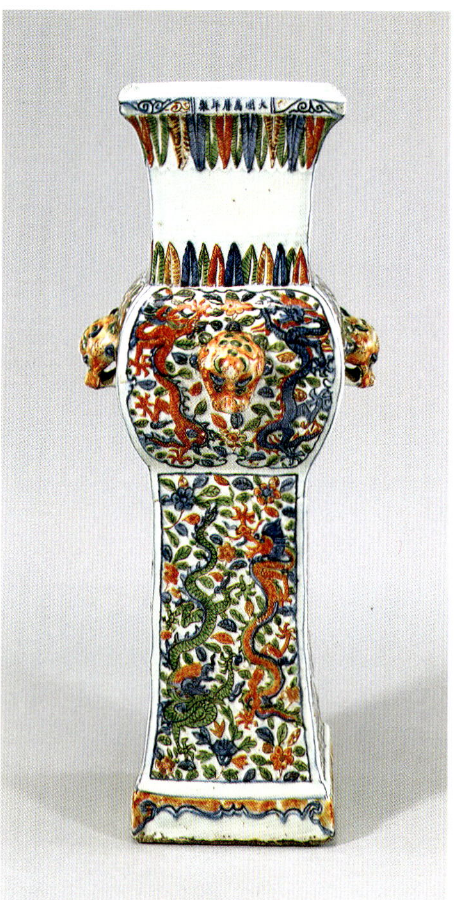

67

ZUN-SHAPED VASE

Jingdezhen ware, *wucai*-decorated porcelain with dragon design

Ming dynasty, Wanli period (1573–1619); Wanli six-character mark, *Da Ming Wanli nian zhi*

H. 58.5 cm (23 in.)

The general shape and animal-mask handles of this monumental vase were distantly derived from the bronze wine container known as a *zun*. The piece is square in section and has a tall foot, a body zone with convex sides, and a high neck flaring to a straight rim, where the reign mark is written in underglaze blue from right to left on one of the four sides. Although the piece was constructed from five horizontal sections luted together, none of the joins corresponds to the natural divisions of the shape. The walls are thick and the foot wide and sturdy; the foot and the slightly recessed base are unglazed, revealing a relatively coarse body with a grayish brown discoloration. The design was first molded in shallow relief on the walls of the vase, a procedure that accounts for the oddly uneven appearance of the surface. Portions were then painted in underglaze blue and the vessel was glazed and fired; the enamel colors were added before a second firing. The bright, greenish-tinged glaze was irregularly applied to the interior of the vessel, where some exposed areas have fired to an orange tone.

Attenuated ascendant and descendant dragons set against a ground of floral sprays decorate each face of the body and foot. The underglaze blue is dark in tone; the overglaze enamels include salmon orange, green, yellow, brown, and black. These same colors alternate on the rising and hanging leaves decorating the extremities of the neck. A classic scroll in underglaze blue appears on the lip, and the base of the foot was painted with contours suggesting the apron of a low table. The overglaze-painted decoration within the three primary zones does not entirely correspond with the molded design: some of the small leaves, for example, have not been colored, and the painting of the stiff leaf bands of the neck does not match the underglaze molding.

The animal heads, each pierced with a horizontal hole, are basically lionine but have horns similar to those on the bovine heads appearing on the shoulder sections of square *zun* of the late Shang to early Zhou periods. The bronze shape has been altered here by the extreme elongation of the foot, which now dominates the form and appears to have compressed the body section. The square *zun* became a useful model for potters when diversity and novelty of shape were consciously pursued in ceramic production, and the historical connotation of the form would doubtless have appealed to the literati class of the time.

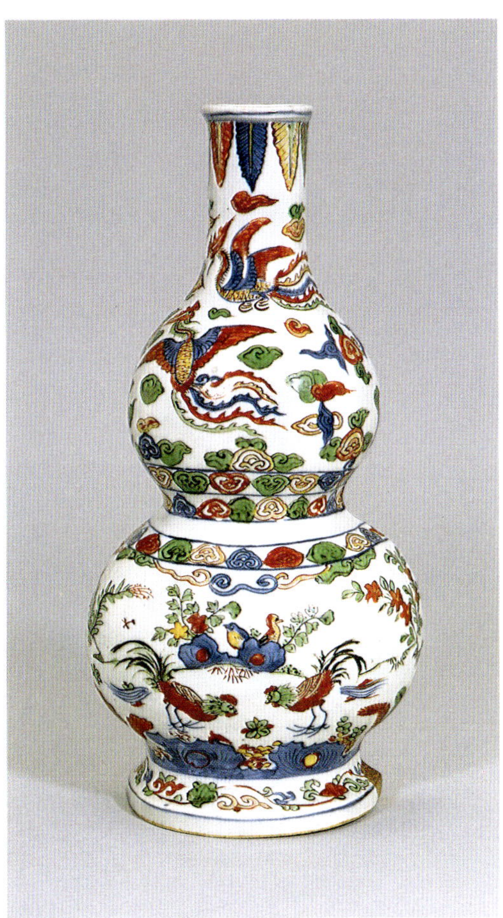

68

GOURD-SHAPED WALL VASE

Jingdezhen ware, *wucai*-decorated porcelain with bird-and-flower design

Ming dynasty, Wanli period (1573–1619); Wanli six-character mark, *Da Ming Wanli nian zhi*

H. 30.6 cm (12 in.)

This gourd-shaped vase is fully rounded in front. The back, which is flat, was pierced with a deep square-shaped depression on the upper section before glazing, allowing the vessel to be secured flush against a wall. The glazed, recessed base, of half-moon shape, is enclosed by a foot whose unglazed rim reveals a dense, white body with few impurities. The six-character reign mark is written in two vertical lines on the back above the depression within a rectangular cartouche, which is supported on a lotus base and topped by a lotus-leaf canopy, all in a subdued and smoothly applied underglaze blue. An underglaze-blue line was drawn along the periphery of the back and front. The front is decorated in *wucai* colors against the bright and slightly grayish-toned glaze.

Stiff banana leaves pendant on the elongated neck and bands of linked *ruyi* heads separating the upper and lower sections of the body are painted in alternating colors, as is the fungus scroll decorating the flaring portion of the foot. The upper bulb displays, appropriately, a scene of the skies and the lower bulb one of the earth: two phoenixes among clouds above and a pair of roosters, smaller birds, and insects among flowers, grasses, and rocks below. Similar vases, with the reign mark written and framed in this peculiar manner, were contemporaneously produced with underglaze-blue designs; their decoration and that of *wucai*-style pieces included dragons and figural scenes. Though contributing little truly new to the repertoire of ceramic decoration, the potters of the Wanli period did create many imaginative and novel shapes. This is evident both from their extant works and from the lengthy inventory of Wanli porcelains given by Zhu Yen in his *Taoshuo* (Discussion of Ceramics), which mentions vases in the form of half-gourds.[1]

1. Zhu Yen, *Taoshuo* (preface, 1774), chap. 6, in *Meishu congshu* (Taiwan ed.), vol. 7, pt. 2, p. 210.

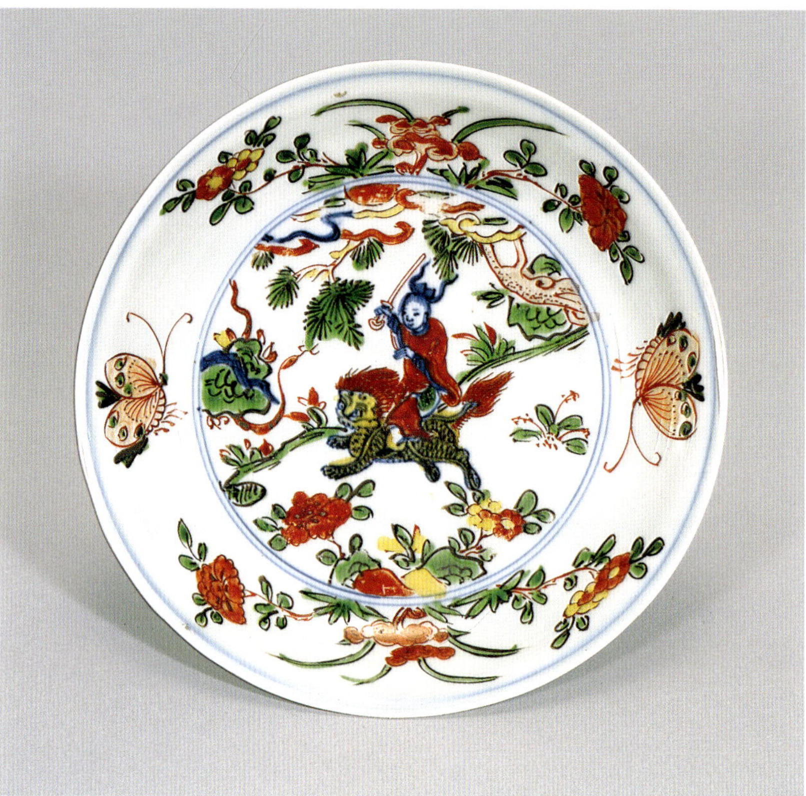

69

SET OF FIVE SMALL DISHES

Jingdezhen ware, *wucai*-decorated porcelain with figure and landscape scenes

Ming dynasty, Wanli period (1573–1619); Wanli six-character mark, *Da Ming Wanli nian zhi*

D. 15.6 cm (6 1/8 in.)

Each of these dishes has low, rounded walls and an everted mouth, a ring foot, and a recessed base, on which the six-character reign mark is written in underglaze blue within a double circle. The decoration varies slightly in color scheme from piece to piece but is otherwise similar. A sword-wielding figure of youthful appearance, mounted on a bushy-tailed lion with scaly body, is about to strike a serpent, which springs from behind a rock. This event takes place in a cheerful setting of swirling clouds, pine, sprightly flowers, shrubs, and flying butterflies. Clusters of fungus framed by grasses and flowers fill the upper and lower quadrants of the cavetto, with two large butterflies in between. The reverse is decorated with two floral sprays and two clumps of grass; a lizard hides in one of the grassy clusters. Bright underglaze blue—which describes the face, hands, and clothing of the figure and the contours and details of the lion as well as a few background elements—is combined with red, yellow, green, and sepia overglaze enamels in an exuberant manner typical of the Wanli period. A number of similarly decorated dishes, of approximately the same size and bearing the Wanli reign mark, add a toad, centipede, and scorpion to the serpent and lizard here, composing the group known as the Five Venomous Animals. This shorthand version of the theme, in which the mounted figure is confronted by only two of the noxious creatures, would have been intelligible to the owner of the dishes, who, by using them, would have been protected from pestilence and disease in the same way that amulets in the shapes of these powerful creatures defended their wearer from harm.

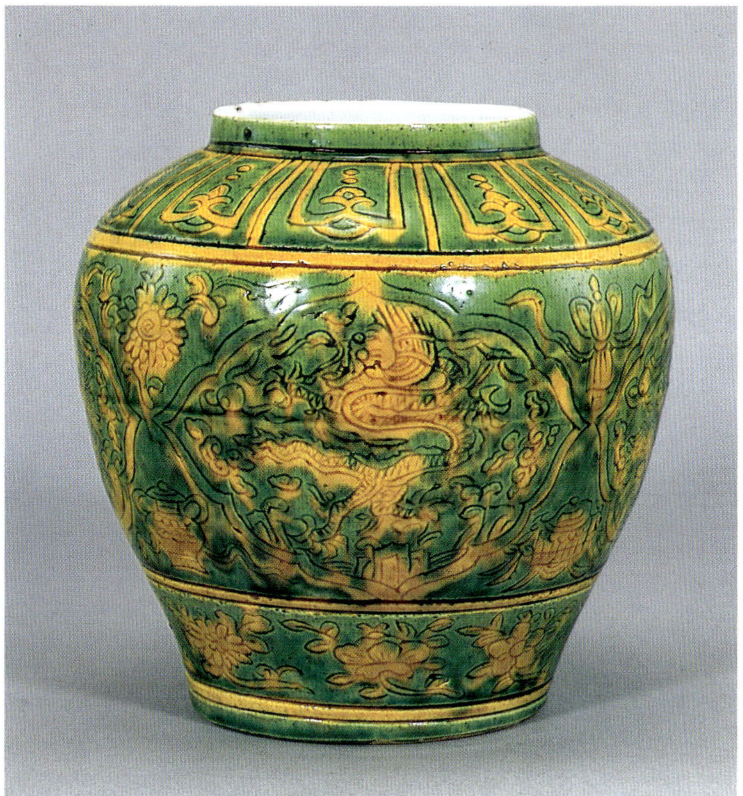

70

JAR

Jingdezhen ware, green-and-yellow enamel-decorated porcelain with dragon design

Ming dynasty, Wanli period (1573–1619); Wanli six-character mark, *Da Ming Wanli nian zhi*

H. 17 cm (6 3/4 in.)

The body of this jar widens from a broad base to high, taut shoulders and is surmounted by a short neck with a rounded mouth rim. The foot rim is unglazed, revealing the iron-specked body; the six-character cobalt-blue reign mark is written within a double circle beneath the grayish white glaze on the recessed base. During the Yuan and Ming dynasties, jars, vases, and bottles were typically constructed by luting together a number of horizontal sections, but during the Wanli period especially, the seams were not sufficiently planed, as seen here in the distinct line around the midsection.

The three-tiered design was incised on the unfired body with firm, deep, and well-controlled lines before glazing and firing. Yellow and green enamels were added, and the piece given a second, lower-temperature firing. Four lobed and pointed panels frame dragons with heads reared, mouths agape, and manes flowing toward pearls in an environment of rocks, waves, and clouds. The triangular open spaces between the panels at the top and bottom are filled with the eight Buddhist emblems, four above and four below. Eight separate floral sprays are arranged in the band above the base, and a conventional lotus lappet band circles the shoulder. If the deeply incised lines were intended to separate the green and yellow enamels, the attempt was unsuccessful. The preliminary neutral glaze had already filled in the incised recesses, allowing the enamels to swim with some abandon over the surface. The original crispness, clarity, and precision of the incised design are lost due to this blending of colors, but an effervescent, mercurial quality was effected in their stead.

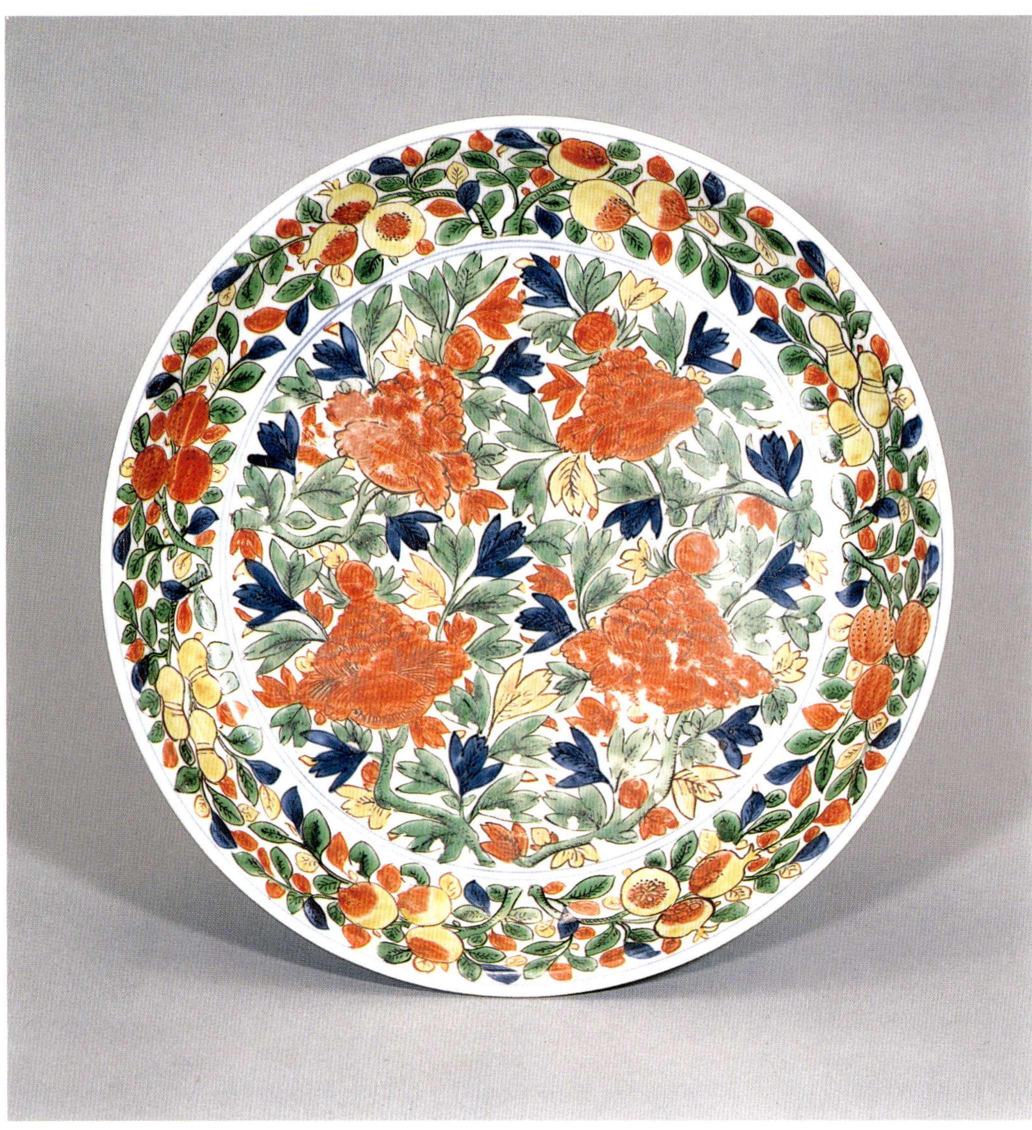

71

LARGE DISH

Jingdezhen ware, *wucai*-decorated porcelain with floral-and-fruit design

Ming dynasty, Wanli period (1573–1619); Wanli six-character mark, *Da Ming Wanli nian zhi*

D. 38.6 cm (15 1/4 in.)

This large dish, sturdily potted from relatively pure white paste, has a rounded cavetto and a slightly everted mouth. The six-character reign mark is written within a double circle in underglaze blue on the convex base. Whatever blemishes exist in the bubbly, grayish white glaze are well masked by the luxuriant design: four large peony blossoms in the center field, fattened pomegranate, peach, gourd, and lichee in the cavetto, and a carpet of verdant leaves throughout both sections. The decoration was painted with overglaze enamels in red, green, and yellow with sepia outlines and brief but compelling passages of bright underglaze blue. A conventional lotus scroll with large, flat blossoms on the outer wall is enlivened by a rapid alternation of these same colors. The condition of the enamels, especially worn away from the peonies on the interior, suggests that this piece was much used in its time.

Though the exterior lotus scroll is standard in ceramic decoration of the later Ming, the interior design, possibly inspired by richly embroidered textile patterns, is quite rare.[1] Its dense, florid appearance, suggesting rampant and impenetrable overgrowth, seems unusual in a Chinese context but is nonetheless governed by the Chinese preference for careful organization and symmetry. As is usual for Wanli-period porcelains, exact counterparts decorated entirely with underglaze blue exist, though these too are rare.[2] The flowers, fruit, and leaves of the interior and exterior of these pieces are rendered in white with blue details and set against a brushed-in background of cobalt blue.

1. A similar example, formerly in the Ataka collection and now in the Oriental Ceramic Museum, Osaka, is illustrated in *Sekai tōji zenshū*, vol. 14, *Ming Dynasty* (Tokyo: Shōgakukan, 1976), pl. 112.

2. An underglaze-blue decorated example is on view in the porcelain section of the Palace Museum in Beijing, and another, in the Topkapi Saray Museum in Istanbul, is illustrated by Regina Krahl in *Chinese Ceramics in the Topkapi Saray Museum, Istanbul*, vol. 2, *Yuan and Ming Dynasty Porcelains* (London: Sotheby's Publications, 1986), pl. 1274, TKS 15/2467.

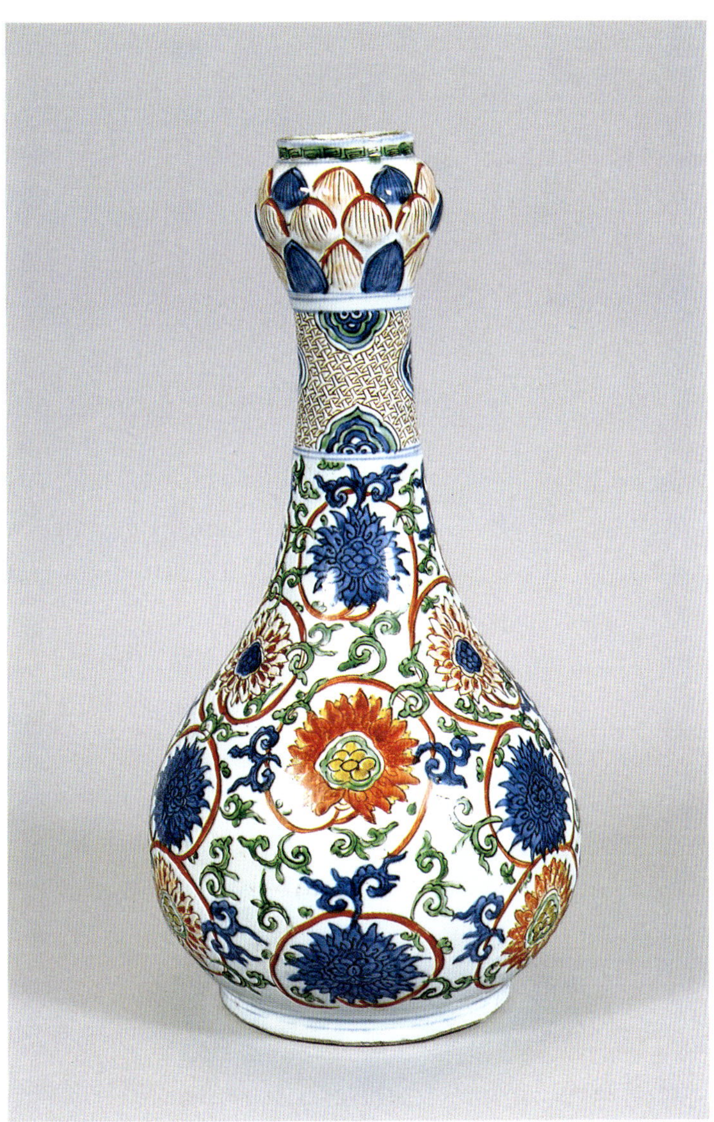

72

GARLIC-HEADED BOTTLE

Jingdezhen ware, *wucai*-decorated porcelain with floral design

Ming dynasty, Wanli period (1573–1619)

H. 40.5 cm (16 in.)

This bottle has a pear-shaped body and a narrow neck. The top, formed like a garlic bulb, is the source of the name *suantouping* (garlic-headed bottle), the term by which this vessel type is known in China. The wide foot, which gives the piece an appearance of weighty stability, and the recessed base are unglazed, revealing a grayish white body flecked with iron. A number of firing cracks on the base were filled in with green enamel.

The *wucai*-style decoration, consisting of underglaze blue and overglaze red and green, yellow, and sepia enamels, is arranged in distinct sections corresponding to the vessel's shape. A formalized lotus scroll with large, flattened blossoms, some in underglaze blue and others in red and yellow, is placed in an austerely symmetrical arrangement on the body; red stems with leafy offshoots circle each blossom. A red diaper pattern on the neck is studded both front and back with *ruyi* heads within small lobed medallions, with half-medallions above and below on the sides. The garlic head, with three tiers of overlapping cloves supporting and enhancing the bulb shape, was molded and then colored. A key fret bands the mouth.

The designs are thematically unrelated to one another and yet are unified by the color scheme, the style of painting, and the geometric regularity of their compositions. The formality of the decoration distinguishes this piece from the numerous Wanli-marked *suantouping* that are less constrained and are decorated with more relaxed and open pictorial schemes.

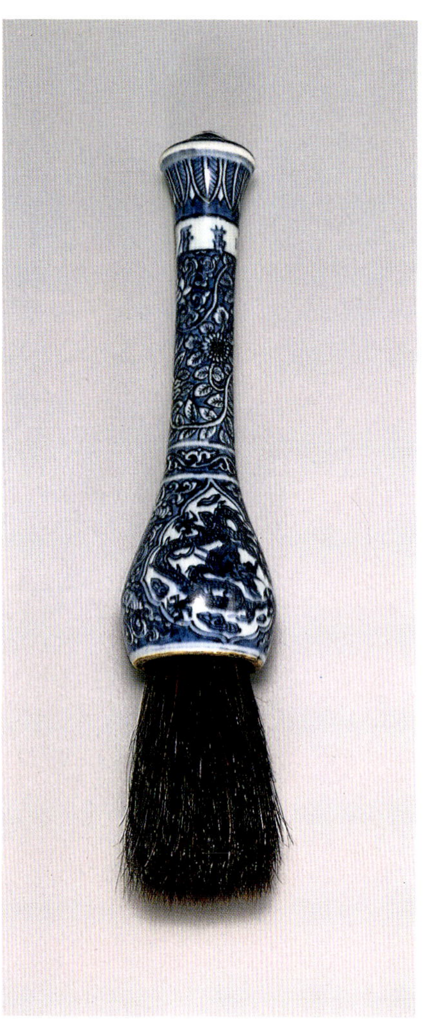

73

BRUSH WITH PORCELAIN HANDLE

Jingdezhen ware, underglaze-blue-decorated porcelain with dragon-and-floral design

Ming dynasty, Wanli period (1573–1619); Wanli six-character mark, *Da Ming Wanli nian zhi*

L. 19.8 cm (7 3/4 in.)

The hollow handle of this brush swells on one end to a wide bulb to cup the hairs and flares slightly at the opposite end, where it is capped by a cone-shaped finial. The underglaze-blue design consists predominantly of white-reserve motifs set against a blue ground, save within the two quatrefoil panels on the bulb and the white horizontal band below the ring of pointed leaves on the narrow end, in which the six-character reign mark is written.

The densely decorated cylindrical section is actually a careful and systematic arrangement of two S-shaped leaf scrolls, varied blossoms, and small, oval-shaped leaves. This area is separated from the bulb by a narrow, horizontal scroll. The quatrefoil panels in the bulb contain dragons and clouds painted in the typical late Ming outline-and-wash technique. The panels are set against a scrolling ground, where lotus bases support coins and other auspicious motifs. The end of the handle is decorated with a floret surrounded by four varieties of flowers with linked stems. The blue is deep and rich in color, and the bright, bubbly, bluish-tinged glaze has a slight orange-peel texture.

Chinese writing and painting brushes were made from animal hair secured by a handle, usually made of wood or bamboo. Also used were materials such as jade, cloisonné, and lacquer, and during the Wanli period, porcelain decorated in either underglaze blue or *wucai* enamels. The careful planning and meticulous execution of the complex decoration of underglaze-blue-decorated brush handles are exemplary. Despite their small size, they rank among the most successful of Wanli-period cobalt-decorated wares. This brush might appear more ornamental than functional, but it was well suited to the limited requirements of the Wanli emperor, and the presence of such brushes in the former imperial collection indicates his access to more than a few of them.

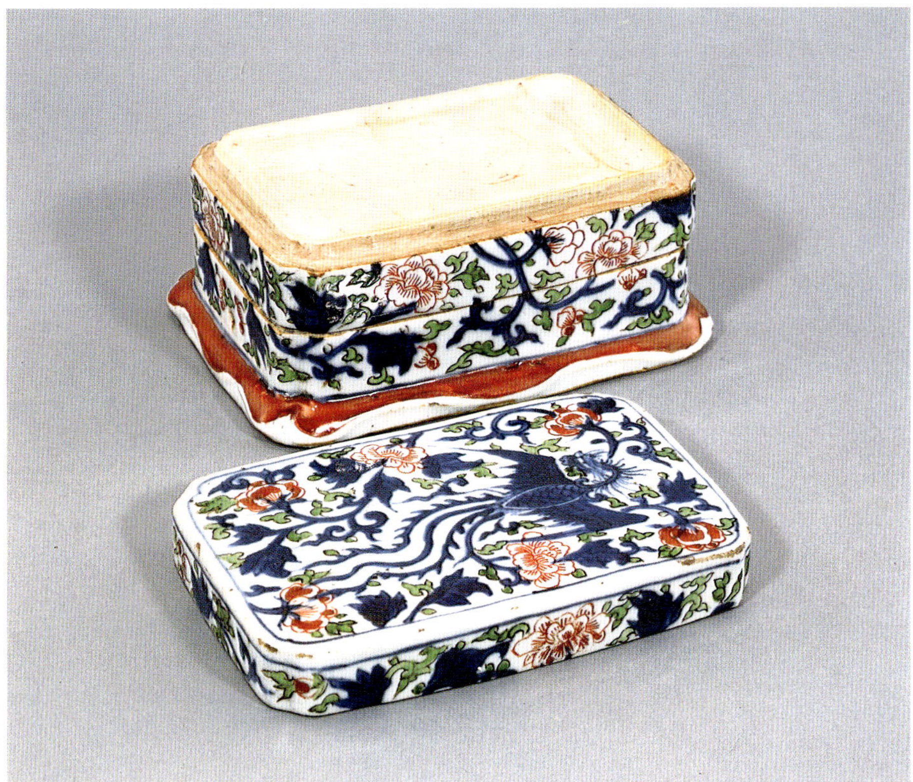

74

INKSTONE

Jingdezhen ware, *wucai*-decorated porcelain with phoenix-and-floral design

Ming dynasty, late 16th to early 17th century

L. 14.8 cm (5 7/8 in.), W. 9.7 cm (3 7/8 in.), H. 8 cm (3 1/8 in.)

This attractively compact, rectangular inkstone has three stacked sections, the bottom one with a strong, slanted foot and a raised, skirtlike flange. The lower and middle sections are inkstones: each has an unglazed upper surface for grinding ink and a depressed well running the width of one end for holding liquid ink. Since the bottom section is a hollow but completely closed form, a small hole was pierced into one side to serve as a gas vent during firing. The interiors of the middle and lid sections as well as the recessed base are coated with a thick, bluish-tinged glaze.

On the flat top, painted in dark underglaze blue in outline and heavy wash, is a single phoenix, with sharply pointed wing feathers and tail streaming in four ribbons, set against a ground of scrolling leaves. This underglaze design is completed by the large red peony blossoms and green leaves painted in enamels over the glaze. A similar but independent floral scroll winds around the exterior, joining the three sections into a single decorative unit; the rhythm of the design continues unbroken around the entire box. The corners, rather than being sharply angled, are gently indented.

Later Ming porcelain inkstones were produced in response to the requirements of a large and active literati class who engaged in scholarly activities both professionally and informally. Stains on the ink-grinding surfaces here indicate that the middle section was used for black ink and the lower reserved for red, which was used while grading examinations and, more generally, in punctuating and annotating handwritten and printed texts.

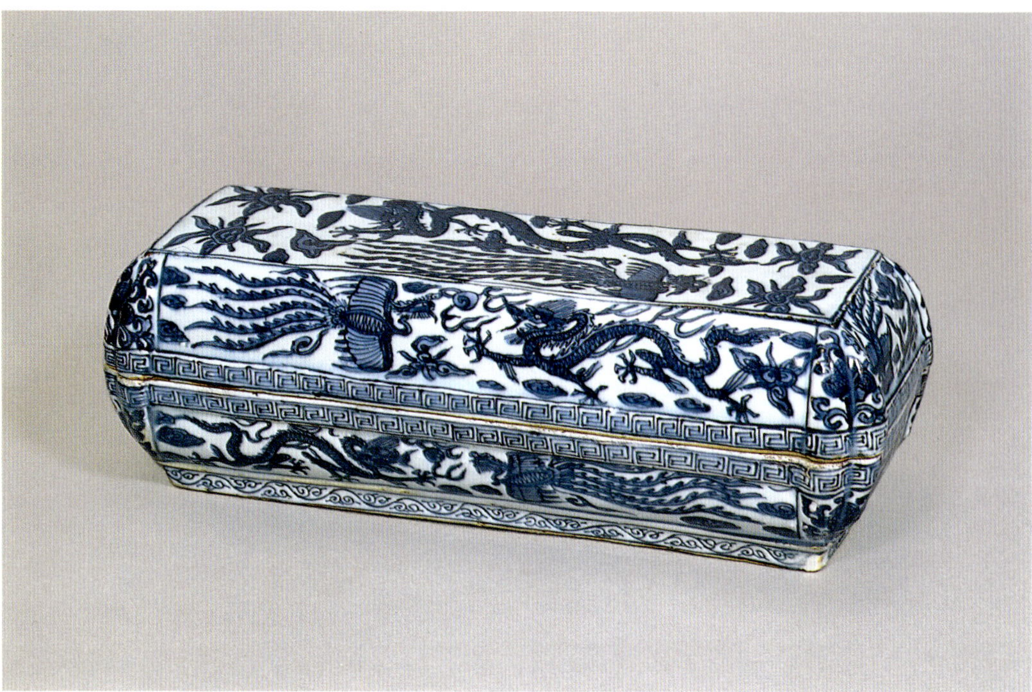

75

BRUSH BOX

Jingdezhen ware, underglaze-blue-decorated porcelain with dragon-and-phoenix design

Ming dynasty, Wanli period (1573 – 1619); Wanli six-character mark, *Da Ming Wanli nian zhi*

L. 30.6 cm (12 in.), W. 11.5 cm (4 1/2 in.), H. 10.2 cm (4 in.)

Long and rectangular, this box has thick walls and is sturdily constructed. Numerous firing cracks are visible on the foot. The six-character reign mark was written in underglaze blue in a single vertical column within a double-lined rectangular panel on the recessed base. The sides of the box and cover are slightly rounded with indented corners. The interior is fitted at one end with an upright wall that dips twice along its upper edge to support brushes laid lengthwise in the box. The glaze is typically bluish, bubbly, and pitted, with irregularities especially evident on the base and the interior of the cover. Also typical is the watery-blue pigment, which is smoothly applied in outline and wash, producing images that are flat and static.

A dragon and phoenix stretch out side by side, facing in opposite directions, on the cover of the box. The large clouds have standard *ruyi*-shaped centers but are otherwise more highly formalized, ornate, and emblematic in character. Smaller clouds puddle here and there and do little more than fill in the blank surface. The dragon-and-phoenix pair are repeated on all exterior walls, in confrontation over a flaming pearl on the long sides and in compressed ascending and descending postures on the short sides. A key fret bands the protruding borders of the lid and the bottom, and a classic scroll decorates the foot. Cloud forms decorate the interior, and the divider, completely coated in underglaze blue, appears by virtue of its shape and color like an undulating bank of water.

Brush boxes such as the present one were made in great quantities during the Wanli period for the literary man's desk. They are consistent in shape, fairly uniform in design, and were produced with overglaze *wucai* decoration as well as with underglaze-blue designs, as seen here.

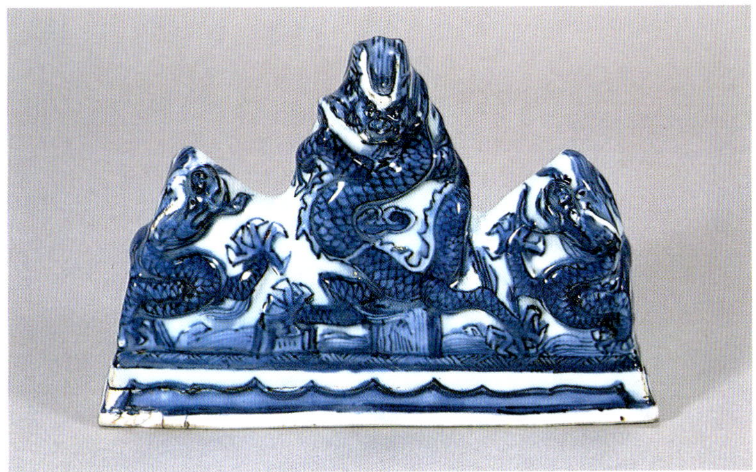

76

BRUSH REST

Jingdezhen ware, underglaze-blue-decorated porcelain with dragon design

Ming dynasty, Wanli period (1573–1619); Wanli six-character mark, *Da Ming Wanli nian zhi*

L. 16.1 cm (6 3/8 in.), H. 10.8 cm (4 1/4 in.)

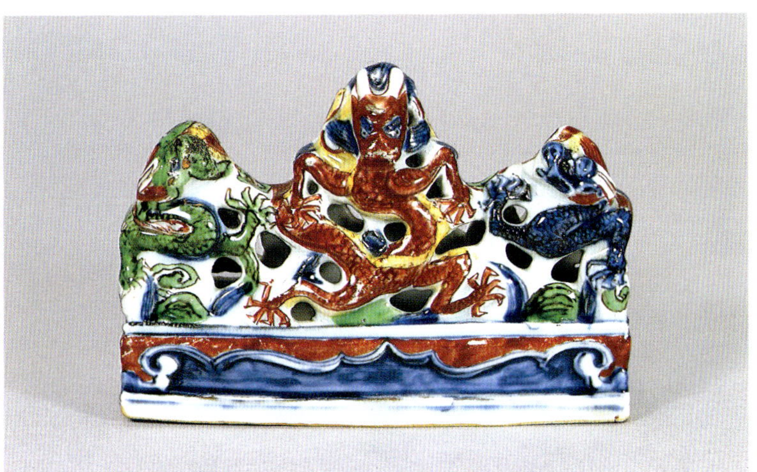

77

BRUSH REST

Jingdezhen ware, *wucai*-decorated porcelain with dragon design

Ming dynasty, Wanli period (1573–1619); Wanli six-character mark, *Da Ming Wanli nian zhi*

L. 15.2 cm (6 in.), H. 10.1 cm (4 in.)

The shape of this brush rest (no. 76) is fundamentally that of the ancient Chinese pictograph meaning "mountain," the valleys between its central and flanking peaks serving as convenient props for writing implements. The forms of the three dragons atop the mountains, part of the original mold-pressed shape, were further defined and enhanced with underglaze-blue painting. The peaks and ocean waves from which the dragons rise were also painted in underglaze blue on both the front and back. The flanking dragons twist from behind, stretching out their huge claws in homage to the central beast. This dragon, with a disarming simian expression, drapes heavily over the peak, grasping it with foreclaws, and is supported from below on giant, crossed legs. A band of waves is an appropriate addition to the sturdy, pedestaled foot. The unglazed, flat base has a coarse, grayish white surface flecked with iron. A rectangular depression in the center contains the reign mark written in blue under the bright, bubbly, bluish-tinged glaze.

Only a limited number of brush rests produced at Jingdezhen prior to the Wanli period are extant. These date back to the *yingqing*-glazed wares of the fourteenth century and include underglaze-blue-decorated porcelains of the fifteenth and early sixteenth centuries. The five-peaked mountain form common in these earlier wares continued to be produced during the Wanli period, contemporaneous with the three-peaked type. The integration of dragons into the basic shape appears to be an invention of the Wanli period, as does the creation of a pictorial space—here a seascape—which contributes to the complexity of the intriguing design.

The molded brush rest (no. 77) is similar in material, form, and design to no. 76 but is more animated due to its deeply modeled surface, pierced walls, and brightly colored *wucai* palette. The dragons, striking formal poses in red, green, and blue, emerge from a mysterious rocky grotto. The pedestal is painted in underglaze blue and a deep brownish red, simulating the form of a low, rectangular table or wooden base supported on *ruyi*-shaped legs. The six-character reign mark is written horizontally in underglaze blue within a double-lined rectangular frame on the recessed and fully glazed base.

This extraordinarily large dish has a slightly rounded, shallow cavetto. The wall above the cavetto slants outward to form a wide, flattened mouth with a foliated rim. The exposed porcelain body on the unglazed base has fired to a grayish brown or pale buff color. Radial chatter marks and spiraling lines from turning remain on the base, and five holes—an identification mark—were subsequently drilled in the central area, an indication that the piece was once in a Near Eastern collection. Only a small amount of kiln grit adheres to the narrow foot. The underglaze cobalt is an intense blue, the glaze smooth and bright.

In the center of the dish, peony and chrysanthemum, fantastic rocks, and a running brook provide an extravagant setting for birds, butterflies, and insects, which appear as if in an imperial aviary. Densely patterned brackets, linked by *ruyi* heads, ornately frame the scene. Eight panels partitioned by diapered and tasseled bands open like petals to halo the central scene and to unify the cavetto and mouth in a single decorative unit. The panels are subdivided into four ornamental pairs that face each other across the dish: peaches, peony blossoms, and brocade-wrapped scrolls fill three of the contraposed pairs; a fly whisk is placed opposite an arrangement with an incense burner in the fourth pair. A brilliant blue was meticulously applied throughout to outline the motifs, which were then colored with various shades of blue typical of the Wanli style. A spare linear design of simplified panels and bands with tassels is sketched on the exterior.

Fuyode (hibiscus style), a word coined in Japan for this style, well conveys the floral nature of the basic dish shape and the open-blossom arrangement of its panels. The term *kraak,* used in the West, comes from the Dutch pronunciation for the Portuguese ships called carracks, which were the primary mercantile link between East and West during the sixteenth century. The cargoes of sunken vessels dating from the early seventeenth century, when Portuguese and Dutch merchants struggled for control of the seaways between the Far East and Europe, have increased our understanding of the development of the ware. Its production spanned the Wanli period and extended at least until the closing years of the Ming dynasty. The Idemitsu piece might have been produced within the first decade or so of the seventeenth century: the elements and composition of the decoration are not unlike those of the single example of Wanli-period *kraak*-style porcelain published in China, a smaller dish discovered in a tomb in Jiangxi province datable to 1603,[1] nor unlike a number of dishes from the remains of a Dutch East India ship, the *Witte Leeuw,* which was lost off the island of St. Helena near the southwest coast of Africa in 1613 and discovered in 1976.[2]

1. See *Wenwu,* no. 8 (1982), p. 5, figs. 4 and 7. The occupant of this tomb, Zhu Yiyin (1537–1603), was a member of the Ming imperial family, enfeoffed as prince of Yi in Jiangxi province in 1581, hailed as a generous benefactor of scholars and artists, and himself a painter and calligrapher, as known from extant examples of his work.

2. See C. L. van der Pijl-Ketel, ed., *The Ceramic Load of the "Witte Leeuw," 1613* (Amsterdam: Rijksmuseum, 1982), p. 54, nos. 4 and 5.

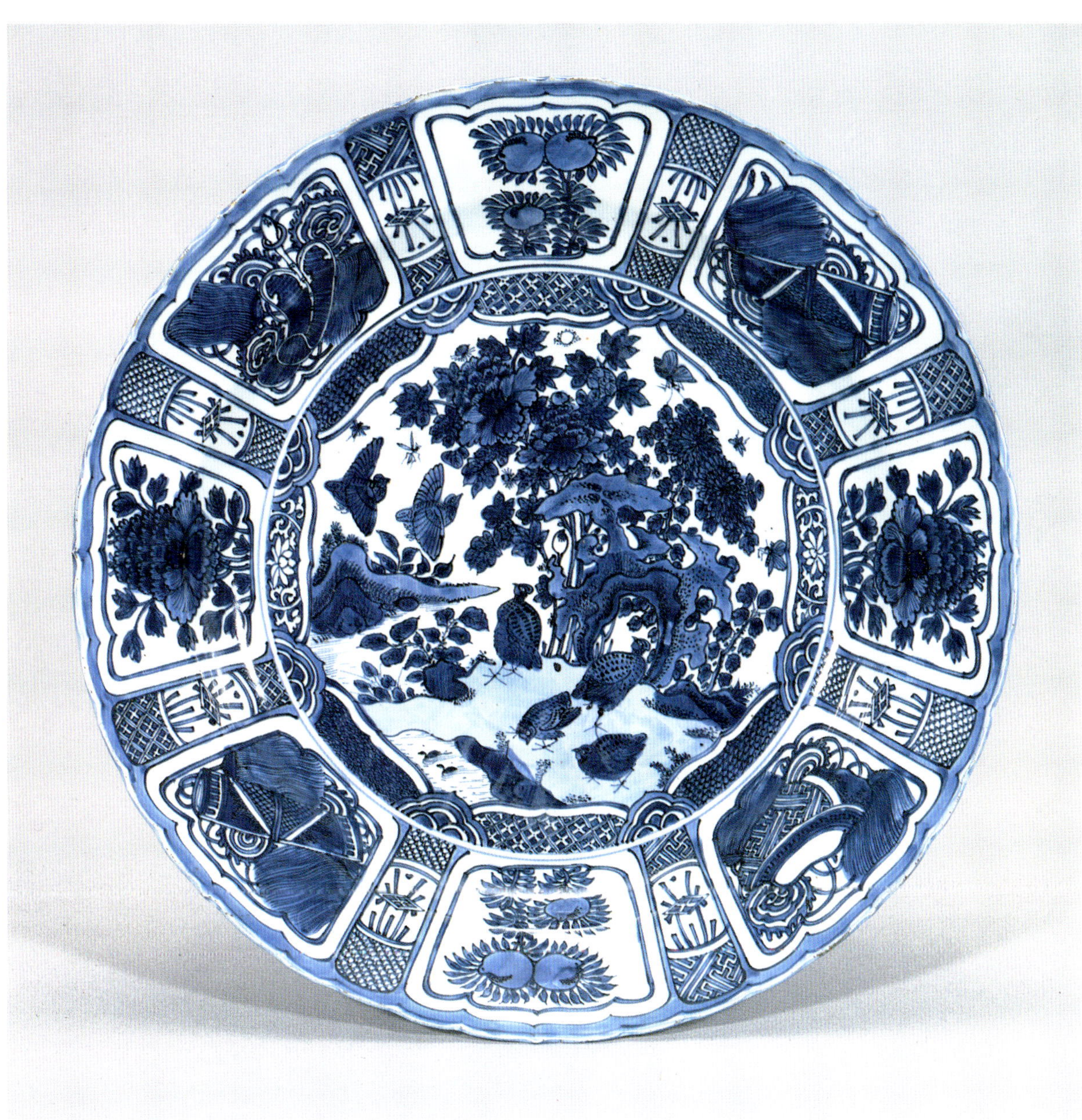

78

LARGE DISH

Jingdezhen ware, underglaze-blue-decorated *kraak* porcelain with bird-and-flower design

Ming dynasty, early 17th century

D. 51.5 cm (20 1/4 in.)

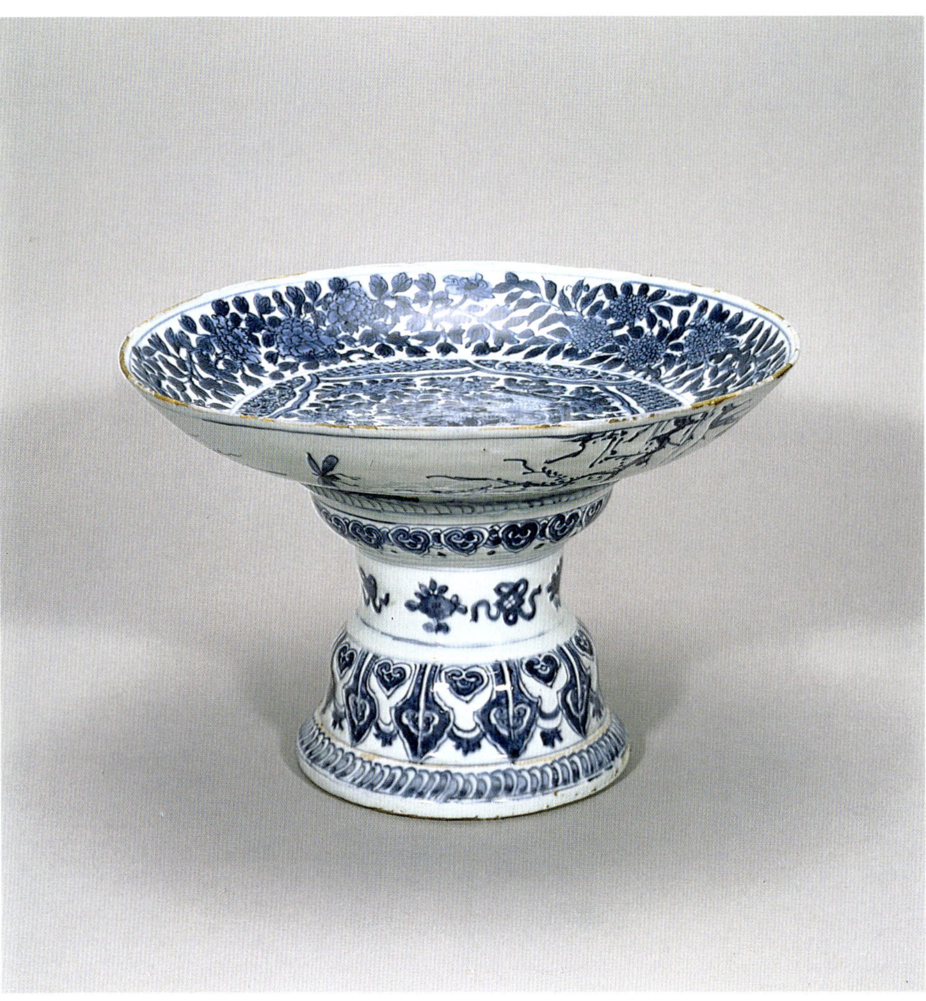

79

FOOTED DISH

Jingdezhen ware, underglaze-blue-decorated porcelain with floral design

Ming dynasty, early 17th century

H. 20.3 cm (8 in.), D. 31.7 cm (12 1/2 in.)

Mounted on an ornately profiled high foot with a bell-shaped lower section, this shallow dish has low, curving sides. The slightly recessed base is pierced by a large circular hole through which the bottom of the dish is visible. The exposed bodies of the dish and base are coarse and have an irregular brown coloration. The glaze is bright, with a bluish tinge, and very bubbly, giving a hazy appearance to the underglaze-blue images. The glaze has chipped from the mouth rim and is gritty around the bottom of the foot.

Two brocade-covered scrolls are almost lost in the dense floral arrangement on the interior bottom of the dish; painted below them is a formation of what appears to be gnarled roots. This scene is framed by eight bracket lobes, four of which contain diaper patterns, and these alternate with lobes containing chrysanthemum scrolls in white reserve against a blue ground. Clusters of flowers are entangled in the abundant leafage of the cavetto. The cobalt blue is dark in color, with a grayish tinge, and was applied in an imprecise outline-and-wash technique. On the outer wall of the bowl, fluid blue strokes render rough designs of old branches, birds, and insects. A ring of typical *ruyi* heads, ribboned auspicious emblems alternating with floral sprays, a geometricized leaf band, and overlapping comma shapes ornament the various sections of the foot. The decoration is thus a mosaic of those late Ming designs encountered most frequently on wares made for export.

Given the plethora of novel, even bizarre forms produced during the late Ming period, this footed dish, though unprecedented in earlier Chinese wares, does not appear out of character. The form is traditionally symmetrical and the shape of the foot reminiscent of earlier ceramic lampstands; its similarity to the footed dishes of Annamese and Sawankalok wares is also notable. During the late sixteenth and early seventeenth centuries—the late Momoyama and early Edo periods in Japan—Japanese taste for the exotic included ceramics produced in Southeast Asia;[1] it is thus possible that these active patrons of the Jingdezhen kilns during the late Ming period were instrumental in the production of the present shape.

1. See George Kuwayama, "Influences of the Wares in Southeast Asia on Japanese Ceramics," *International Symposium on Japanese Ceramics* (Seattle: Seattle Art Museum, 1973), pp. 171–77.

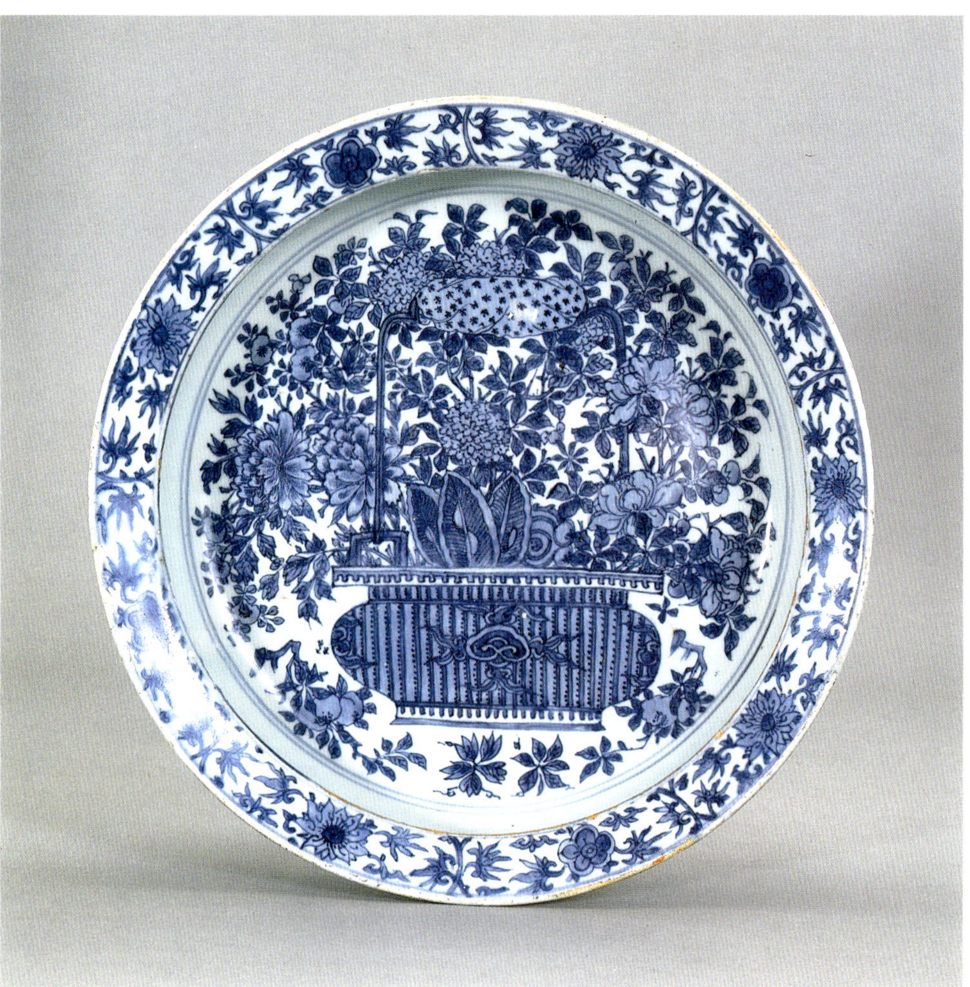

80

BASIN

Jingdezhen ware, underglaze-blue-decorated porcelain with flower-basket design

Ming dynasty, Tianqi period (1620 27); Tianqi six-character mark, *Da Ming Tianqi nian zhi*

D. 33 cm (13 in.)

This deep basin has rounded sides, which contract below the everted mouth rim. The perfunctory foot curves to a slightly recessed base, unglazed aside from a circular depression containing the six-character reign mark in underglaze blue. Grit is clustered in this glazed area as well as on the bottom of the exterior wall. The exposed body has a pale buff coloration. The thick and bright bluish-tinged glaze has numerous surface irregularities and has peeled from the protruding edges of the mouth rim.

The broad circular field of the interior bottom of the basin is decorated with a design of a basket, its upright handle wrapped in a patterned textile. This flat and symmetrically oriented image stabilizes the riotous arrangement of flowers and fruit sprays. Included among the usual peonies are the less frequently depicted rose and hydrangea. Pomegranate and free-floating flowers are dispersed to fill the remaining space. The rim contains alternating lotus and five-petaled flowers surrounded by stylized leaves within partial frames, which are formed by an interrupted scroll sprouting leaves. The careful outline-and-wash technique of the interior contrasts with the spontaneously brushed branches and birds placed in three areas on the reverse and with the limpid scroll beneath the mouth rim. Although the dense decoration and painting style of the interior are closely related to porcelains of the preceding Wanli period, the sparser and more spontaneous style of the exterior design is closer to that of wares produced during the Tianqi period for the Japanese market. The piece thus embraces the stylistic extremes of this short but creative period and is among the very few surviving pieces that bear the Tianqi reign mark.[1]

1. A similar example of this unusual type is in the Nezu Art Museum, Tokyo, and is illustrated in *Sekai tōji zenshū*, vol. 14, *Ming Dynasty* (Tokyo: Shōgakukan, 1976), pl. 115, and also bears the six-character Tianqi reign mark. A related example with an apocryphal Chenghua mark is illustrated by Regina Krahl in *Chinese Ceramics in the Topkapi Saray Museum, Istanbul*, vol. 2, *Yuan and Ming Dynasty Porcelains* (London: Sotheby's Publications, 1986), pl. 1514, TKS 15/2279.

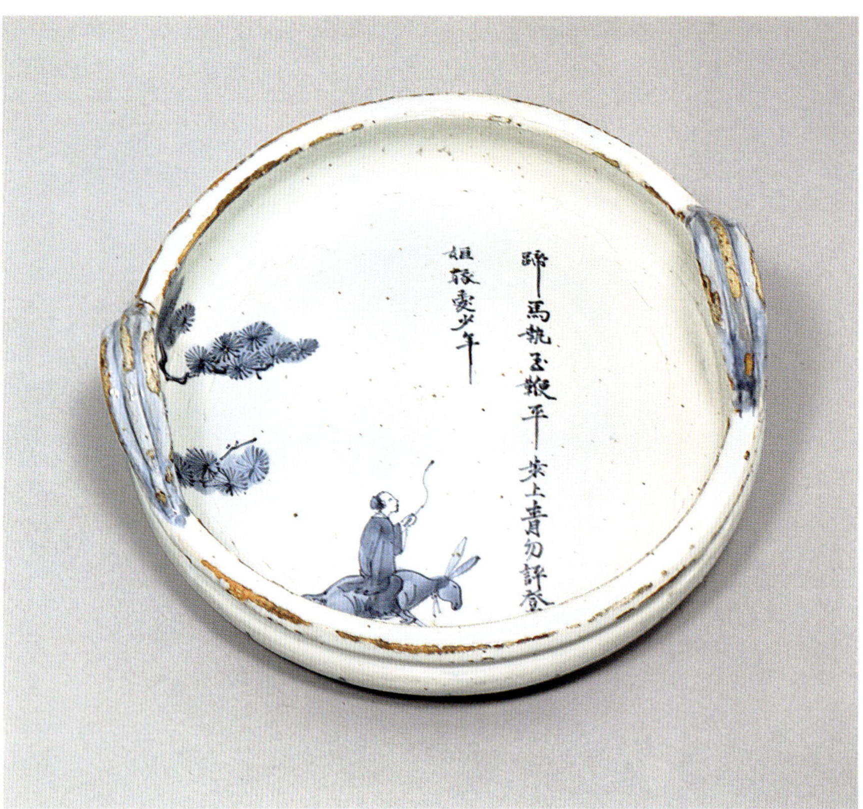

81

LARGE TWO-HANDLED BASIN

Jingdezhen ware, underglaze-blue-decorated porcelain in *kosome-tsuke* style with figure, tree, and poem

Ming dynasty, early 17th century, probably Tianqi period (1620–27)

D. 28.5 cm (11 ¼ in.)

The curved sides of this large, sturdy basin contract below the wide, thickened mouth, where two upright, ribbed handles are attached. The walls are thick, the piece heavy, and the shape distorted. The unglazed recessed base was raggedly scraped out, leaving a coarse surface that has burned a rusty brown. Kiln grit adheres to the vestigial foot. The relatively bright, bluish-tinged glaze is uneven, pitted and cracked, and dotted with dark iron spots. The glaze has separated and peeled extensively from the mouth rim and handle edges. The deep blue of the main decoration contrasts with the fainter blue thinly brushed over the handles and rim. Simple pointed leaves overlap in a broad band around the base, and on the interior is a pine tree, a scholar mounted on a donkey, and a poetic inscription, which reads: "The horse's hooves are controlled, the jade whip idle; step by step he advances to the green, but don't criticize his ascent—Chang E loves young men."[1]

During the late Ming dynasty the Chinese potter was tasked with producing wares for Japanese arbiters of fashion whose taste in ceramics was antithetical to that held by discriminating Chinese. This eccentric breed of coarsely potted and glazed porcelains, which flourished during the Tianqi period, is known even in the West by the Japanese term *kosome-tsuke* (old blue-decorated ware), and the characteristics of the present dish are a fair summary of its technical features and particular aesthetic. The deformities in shape, such as the bowed interior, were probably fortuitous, but the handles might have been encouraged to tilt to avoid a symmetrically balanced form. Although substantial contortions were sometimes purposely imposed on a shape, the final outcome after firing was unpredictable; no two pieces were exactly alike. During the previous century in Japan, tea masters were drawn to the natural imperfections and rugged beauty of the humble utilitarian ceramics of their own native kilns, and under the influence of their sophisticated taste, Japanese potters consciously cultivated these characteristics. Not only were the general aesthetic peculiarities of the Japanese wares captured by Chinese potters in the production of *kosometsuke* wares, but even specific shapes were derived from Japanese models. In the present case a two-handled stoneware basin produced at the Bizen kilns could have provided the prototype.

Although the underglaze design here is stunningly composed and skillfully painted, the effect is one of simplicity, even naiveté. The lone pine and the single mounted figure who gazes at the poetic inscription in the silence of the vacant ground creates a deeply evocative mood, one splendidly suited to a tea ceremony vessel.

1. "Green" symbolizes a brothel; Chang E is the Goddess of the Moon.

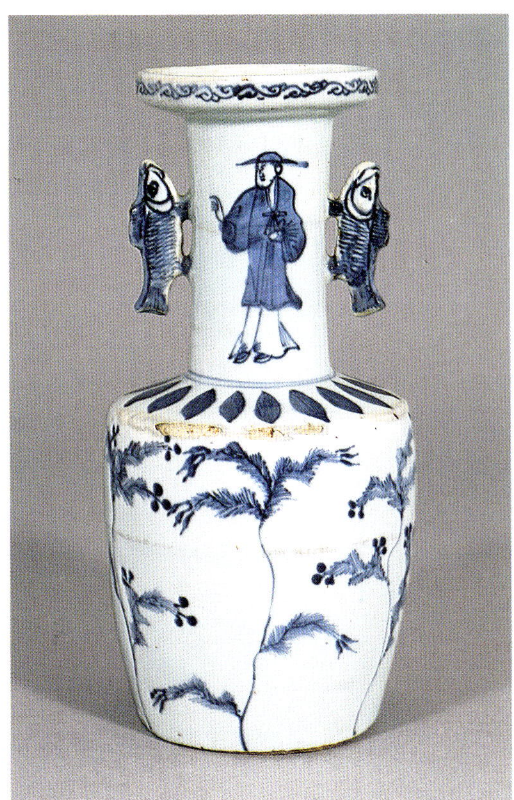

82

VASE

Jingdezhen ware, underglaze-blue-decorated porcelain in *kosome-tsuke* style with *takasago* theme

Ming dynasty, early 17th century, probably Tianqi period (1620–27)

H. 26.1 cm (10 1/4 in.)

This vase has a slightly tapering cylindrical body, a straight cylindrical neck, a dish-shaped mouth, and handles molded in the shape of fish. It was made from an unrefined porcelain paste, which is visible on the darkly discolored, gritty foot rim and where the glaze has peeled from the slanted shoulder. The body join remains visible as a horizontal line around the center. A female and a male figure are painted in bright blue on the neck, pine branches on the body, oval leaves on the shoulder, a scroll on the mouth rim, and a band of linked triangles around the interior of the mouth. The flat handles are detailed in underglaze blue to enhance their fish forms. The typical late Ming outline-and-wash technique has been used throughout save for the scroll and the pine boughs, whose spindly branches and needles are linearly drawn with some spots of blue added. The painted images blur where the bubbly glaze is particularly thick.

With the exception of the handles, the distinctive shape of this vase resembles that of the wooden block (*kinuta*) used for beating clothes and bedding. During the Kamakura period in Japan (1185–1333), this shape numbered among the late Song and early Yuan celadons imported from the Longquan kilns of China. (A *kinuta*-shaped celadon vase of a much admired shade of bluish green inspired the adoption of the name *kinuta* for any celadon of that prized color, regardless of its shape.) During the early seventeenth century, the porcelain vases were often decorated in underglaze blue with two legendary Japanese figures: Jo, who wears a broad-rimmed hat, and Uba, who carries a broom or a staff. The story of this virtuous couple, whose spirits appear on moonlit nights to sweep the ground beneath the pine in which they dwell, has been enacted from the fifteenth century until today in the Noh drama *Takasago*. Chinese vases decorated with this theme, clearly intended for the Japanese market, are thus called *takasago* vases. The secondary motifs are drawn from the traditional Chinese decorative repertoire, but the old pine branches are obvious references to the Japanese tale. The physical and technical characteristics, while appealing to a taste for the rough and imperfect held by early Edo-period aesthetes, in fact have much in common with standard late Ming underglaze-blue-decorated wares produced for lower-class consumption at home, and such domestic wares are likely the ultimate source for the *kosometsuke* style.

1. See Masahiko Kawahara, *Ko-Sometsuke* (Kyoto: Shoin, 1977), 2 vols., for a comprehensive illustrated catalogue of the porcelains exported to Japan, and for related Chinese domestic wares see *Mingdai minjian qinghua ci hua*, compiled by Wang Zhimin (Beijing: Xinhua shudian, 1958).

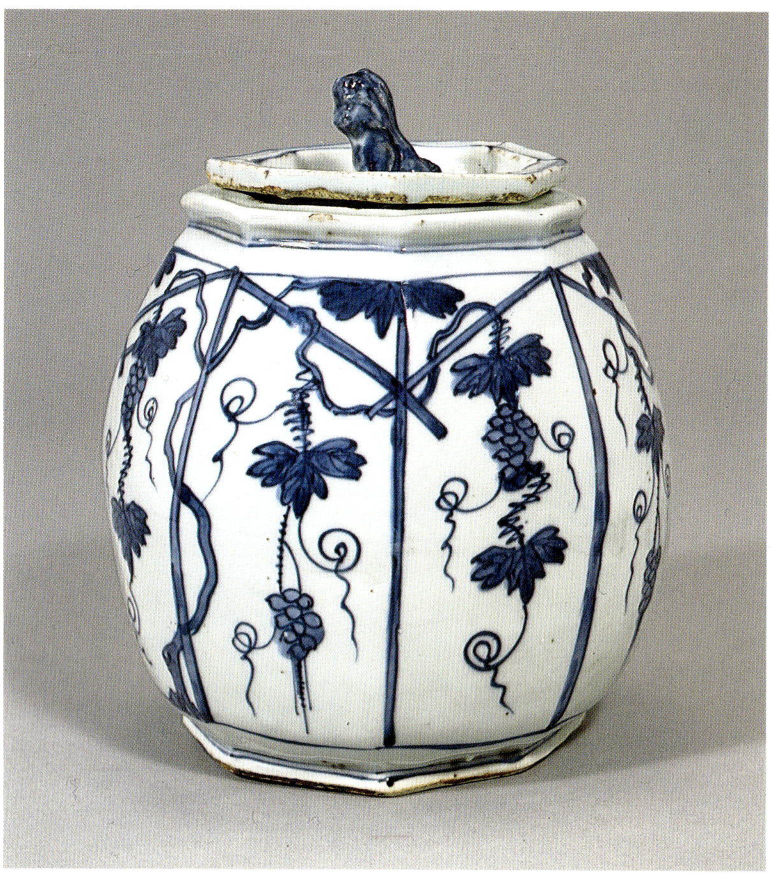

83

WATER JAR

Jingdezhen ware, underglaze-blue-decorated porcelain in *kosometsuke* style with trellis-and-grape design

Ming dynasty, early to mid 17th century, Tianqi (1620–27) or Chongzhen period (1628–44)

H. 21.8 cm (8 5/8 in.)

The rounded octagonal shape of this covered jar was produced by a series of facets cut vertically into the curving walls of the heavy body. The vessel rests stably on a flat base, contracting above the base and below the bold mouth rim. The paste revealed on the unglazed base, which has the remains of a lacquer coating applied in Japan, is white and dense. The octagonal lid, which sits awkwardly on the rim, has a sunken center and is surmounted by a casually modeled lion. The reverse of the lid is unglazed and has a rough, fissured, buff-colored surface.

The divisions of the octagonal shape are reinforced by an underglaze-blue painted trellis, which consists of eight upright posts joined at the top by diagonally tilted crossbars. Grapevines twine up two posts on opposite sides of the vessel and weave horizontally through the crossbars above, dangling bunched grapes, leaves, and tendrils into the spaces below. This brilliant composition, perfectly suited to the faceted, swelling form, is matched by the deft outline-and-wash execution of the motifs in vibrant blue and by the facile linear calligraphy of the curling tendrils. The richness of the blue is enhanced by the thick, bright glaze, which appears pure and colorless.

The covered vessel (*mizusashi*) from which fresh water is ladled to replenish the kettle during the Japanese tea ceremony was among the various underglaze-blue-decorated porcelains known as *kosometsuke* (old blue-decorated ware), produced by Chinese potters during the later decades of the Ming period for the Japanese market. A similar grapevine-and-trellis water jar, ovoid in shape and less stunning in design, has a four-character reign mark, *Tianqi nian zhi,* written vertically on the exterior and is one of the few marked pieces providing the basis for dating the entire *kosometsuke* group to the Tianqi period.[1] However, the technical and aesthetic range of the group suggests a more lengthy production period than the mere six years of the Tianqi emperor's reign.

1. Illustrated in *Tōji taikei,* vol. 44, *Kosometsuke/Shonzui* (Tokyo: Heibonsha, 1972), p. 98, fig. 23.

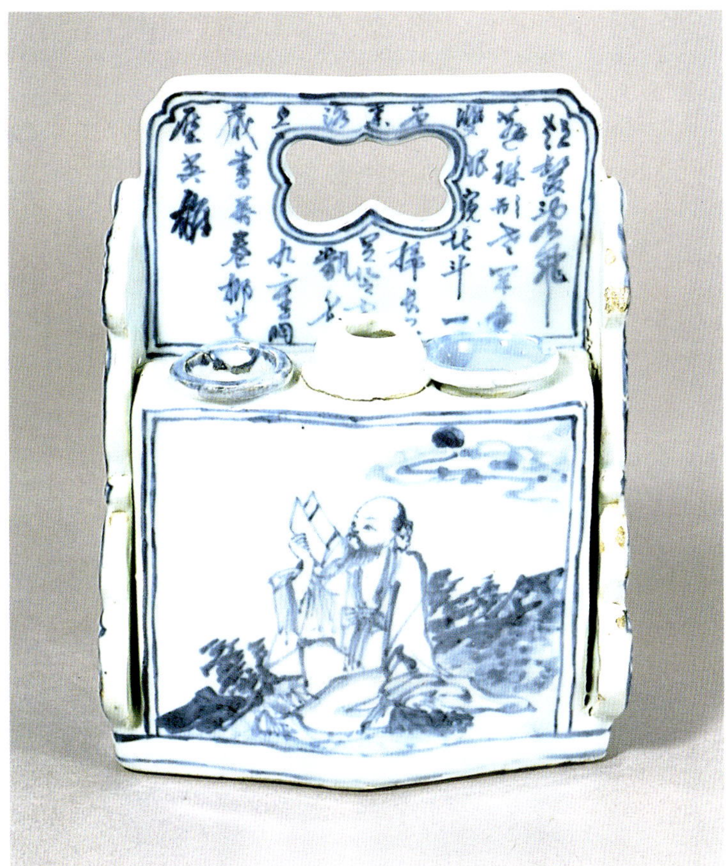

84

BRUSH HOLDER

Jingdezhen ware, underglaze-blue-decorated porcelain with figural design

Ming dynasty, early to mid 17th century

H. 15.7 cm (6 1/4 in.)

This engaging brush holder was fashioned as a miniature standing screen with elaborate leaf-shaped side panels and pictorial decoration on its front and back faces. The top of the hollow box in front was pierced with three round holes, into which small, bottomless receptacles for holding brushes were glazed in place. This section is backed by an upright, rectangular slab of clay perforated with an ornamental cartouche. The thick, unglazed base is flat, aside from a rectangular depression in the center which might have been intended for a reign mark.

The painted decoration and calligraphy, produced with a pale but tonally varied blue, is accomplished and assured yet unrestrained. The figure in repose on an earthy slope with moon and clouds above is gazing at a scroll; the poem above is perhaps to be understood as emanating from his thoughts. Filling the rectangular field on the reverse is a representation of Kui Xing, one of the four attendants of the Chinese god of literature, in his usual guise "… with the visage of a demon, holding a writing brush in his right hand and a *tou* (measure) in his left, one of his legs kicking up behind—the figure being obviously intended as an impersonation of the character *k'uei* (demon)."[1] Kui Xing is shown amid a flurry of wind-blown clouds, the constellation above him marking his stature as a stellar deity; the books airborne behind him recall his function as distributor of literary degrees, a role that accounts for his invocation on a number of similar brush holders of the late Ming period.

The side panels are painted with chrysanthemum florets and a type of frilly-leafed lotus scroll known from other porcelains of the post-Wanli period. The bluish-tinged and bubbly glaze, which created a slight haze over the decoration, has peeled from several of the protruding edges. The technical and stylistic features of this object are not unrelated to those of the *kosometsuke* wares (see nos. 81–83) produced for the Japanese market in the latter decades of the Ming dynasty; this piece can be similarly dated.

1. E. T. C. Werner, *A Dictionary of Chinese Mythology* (New York: Julian Press, 1969), p. 557.

This unassuming flower vase, narrow and pear-shaped in form and decorated in underglaze blue and overglaze enamels, seems informal, even homespun. The glaze is unevenly applied and has peeled from the mouth rim. The flat base is unglazed, discolored to a dark brown, and marked by concentric lines from the potter's wheel. The four underglaze-blue butterflies look a bit out of focus, and the red, yellow, and brown butterflies and floral sprays and florets were drawn with an undisciplined hand. The motifs are by no means haphazardly arranged, yet they appear free-floating and random.

Related butterfly-and-flower compositions appear on pear-shaped vessels decorated in underglaze blue from late Ming tombs datable to the Chongzhen period: two vases from a tomb dated to 1628 were discovered at Nancheng in Jiangxi province, and a similar vase came from a tomb, also in Nancheng, dated to 1634. These pieces are stouter in proportion than the Idemitsu vase and were finished with shallowly cut feet.[1]

A small dish in the Shanghai Museum, decorated with the same motifs and using a similar *wucai* palette and painting style as seen here, bears on its base a four-character *Tianqi nian zhi* reign mark written in underglaze blue.[2] A production date during the later decades of the Ming, when private kilns served domestic and foreign markets alike with a prodigious range of wares, is thus reasonable for this vase.

1. One of the pair from the 1628 tomb, now in the Jiangxi Provincial Museum, is illustrated in *Zhongguo taoci quanji,* vol. 19, *Jingdezhen minjian qinghua ciqi* (Kyoto: Shanghai People's Art Publishing House and Bi-no-Bi, 1983), pl. 177. The vase from the 1634 tomb is illustrated in *Wenwu,* no. 2 (1983), pl. 5, fig. 2.

2. *Zhongguo taoci quanji,* vol. 21, *Jingdezhen caihui ciqi* (Kyoto: Shanghai People's Publishing House and Bi-no-Bi, 1981), pl. 49.

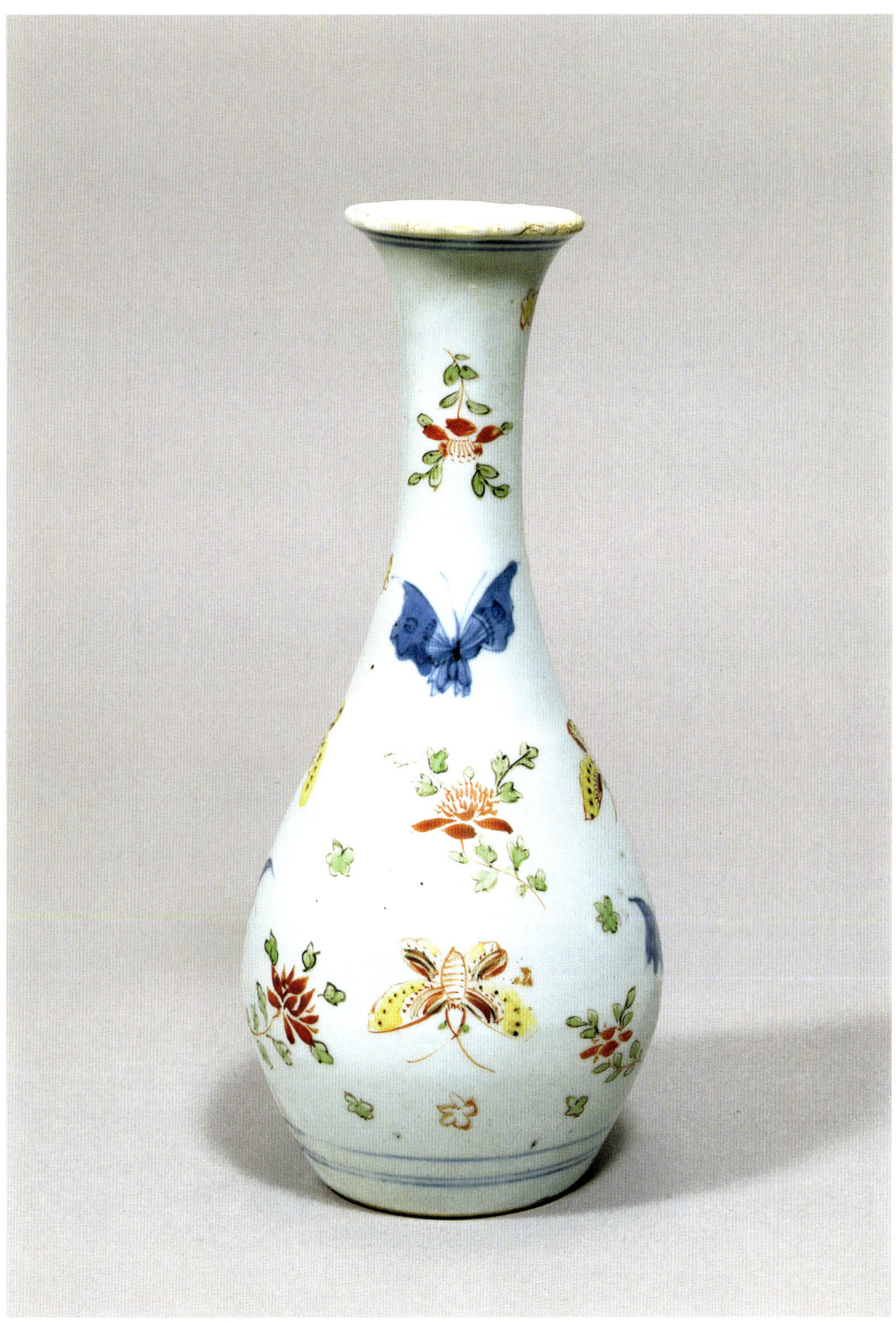

85

PEAR-SHAPED VASE

Jingdezhen ware, *wucai*-decorated porcelain with butterfly-and-flower design

Ming dynasty, first half 17th century, Tianqi (1620–27) or Chongzhen period (1628–44)

H. 22.9 cm (9 in.)

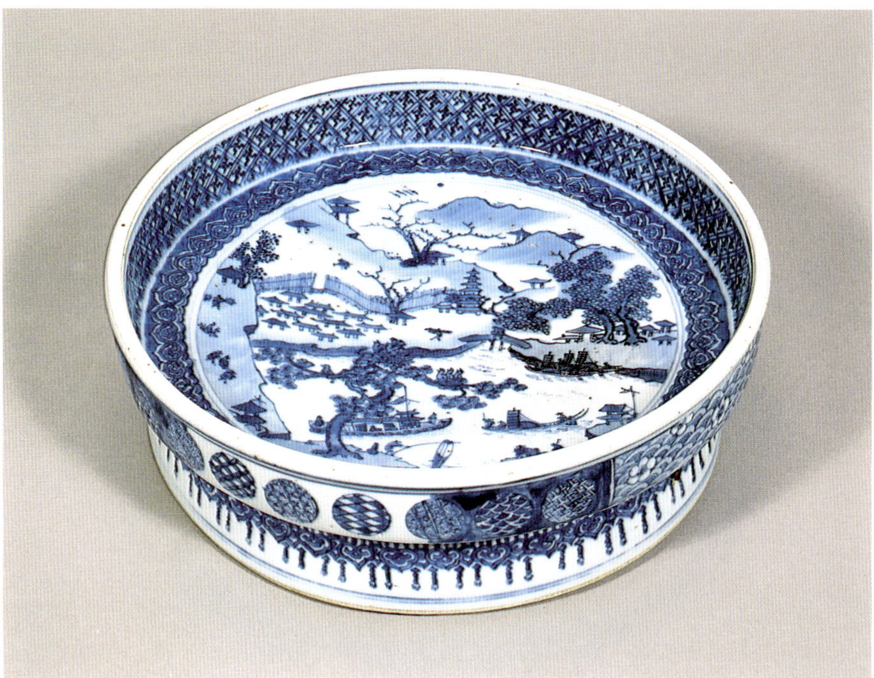

86

FOOTED DISH

Jingdezhen ware, underglaze-blue-decorated *shonzui*-style porcelain with scene of river village

Ming dynasty, Chongzhen period (1628–44); eight-character inscription, *Wuliang dafu Wu Xiangrui zao*

D. 23.5 cm (9 1/4 in.), H. 7.6 cm (3 in.)

Shallow, straight sides and a broad, high foot that slants slightly outward characterize this strongly potted dish. The underglaze-blue eight-character inscription is written on the deeply recessed base in two four-character columns. The white paste has a slight grayish tinge, and the bright glaze has an orange-peel texture. On the flat interior of the dish is a scene of a river village, executed in spirited detail with consummate painterly skill. The swaying boughs of a foreground pine harbor nests of chirping birds; immediately below, a fisherman pulling in his catch has caught the attention of three figures on the far bank. A fancy pleasure boat drifts lazily on the lake while a sailboat plies more rapidly nearby. A gentleman crosses the bridge, and beyond, a thatch-laden worker makes his way to the main group of village houses; at the left several figures descend the slope, and another can be seen hoeing in the fields beyond the village, which has as its prized building a seven-storied pagoda. The intriguing scene is framed by linked *ruyi* heads, which abut the fastidiously drawn swastika diaper band in the cavetto. On the exterior, separated fields are patterned with diaper and cherry-blossom designs and circular medallions containing either geometric patterns or scenes of figures in landscape settings. The foot is decorated with pendant *ruyi* heads supporting hanging tassels.

The distinctive group of underglaze-blue-decorated porcelains produced for use in the Japanese tea ceremony and known as *shonzui* ware is defined by common technical and stylistic features: fine, strong potting and careful finishing; the use of high-grade cobalt blue; inventive shapes; designs employing geometric patterns, medallions, and often, figures in landscape scenes. These characteristics suggest a production period during the very late Ming period and perhaps even somewhat later.

The term *shonzui* is taken from the Japanese pronunciation of the Chinese name Xiangrui, which appears in the eight-character inscription, *Wuliang dafu Wu Xiangrui zao,* written on a number of such pieces. There is yet no general agreement as to how this inscription should be translated, nor even if it should be read in Chinese or in Japanese. If read in Chinese (there is no precedent in Chinese ceramic history to suggest we do otherwise), one possible translation is: "Made by Wu Xiangrui, the Great Originator in Art."[1] Although historical records have been mute concerning this extraordinary artist, he speaks to us directly and eloquently through his work and, more distantly, through the family of wares his creations inspired.

1. *Wu* is a common Chinese surname, and *Xiangrui,* "Auspicious Omen," is an acceptable *hao* or by-name. *Wuliang* might refer to the five virtues of ritual, knowledge, courage, talent, and art, or solely to the fifth virtue of art. *Fu* means "great, large, eminent, or to begin," but to avoid redundancy when used with *da,* "great," the second usage is preferred, yielding "Great Originator." Other theories concerning *shonzui* ware and the meaning of the inscription are discussed by Soame Jenyns in "The Chinese Ko-sometsuke and Shonsui Ware," *Transactions of the Oriental Ceramic Society,* vol. 34 (1962–63), pp. 13–50.

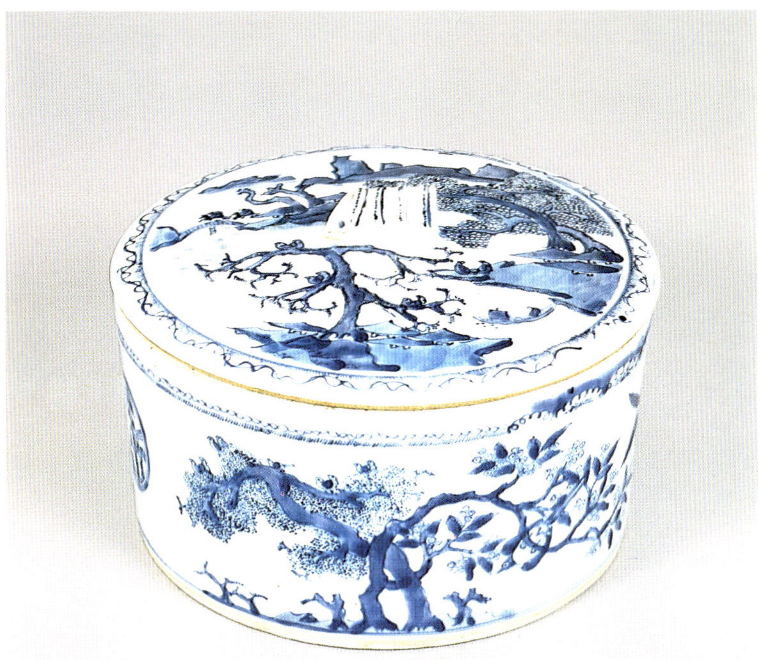

87

WATER JAR

Jingdezhen ware, underglaze-blue-decorated *shonzui*-style porcelain with bird, bamboo, tree, figure, and landscape scenes

Ming dynasty, probably Chongzhen period (1628–44)

H. 13 cm (5 1/8 in.), D. 19.3 cm (7 5/8 in.)

This strongly potted covered jar is supported on a rounded foot enclosing an unglazed, slightly recessed base. The bright and bluish-tinged glaze has a network of widely spaced, long crackles. The cover fits securely into the jar and is surmounted by a bamboo-shaped knob. The form of the vessel, which at first appears to be simply a broad cylinder, might have been meant to suggest, through the slight constriction of the body, a segment of bamboo, a notion in harmony with the bamboo design painted on the interior and exterior of the jar and cover.

The underglaze-blue decoration combines pictorial scenes with geometric motifs. Numerous small birds perch in the crab-apple and peach trees on opposite sides of the vessel, and a giant magpie balances on a single stalk of bamboo. Three circular medallions—one with a geometric wheel motif, one with men in a boat, and the other with bird and bamboo—interrupt the lively naturalism but are neither discordant nor intrusive. The themes set here are repeated in the decoration of the lid: on the exterior is a more complete and spacious landscape scene, and on the interior a central geometric medallion is surrounded by figures in landscape and bird-and-bamboo scenes. The interior of the jar is decorated with three irregularly shaped medallions that suggest the visual distortion of images viewed through water and must have been particularly pleasing when the vessel was filled.

The brushwork is bold and varied, especially the stippling of the branches, and the blue dark and rich. In contrast to the skillfully drawn main designs, the neck band decoration, which looks like a stretched coil of wire, and the lazy rambling lines surrounding the lid appear naive and awkward. This inconsistency is understandable given the artistic heritage of *shonzui*-type wares. The potters and painters worked essentially in the ingenious style created by Wu Xiangrui but were also the artistic descendants of those who produced *kosometsuke* and popular domestic wares in the earlier seventeenth century.

This dish has shallow, rounded sides, a flat rim thickened at the edge and dressed with a brown wash, and a buff-colored gritty foot with three sections cut out (perhaps to accommodate a stand), and a recessed glazed base. The apocryphal reign mark, followed by the character *fu* (good fortune) within a square frame, was written in underglaze blue on the base in the grass-script writing style. The piece is light in weight and warped.

The interior is divided into a central landscape-and-figure scene surrounded by a six-sectioned, geometrically decorated cavetto, with a meandering vine sprouting leaves and flowers on the rim. The main scene was broadly brushed using bright underglaze blue and enlivened by the addition of red, green, yellow, and sepia overglaze enamels. A fisherman clad in green casts his line in waters roughly depicted by short underglaze-blue and overglaze-red lines; another figure has just crossed a precariously tilted bridge and approaches two simple dwellings partially hidden by large rocks. Another boat with a figure is adrift in the background waters, and a distant mountain with a red moon above rounds off the scene. The brightly colored enamels that float and puddle in the landscape scene are repeated in the simple geometric patterns appearing in the cavetto and on the exterior, which was rapidly decorated with cursorily rendered birds perched on underglaze-blue bamboo leaves, naively depicted fruiting branches, and butterflies and insects.

Among the overglaze-enameled wares that reached Japan during the late Ming period were those termed *iro-shonzui* (colored *shonzui*) because of the similarity they bore to underglaze-blue *shonzui*-style porcelains. Here, for example, the wide cavetto is given over entirely to geometric diaper fillers, and the central scene is a rustic landscape. In contrast to the usual fastidiousness of the underglaze-blue-decorated wares, however, the decoration was hastily done and little care was given to details; the diaper patterns of the cavetto spill over their boundaries in some areas, and the underglaze-blue tree of the central area blunders obliviously into the diaper ground above. Despite these and other shortcomings, however, the historical significance of such late Ming ceramics is assured by the important influence they had on the development of porcelain decoration in seventeenth-century Japan.

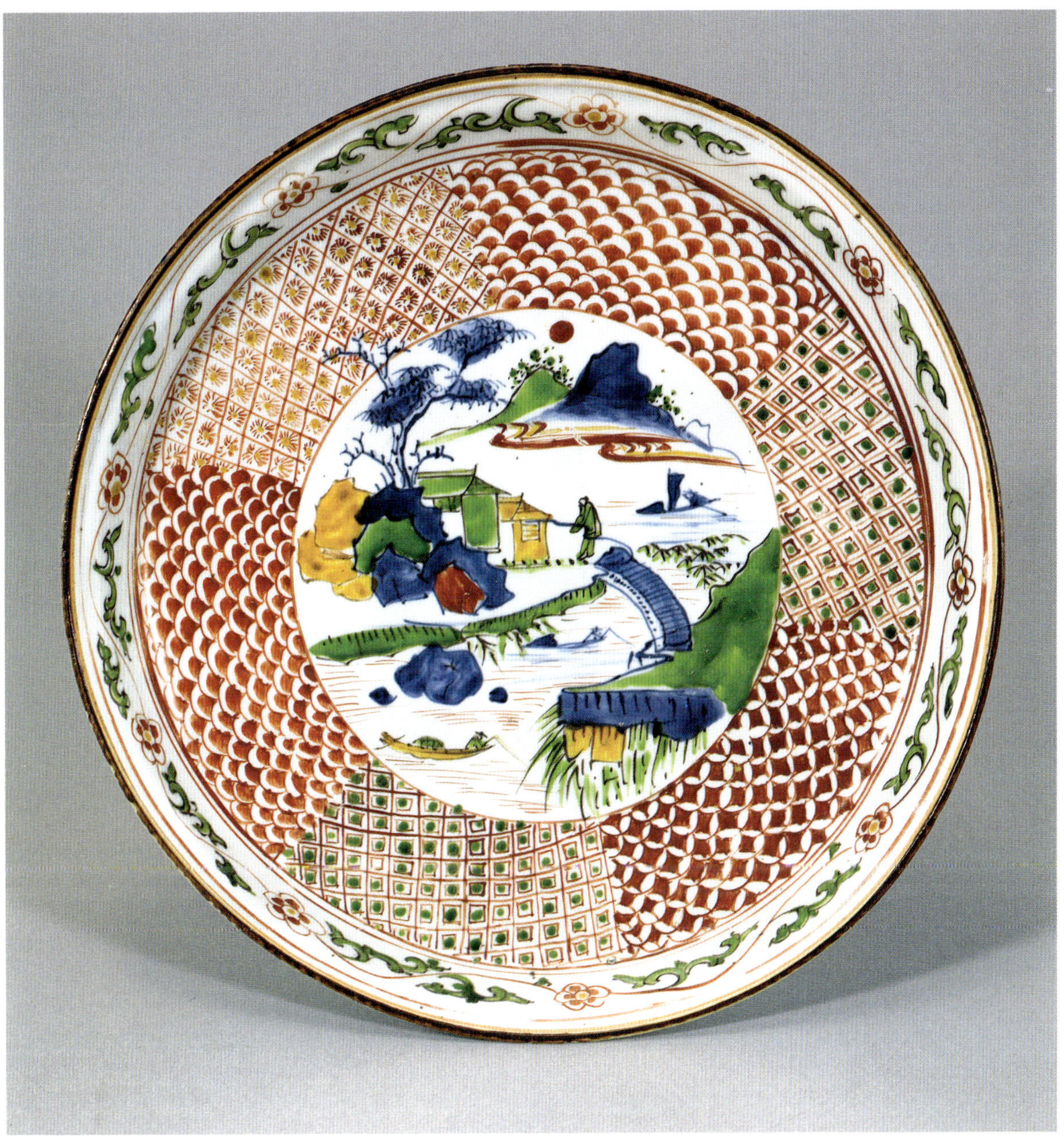

88

DISH

Jingdezhen ware, *wucai*-decorated porcelain in *iro-shonzui* style with scene of figures in landscape

Ming dynasty, probably Chongzhen period (1628–44); apocryphal six-character mark, *Da Ming Jiajing nian zhi*

D. 27.1 cm (10 5/8 in.)

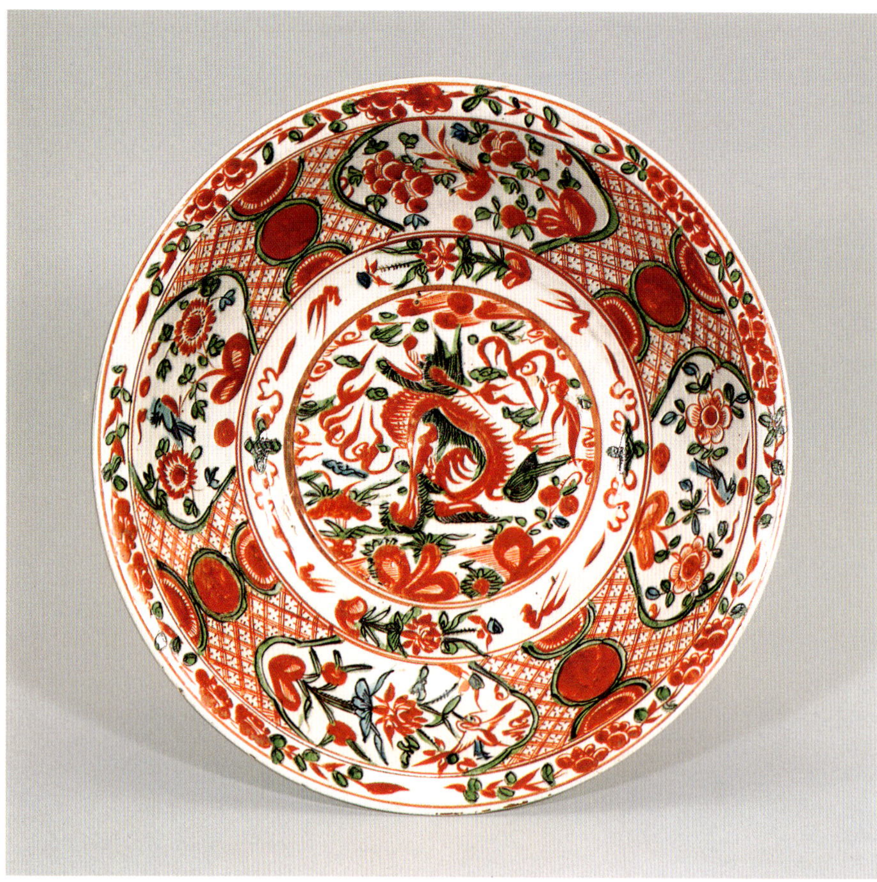

89

LARGE DISH

Swatow ware, overglaze-enamel-decorated porcelain with *qilin* design

Ming dynasty, late 16th to first half 17th century

D. 42.8 cm (16 7/8 in.)

The shape of this deep dish with a large cavetto sweeping to a flat, slanted mouth is very common among the wares known in the West as Swatow. The consistent technical features of the group are present here, including a coarse body that became highly discolored on exposed areas during firing, an opaque glaze with an irregular surface marred by pits and iron spitouts, a foot that slants inward and is steeply cut on the interior, a base roughly splashed with glaze, and an excessive amount of gravelly kiln grit adhering to the foot and base. The rapidly executed, bold, and colorful designs of polychrome Swatow ware—usually dominated by overglaze red and green enamels with turquoise and black—lack precision but are in perfect harmony with the potting and general physical character of these ceramics.

The creature in the center of this dish, which to the occidental eye might look like a dog baying at the moon, is more likely a *qilin*, known together with the dragon, the phoenix, and the tortoise as the *siling* (four supernatural creatures) in Chinese mythology. This composite animal combines the body of a stag, the head of a dragon, and a lion's bushy tail. It is regarded as a happy portent, a symbol of longevity, felicity, and illustrious offspring, with its soft fleshy horns a sign of its virtue and benevolence. The elevated center of the dish, which rose to a hump during firing, gives the body of the beast some added corporeality.

Certain features of the decoration, such as the diaper ground studded with red medallions, are similar in concept, if not in actual execution, to *kinrande* porcelain designs, and not surprisingly, underglaze-blue-decorated Swatow wares bear a strong decorative resemblance to *kraak* porcelain. The Swatow style indeed owed a tremendous amount to the export wares produced at Jingdezhen. During the Song dynasty, to cite a precedent example of the influence at work here, the flow to foreign markets of *yingqing* wares from Jingdezhen and of celadons from the Longquan area stimulated local production in port regions of both imitations and new versions of these major commercial wares. A large portion of Swatow ceramics can likewise be regarded as a provincial manifestation of popular export styles, in this case those emanating from Jingdezhen. No kiln site producing the polychrome wares has so far been reported, but it is believed that the kilns were located in southern Fujian and northern Guangdong provinces; the name Swatow is in fact an old romanization for Shatou, a port in northeastern Guangdong. To date, however, excavations in these areas report the discovery of mainly underglaze-blue-decorated wares.

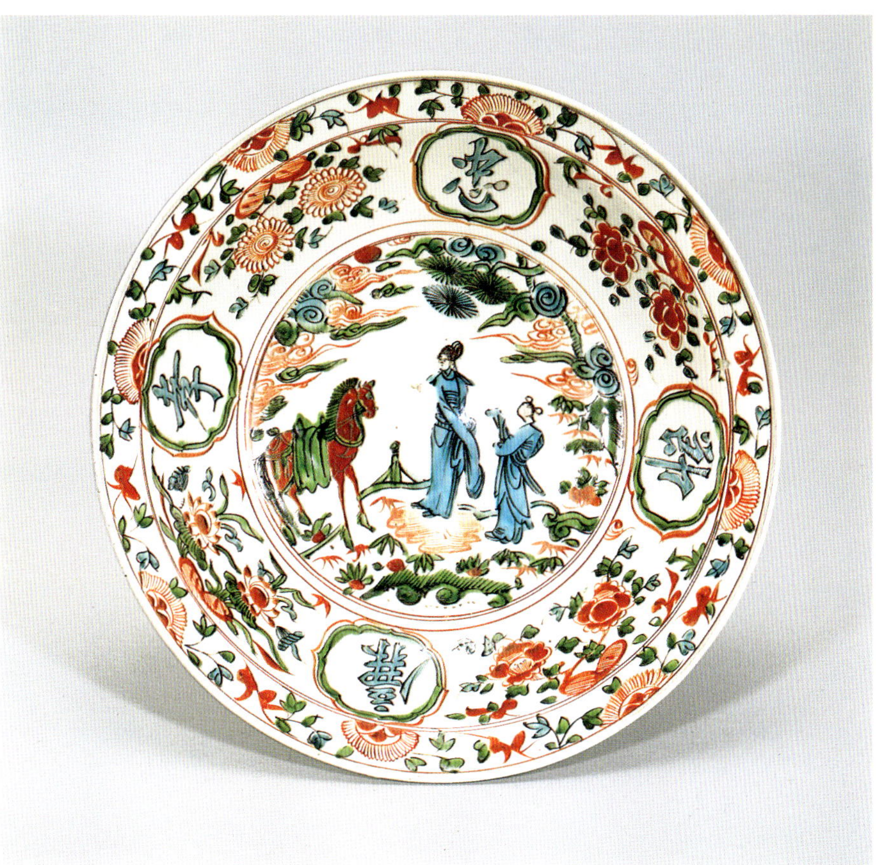

90

LARGE DISH

Swatow ware, overglaze-enamel-decorated porcelain with figural scene

Ming dynasty, late 16th to first half 17th century

D. 39 cm (15 3/8 in.)

This large dish has an expansive cavetto opening to a slanted rim, a foot tilted sharply inward, a recessed base roughly splashed with a milky, opaque glaze, considerable gravelly adhesion on the foot and base, a coarse paste strongly discolored on exposed areas, and a thick-walled, heavy body. Technically it is a standard Swatow dish; the arrangement of its decoration to cover the three concentric zones of the interior, the majority of motifs, and the lively enamel palette are typical. Within the cavetto four quatrefoil cartouches frame characters outlined in black and filled in with turquoise enamel: *zhong* (loyalty), *xiao* (filiality), *lian* (purity), and *jie* (modesty). Between these decorative images, clusters of flowers—lotus, peony, camellia, and chrysanthemum—grow in pairs from simplified and highly abstracted rockeries. Half-chrysanthemum motifs connected by leafy tendrils decorate the flattened mouth, and swiftly brushed scroll elements skim the exterior wall.

Within the extant body of Swatow wares, this central scene is stunningly individualistic. Compared to the drawing usual in Swatow decoration, which is at best spontaneous and freewheeling but often simply slapdash, the captivating fiery-red horse and human figures are distinguished by a far more thoughtful execution. The turquoise-blue enamel has been applied with great care within the sharp black outlines of the flowing garments of the stately female figure and the youth at her side, and the green of the horse's mane, hooves, saddle blanket, and trappings was also applied with restraint. A small number of Swatow dishes are closely related to the Idemitsu piece not only by similar rim and cavetto decorative schemes but by well-painted and individualistic figural scenes in the central zone. One has the eccentric Chan Buddhist monk Shide with a broom in hand laughing at the moon, another a scholar on a riverbank awaiting a figure who approaches in a boat, and a third the Daoist divinity Lan Caihe carrying two baskets of flowers.[1] Given the resemblance between these pieces, it is possible that all were produced by the same workshop and the central scenes by the same artist. The figural subject of the present piece was likely based on a specific historical or dramatic event, but even if the scenes depicted on the dishes were not easily identifiable nor the written characters in the cartouches understandable to the non-Chinese, for whom these wares were in most cases destined, the sheer vitality of the decoration surely would have been captivating and the porcelains themselves irresistible.

1. *Gosu aka-e zukan* (Tokyo, 1952), pls. 24, 23, and 22, respectively.

Suggested Reading

Addis, John. *Chinese Ceramics from Datable Tombs*. New York and London: Sotheby Parke Bernet, 1978.

Ayers, John. *The Baur Collection: Chinese Ceramics*. 2 vols. Geneva: Collections Baur, 1968.

Chinese Ceramics in the Idemitsu Collection. Tokyo: Heibonsha, 1987.

Garner, Harry. *Oriental Blue and White*. London: Praeger, 1954; 3rd ed., 1970.

Jenyns, Soame. *Ming Pottery and Porcelain*. London: Faber and Faber, 1953.

Krahl, Regina. *Chinese Ceramics in the Topkapi Saray Museum, Istanbul*. 3 vols. London: Sotheby's Publications, 1986.

Little, Stephen. *Chinese Ceramics of the Transitional Period: 1620–1683*. New York: China Institute in America, 1974.

Medley, Margaret. *The Chinese Potter: A Practical History of Chinese Ceramics*. New York: Scribner's, 1976.

———. *Illustrated Catalogue of Celadon Wares*. London: Percival David Foundation, 1977.

———. *Illustrated Catalogue of Ming and Ch'ing Monochromes in the Percival David Foundation of Chinese Art*. London: School of Oriental and African Studies, 1973.

———. *Illustrated Catalogue of Ming Polychrome Wares*. London: Percival David Foundation, 1978.

———. *Yuan Porcelain and Stoneware*. London: Faber and Faber, 1974.

Mino, Yutaka. *Freedom of Clay and Brush through Seven Centuries in Northern China: Tz'u-chou Type Wares, 960–1600 A.D.* Bloomington, Ind.: Indiana University Press, 1980.

——— and Katherine Tsiang. *Ice and Green Clouds, Traditions of Chinese Celadon*. Bloomington, Ind.: Indiana University Press, 1986.

Oriental Ceramics: The World's Great Collections. 11 vols. Tokyo: Kodansha, 1975–.

Pope, John A. *Chinese Porcelains from the Ardebil Shrine*. Washington: Freer Gallery of Art, 1956; rev. ed., 1981.

———. *Fourteenth-Century Blue-and-White: A Group of Chinese Porcelains in Topkapu Sarayi Muzesi, Istanbul*. Washington: Freer Gallery of Art, 1952; rev. ed., 1970.

Porcelain of the National Palace Museum. 20 vols. Hong Kong: National Palace Museum, 1963.

Sekai tōji zenshū. 22 vols. Tokyo: Shōgakukan, 1975–.

Sinan haeja yumul (Sinan Seacoast Cultural Relics). Seoul: National Museum of Korea, 1977; Ministry of Culture and Information of Korea, 1985.

Trubner, Henry, et al. *Chinese Ceramics from Japanese Collections*. New York: Asia Society, 1977.